On Every Front

THE NORTON ESSAYS IN AMERICAN HISTORY
Under the general editorship of
HAROLD M. HYMAN
William P. Hobby Professor of American History
Rice University

On Every Front:

The Making of the Cold War

Thomas G. Paterson

W · W · NORTON & COMPANY
New York · London

Library of Congress Cataloging in Publication Data
Patterson, Thomas G.   1941–
    On every front.
    (The Norton essays in American history)
    Bibliography: p.
    Includes index.
    1.   United States—Foreign relations—1945–
2.   Russia—Foreign relations—1945–   3.   United
States—Foreign relations—Russia.   4.   Russia—Foreign
relations—United States.   5.   World politics—1945–
I.   Title.
E744.P312   1979   327.73'047   79-4509

ISBN 0-393-01238-7
ISBN 0-393-95014-x pbk.

2 3 4 5 6 7 8 9 0

For Stephen W. C. Paterson

Contents

Preface

THE WORLD, Winston Churchill told President Truman in early 1946, was "bewildered, baffled, and breathless."[1] With his dramatic "Iron Curtain" speech just a little over a month ahead, the former British prime minister, always the phrasemaker and forthright analyst, believed that he knew why international affairs had descended so precariously from the Grand Alliance into what would soon be called the Cold War. If less eloquent than the venerable Churchill, scholars have also penned their commentaries on the postwar crisis. We have learned much from most of them—from monographs that plumb particular issues, from descriptive narratives that tell an engaging story, and from ambitious overviews that subordinate vast data to overarching themes.

This book attempts a modest synthesis of the voluminous historical literature and different schools of thought. It presents new research in rich archival sources that have become available to scholars only in recent years. More, it studies both American and Soviet diplomacy and, drawing upon theoretical works on international relations and the behavior of large nations, takes an interdisciplinary tack. My study of the "bewildered, baffled, and breathless" state of postwar world affairs seeks a multifaceted explanation—one more complex than that which Churchill offered in March 1946, to his Fulton, Missouri, audience or that which Truman contemplated (and later acted upon) as he sat on the stage listening to the message that Churchill had assured the president he would "very likely" find agreeable.[2]

1. Winston S. Churchill to Harry S. Truman, January 29, 1946, Box 115, President's Secretary's File, Harry S. Truman Papers, Harry S. Truman Library, Independence, Mo.
2. *Ibid.*

The Cold War derived from three closely intertwined sources: the conflict-ridden *international system*, the divergent *fundamental needs and ideas* of the major antagonists, America and Russia, and the diplomatic conduct or *tactics* of American and Soviet leaders. To reduce the conflict inherent in the postwar structure, to satisfy their strategic and economic needs and ideologies, and to conduct diplomacy true to their individual personalities and domestic political environments, officials in Washington and Moscow abandoned any quest for a community of nations and instead built competing spheres of influence. They thereby expanded and protected what they respectively perceived to be their interests, divided the world, and stimulated more conflict, which took the form of a "prolonged armed truce," to use the words of Soviet diplomat Maxim Litvinov.[3]

The first chapter introduces the world of 1945, reeling from the dislocations of the global war. Chapter 2 identifies the characteristics of the unstable international system, which afforded the great powers opportunities to extend their influence but also placed restraints on them. Chapter 3 surveys the events of the immediate postwar years, when the United States and the Soviet Union constructed their respective spheres of influence and launched the Cold War. Subsequent chapters attempt to explain why the two powers acted as they did, although the severe restrictions on the use of Soviet documents dictate that American policies will receive more attention. Chapter 4 studies the wellsprings, or fundamentals, of American foreign policy—those internal stimuli that induced the United States to undertake an activisit, global diplomacy. Chapters 5 and 6 investigate the "tactics" of American leaders: how they conducted their diplomacy, made their decisions, and functioned within the boundaries of their national politics. The seventh chapter, with necessary speculation because of the scarcity of Soviet sources, seeks to fathom the fundamental and tactical ingredients of Soviet for-

3. Department of State, *Foreign Relations of the United States, 1946*, VI, 763. (The *Foreign Relations* series is published at irregular intervals by the Government Printing Office in Washington, D.C., in multiple volumes for each year. Hereafter cited as *Foreign Relations*, year, volume, page.)

eign policy in order to explain why the Soviets behaved in such a way after World War II as to arouse fears that they were ruthless, callous aggressors challenging the United States in an unrelenting global contest. The last chapter is a brief conclusion, sketching the configuration of the Cold War in mid-1950, on the eve of the Korean War. The appendix provides a chronology of Cold War events.

My work has always benefited from the counsel and assistance of others. The many scholars cited in the footnotes and bibliography provided ideas and information through their books and articles, and I am eager to thank them. Helpful librarians and archivists in the depositories cited throughout facilitated the search for sources and responded generously to inquiries. Selma Wollman expertly typed the final draft. My students at the University of Connecticut have listened, questioned, and debated; in ways one cannot measure they have shaped this book. Among them, Jean-Donald Miller, James Gormly, Eduard M. Mark, Thomas G. Smith, Stephen Rabe, and Robert McMahon provided me with documents that they unearthed in their doctoral research. I also appreciated the research assistance of Mary Pain, Robin Beveridge, and Charlton Brandt. The Research Foundation of the University of Connecticut, the Harry S. Truman Institute, and the Eleanor Roosevelt Institute provided financial resources for travel in the United States and to Great Britain. Scholars who must seek their materials in distant archives know how much these grants-in-aid are appreciated. A fellowship from the National Endowment for the Humanities made the writing of the first draft possible, and I thank that valuable institution.

My editors, Harold Hyman of Rice University and Robert Kehoe and Jane Lebow of W. W. Norton and Company made useful suggestions for improvement. To my friend and colleague, J. Garry Clifford, always the perceptive reader and intelligent critic, I owe special thanks. He helped me to break through organizational and analytical roadblocks and his red (sometimes green) pen cut a path through literary overgrowth. Thomas Zoumaras also read the manuscript and provided me with a rewarding critique. My wife, Holly Izard Paterson, researched the documents with me, typed drafts of the manuscript, and quietly suffered the absences and preoccupations common to book writing. She always lifted the spirits, offering in her gentle manner the encouragement and understanding that sustain. This book is dedicated to Stephen, who knows the specialness of a dedication.

THOMAS G. PATERSON

Storrs, Connecticut

On Every Front

"It seems to me that we might just as well begin to face the Communist challenge on *every* front."

Senator Arthur Vandenberg
1947

1

Rubble: The World in 1945

WINSTON S. CHURCHILL WORE his usual bulldog visage. The ever-present cigar and hunched gait, other familiar trademarks of the British prime minister, also drew the crowd's attention on that very hot day of July 16, 1945. He was surveying the dusty remains of the Nazi capital—"that rubble heap near Potsdam," murmured one Berliner.[1] This time a preoccupied Churchill evinced little interest in his curious onlookers. What captured Churchill's regard was the grisly aftermath in Berlin of heavy Allied bombing and artillery fire and stout German resistance. He and the passengers in his motorcade grew sick, utterly stunned by the stark display of carnage in the German city.

"There is nothing to do here," sighed a dispirited Berliner.[2] Old men, women, and children trudged along, aimlessly pushing wheelbarrows. Over a million people lived in cellars, ruins, and makeshift suburban shacks, trading what they could for precious scraps of food to support their meager diet. Sixty-five to 75 percent of the city was levelled or damaged. The once-prized chariot of victory on the Brandenberg Gate had been reduced to a gnarled mass of molten metal. The Reichstag was a hollow shell. Some *"Nicht fur juden"* signs were still posted, ugly reminders of the German extermination of European Jews. Industrial equipment which survived the bombings had been torn from its

---

1. Quoted in Oscar Jacobi, "Berlin Today," *New York Times Magazine*, September 24, 1944, p. 5.
2. Quoted in Charles M. W. Moran, *Churchill: Taken from the Diaries of Lord Moran* (Boston, 1966), p. 289.

foundations by the Russians as war booty, leaving stripped, hull-like factories. Partially buried corpses lay rotting in the sun. Visitors and citizens alike recoiled from the stench of death that hung everywhere.[3] Lord Moran, who accompanied Churchill in Berlin, "felt a sense of nausea." Worse, "it was like the first time I saw a surgeon open a belly and the intestines gushed out."[4]

The curious prime minister entered what was left of Adolf Hitler's Chancellery. The Führer's marble-topped desk lay in a thousand pieces. Iron Crosses, military ribbons, and papers littered the floor. Uncharacteristically, Churchill said little as the descent into Hitler's damp hideaway apparently induced quiet reflection. Members of the prime minister's party picked up souvenirs; one pocketed a fragment of Hitler's world map. Depressed by what he saw, General H. L. Ismay hurried away to his villa to take a hot bath and a strong drink.[5] That night Churchill finally talked about his visit to the Chancellery. "It was from there that Hitler planned to govern the world," he mused. "A good many have tried that; all failed."[6] Savoring the Allied victory, the prime minister smiled contentedly and went to bed.

The president of the United States, Harry S. Truman, surveyed Berlin that same day. After reviewing the American 2nd Armored Division, the president led his entourage down the Wilhelmstrasse to the Chancellery of the Third Reich, all the while

3. The description of Berlin is drawn from Michael Balfour and John Mair, *Four-Power Control in Germany and Austria* (London, 1956), pp. 7–8; Lucius D. Clay, *Decision in Germany* (Garden City, N. Y., 1950), pp. 21, 31–32; Eugene Davidson, *The Death and Life of Germany* (New York, 1959), p. 66; David Dilks, ed., *The Diaries of Sir Alexander Cadogan, 1938–1945* (New York, 1971), pp. 761–764; Hastings Ismay, *The Memoirs of General, the Lord Ismay* (London, 1960), pp. 401–402; Richard Mayne, *Recovery of Europe, 1945–1973* (Garden City, N. Y., 1973), pp. 34–45; Moran, *Churchill*, pp. 288–291; Robert Murphy, *Diplomat Among Warriors* (Garden City, N.Y., 1964), pp. 257, 264; Alexander Werth, *Russia at War, 1941–1945* (New York, 1964)), pp. 890, 892; *New York Times,* July 5, 1945; Jacobi, "Berlin," p. 5; *Life,* XIX (July 23, 1945), 19–27.

4. Moran, *Churchill*, p. 289.

5. Churchill's tour is described in *ibid.*, pp. 290–291; Ismay, *Memoirs*, p. 402; Dilks, *Diaries of Cadogan*, pp. 763–764.

6. Quoted in Moran, *Churchill*, p. 291.

growing more awestruck by the destruction of the city. "That's what happens," he remarked, "when a man overreaches himself." For two hours Truman rode through Berlin's streets. "I was thankful," he noted later, "that the United States had been spared the unbelievable devastation of this war."[7] Berlin had actually appeared worse a month earlier, before Berliners, under the stern guidance of Russian and other Allied soldiers, began to stack bricks and shovel ashes. American diplomat Robert Murphy found that "the odor of death was everywhere." Indeed, "the canals were choked with bodies and refuse."[8] General Lucius Clay, who would soon become the military governor of the American zone, was also stunned. "The streets were piled high with debris which left in many places only a narrow one-way passage between mounds of rubble, and frequent detours had to be made where bridges and viaducts were destroyed. . . . It was like a city of the dead."[9]

From urban center to rural village, Germany looked charred and ravaged. Bomb-gutted Cologne and Nuremberg were hardly recognizable. Ninety-three percent of the houses in Düsseldorf were totally destroyed. Hamburg, Stuttgart, and Dresden had been laid waste by firebombs and firestorms. In Dresden mounds of bodies had to be bulldozed into mass graves or burned on huge makeshift grills, so great was the toll and the fear of epidemic disease. An American Army Air Corpsman flying low over the country at the end of the war could not spot streets or homes in Mannheim—only tossed dirt. "Aachen," he observed, "lay bleaching in the sun like bones on a desert." A disbelieving companion gazed at the pulverized land below and asked, "Where do the people live?"[10]

Hospitals, schools, and churches throughout Germany felt the war's fury. Fourteen of the nation's twenty-three universities were severely damaged. Transportation and communication sys-

7. Harry S. Truman, *Memoirs* (Garden City, N.Y., 1955–56; 2 vols.), I, p. 341.
8. Murphy, *Diplomat*, p. 257.
9. Clay, *Decision*, p. 21.
10. Quoted in W. D. Jacobs, "Where Do the People Live?" *Commonweal*, XLIII (January 18, 1946), 354.

tems were disrupted. Untreated sewage flowed into waterways, spreading disease. Water traffic on the Rhine River, which before the war had been greater than that of the Suez or Panama Canals, was now negligible; demolished bridges and sunken vessels blocked the artery. Industrial plants, once the marvel of Europe, lay prostrate. The Ruhr, which had produced 400,000 tons of coal a day, could manage only a paltry 25,000 in 1945. "If we had then realized the confusion and chaos which existed," General Clay wrote five years after the war, "we would indeed have thought ours a hopeless task."[11]

In Churchill's country the war claimed a frightful toll. Some observers after V-E Day made the grim observation that the Germans looked better fed and less ragged than the British. The air blitz which struck London, Coventry, and other cities in 1940–41, and then subsided somewhat, began anew in 1944 with German V-1 and V-2 rockets which indiscriminately pounded buildings and people. Major sections of London were badly mangled, turning that regal city into a shabby, battered replica of itself. The Foreign Office building lost most of its windows and doors, and No. 10 Downing Street had no windows and few tiles in place. After one attack, it took workmen six hours to free a woman from a tumbled row house on Stepney High Street. She was asked if she had a husband. "Yes," she snapped. "He's at the front, the dirty coward."[12]

The "front" constantly shifted with the fortunes of war, and few European nations were spared from marauding armies and death-dealing bombers. In Greece in 1945 a million people were homeless. About one-quarter of the nation's buildings were damaged or destroyed, and farm yields were down by 50 percent. One-third of all cattle were lost. Eighty percent of railway roll-

11. Clay, *Decision*, p. 16. For immediate postwar conditions in Germany, see *ibid.*, pp. 15–16, 31–32; Mayne, *Recovery*, pp. 35–45; Balfour and Mair, *Four-Power Control*, pp. 7–14; Jacobs, "Where Do the People Live?" pp. 354–355; David Irving, *The Destruction of Dresden* (New York, 1963).

12. Quoted in Marquis Childs, "London Wins the Battle," *National Geographic*, LXXXVIII(August 1945), 129. The material on Britain is drawn from *ibid.*, pp. 129–152; Balfour and Mair, *Four-Power Control*, p. 12; and Dilks, *Diaries of Cadogan*, p. 607.

ing stock and three-quarters of the ocean shipping fleet were incapacitated. Before leaving Greece the Germans blasted the walls of the Corinth Canal, filling it with 900,000 cubic yards of earth. The modern port facilities of Piraeus lay in ruins. Gravely undernourished people found hospitals overcrowded. Five hundred thousand registered cases of tuberculosis spelled epidemic. An American doctor who tried to work at the Athens Red Cross Hospital in early 1945, during an outbreak of civil war, found that the "operating room had been blown up with all the glass gone and even the surgical instruments had been melted by the magnesium bombs and were lying around in heaps of molten metal."[13]

In neighboring Yugoslavia the retreating Germans had devastated the countryside, causing starvation in some regions. Upon liberation only one of Yugoslavia's seven large power stations was operating, and the rails running through the Danube valley, which linked the nation to other European states, were rendered useless. In the Hungarian capital of Budapest, the splendor of the Hapburgs had given way inelegantly to the specter of death. All the bridges over the Danube were demolished, houses were flattened, and the 860-room royal palace of Maria Theresa and Franz Josef stood only as a maze of walls. In Austria German fires and Allied bombs had gutted 70 percent of the center of Vienna, not even sparing the seven-hundred-year-old St. Stephen's Cathedral. Women searched for sticks in the Vienna Woods, there being no coal for fuel. Elderly Viennese men and women looked pallid; young people were listless as they begged for GI rations. In Czechoslovakia and Italy, Prague and Rome had mercifully escaped large-scale devastation, but such blessings were rare. Italian agricultural production was down 50 percent. People in Naples clawed like cats through garbage cans for tidbits of food. Before abandoning that city, the Germans had wrecked the gas, electric, and water systems and put the torch to the university. In the Netherlands, 540,000 acres were flooded and Rotterdam was battered. As for France,

13. Paul K. French, "William E. Brown, Dean of UVM's Medical College, 1945–52: An Oral History Interview," *Vermont History*, XLI (Summer 1973), 170.

Paris had largely been spared, but almost 20 percent of the buildings in the entire country were destroyed—twice the number demolished in World War I. Ninety percent of French trucks were out of action, and much of the French fleet rested on the bottom of the harbor at Toulon.[14]

John Hersey, whose book *Hiroshima* was to expose the ghastly details of the Asian atomic holocaust, also witnessed the tragedy of Warsaw, Poland—"destroyed, systematically, street by street, alley by alley, house by house. . . . Nothing is left except a mockery of architecture." Travelling with a Polish officer who was returning from battle to his native city, Hersey watched as desperate Poles scratched at the flesh of a fallen army horse, quickly leaving a steaming skeleton. "God, my God, God," whispered the horrified officer.[15] Almost six million Poles died in World War II. Polish Jews had been deliberately exterminated, with the Auschwitz concentration camp setting barbaric records in human cremation. The cities of Gdynia, Danzig, and Stettin were mauled. In this predominantly agricultural nation, one-sixth of the farms were inoperable, 70 percent

14. For details of the destruction in Europe here and in succeeding paragraphs, see United Nations General Assembly, *Preliminary Report of the Temporary Sub-Commission on Economic Reconstruction of Devastated Areas* (London, 1946); UNRRA, European Regional Office, *Post-War Public Finance in Greece* (London, 1947), pp. 1–2; Francis F. Lincoln, *United States' Aid to Greece, 1947–1962* (Germantown, Tenn., 1975), p. 53; George Woodbridge *et al.*, *The History of the United Nations Relief and Rehabilitation Administration* (New York, 1950; 3 vols.), II, 94–97, 138–139; "Allies Enter Vienna," *Life*, XIX(September 3, 1945), 34; Thomas R. Henry, "Tale of Three Cities," *National Geographic*, LXXXVIII(December 1945), 641–669; "Building Damage and Reconstruction in France," *Monthly Labor Review*, LXI(November 1945), 925–929; R. G. Hawtrey, "The Economic Consequences of the War," in Arnold J. Toynbee, ed., *The Realignment of Europe* (London, 1955), pp. 36–51; Katharine Duff, "Italy," in *ibid.*, pp. 440–441; Mayne, *Recovery*, pp. 35–45; Gordon Wright, *The Ordeal of Total War* (New York, 1968), pp. 234–267; Alan S. Milward, *War, Economy and Society, 1939–1945* (Berkeley, Cal., 1977); John Horne Burns, *The Gallery* (New York, 1947); House of Representatives, Committee on International Relations, *Problems of World War II and Its Aftermath* (executive session hearings; historical series; Washington, D.C., 1976), Vol. II, Part 2, pp. 465–494.
15. John Hersey, "Home to Warsaw," *Life*, XVIII(April 9, 1945), 16, 19.

of the horses gone, and one-third of the cattle dead.[16] American Ambassador Arthur Bliss Lane flew into Warsaw on an Army C-47 in July 1945. The seven-mile trip from the airport to the center of the city gave him the "chill of deep depression:"

I could see only a handful of houses left unharmed; all others were bombed or gutted by fire. The smoky smell of long-dead fires hung in the air. The sickening sweet odor of burned human flesh was a grim warning that we were entering a city of the dead. . . . The scene was depressingly lacking in the normal bustle and movement of a city. . . . But the most terrible sight of all was that of the one-legged children.[17]

To the east the Ukraine ranked high in the gruesome tally of war losses. This area of 181,000 square miles, before the war a mainstay of the Soviet economy, with its large production of coal, pig iron, steel, and manganese, as well as farm goods, now lay denuded by the Soviet scorched-earth policy and the German rampage. Mines were blown up and flooded, the Dnieper Dam blasted, whole farm villages razed, tractors wrecked, and livestock massacred or driven off. The modern Zaporozhal steel plant near the Dnieper Dam was reduced to acres and acres of tangled debris. In the Brovary district alone, 12,099 out of 16,000 prewar farm buildings were destroyed. Famine and starvation were widespread in this drought-stricken region. The Soviet Socialist Republic of Byelorussia fared no better. Minsk looked like Warsaw. Five miles beyond that city, thirty-four pits held the corpses of 150,000 people murdered and buried by the Germans. The much fought-over province of Vitebsk counted 300,000 dead.

Correspondent Harrison Salisbury called Sevastopol "a city of the dead." Of the city's 15,000 houses, only 500 remained standing after the German retreat. "If a room has three walls and a ceiling," the mayor told Salisbury, "we count it in good shape."[18] Another reporter, Alexander Werth, passed through

16. For Poland, see Woodbridge, *UNRRA*, II, 200–202.
17. Arthur Bliss Lane, *I Saw Poland Betrayed* (Boston, c. 1948 [1965]), pp. 4, 9.
18. Quoted in Harrison Salisbury, *Russia on the Way* (New York, 1946), p. 318.

Istra, west of Moscow, and saw nothing but a "forest of chimney-stacks."[19] As for Stalingrad, American ambassador W. Averell Harriman viewed "a desert of broken brick and rubble, the survivors huddling in cellars or tar-paper shanties."[20] The people of Moscow looked haggard as they piled rubble. The domes of the Kremlin, blackened with war paint, still cut the skyline, but its occupants now governed a Russia which had suffered the awesome wartime loss of 15 to 20 million dead. Visiting Russia less than a year after the close of the war, the Secretary General of the United Nations found "the chaos of charred and twisted villages and cities . . . the most complete exhibit of destruction I have ever witnessed."[21]

Europe lost more than 30 million people in the Second World War. The grisly statistical gallery ranked Russia an uncontested first. Then came Poland with 5.8 million dead; Germany, with 4.5 million; Yugoslavia, 1.5 million, France, 600,000; Rumania, 460,000; Hungary, 430,000; Czechoslovakia, 415,000; Italy, 410,000; Britain, 400,000; and the Netherlands, 210,000. C. Day Lewis's "War Poem" read:

> They lie in the Sunday Street
> Like effigies thrown down after a fête
> Among the bare-faced houses frankly yawning revulsion,
> Fag ends of fires, litter of rubble, stale
> Confetti sprinkle of blood. . . .[22]

19. Werth, *Russia at War,* p. 353.
20. W. Averell Harriman and Elie Abel, *Special Envoy to Churchill and Stalin, 1941–1946* (New York, 1975), p. 257.
21. The foregoing details on the U.S.S.R. are taken from Diary, November 10, 1944, vol. 49, Henry L. Stimson Papers, Yale University Library; "First Monthly Report," by Marshall MacDuffie (Chief, UNRRA Mission to Ukraine), April 2, 1946, Box 59,000, UNRRA Records, United Nations Library, New York; Statement by Richard Scandrett, (n.d., but 1946), Box 58,000, UNRRA Records; Woodbridge, *UNRRA,* II, 231–232; Werth, *Russia at War,* pp. 350–353; John R. Deane, *The Strange Alliance* (New York, 1947), pp. 3–7; William McNeill, *America, Britain, Russia* (London, 1953), pp. 441n, 670; Thomas P. Whitney, *Russia in My Life* (London, 1963), pp. 65, 69.
22. In Joy Davidman, ed., *War Poems of the United Nations* (New York, 1943), p. 33.

As for the living, they had to endure food shortages, closed factories, idle fields, cold stoves, currency inflation, festering wounds. In West Germany alone, two million cripples hobbled about. Thirty-four percent of the Germans born in 1924 were badly mutilated in some way by 1945. The sad photographs of ill-clad, skeletal bodies struggling for life in Germany's concentration camps provided evidence enough of the human depredation. Displaced persons (DPs) provided another picture. "The wind will tell you what has come to us; /It rolls our brittle bones from pole to pole," went "The Refugees' Testament."[23] Many dazed refugees wandered helplessly through Europe, searching for relatives, for friends, for a livelihood, for a ride home. The words of British writer Richard Mayne have poignantly depicted the lives of Europe's survivors:

To many of the troops who first encountered them, the people in parts of Europe seemed a population of cripples, of women and children and the very old. Some were starving; some were sick with typhus or dysentery. . . . The survivors, gray-faced ghosts in parodies of clothing, trundled their salvaged belongings in homemade handcarts—rugs, threadbare overcoats, a kettle, an alarm clock, a battered toy. They waited at stand-pipes for a dribble of brown water; they queued for bread and potatoes; they rummaged for sticks and scraps. For them, this waste land of rubble, rags, and hunger was a prison without privacy or dignity; and like all prisons, it smelled. It smelled of dust, oil, gunpowder, and greasy metal; of drains and vermin; of decay and burning and the unburied dead.[24]

So it was in parts of Asia as well, where Japanese forces had been beaten back to their small imperial islands and finally battered with fire-bombs and two monumental atomic blasts. The lush vegetation of the Philippines and numerous Pacific islands was singed and burned, whole jungles disappearing. A British official who stopped at Okinawa remarked that it looked like the Somme after World War I. China had known population pressure, famine, and epidemics before the war. But Japanese plunder, the destruction of cities, disruption of vital agricultural production, and the displacement of its people increased the bur-

23. Frederick Brainin, "The Refugees' Testament," in *ibid.*, p. 6.
24. Mayne, *Recovery*, pp. 36–37.

dens that the Chinese had to bear in the postwar period. Hunan and Kwangsi were devastated. Along with Kwangtung, these provinces were visited by famine; millions suffered malnutrition and outright starvation. Cholera, plague, tuberculosis, smallpox, and malaria struck a population which had only 12,000 physicians—one for every 40,000 people. In 1938 the key dikes along the Yellow River—"China's Sorrow"—were blown up, killing thousands and flooding three million acres of fertile land. China's rivers now rampaged in the Spring and Summer through vulnerable villages. Manchuria's industrial plants were destroyed or dismantled, and China's small railroad network was a shambles. Some 1.32 million Chinese soldiers died; incalculable civilian losses were greater.[25] Kiang Ling's "The Chinese Refugee" captured the times:

> Weeping I left my loved hills;
> Now by this flat long river
> Wandering, homeless, fleeing, fearing . . .
> Wandering till what time?
> Fleeing to what clime?
> Today's riches are ashes tomorrow;
> In a moment joy turns into sorrow.
> How call this yours or mine,
> How rich and poor define?
> In the eyes of death and flame
> Rich and poor are all the same.[26]

For defeated Japan, the bitter results of imperial dreams could be measured in the loss of 2 million lives. Tokyo's population was reduced from 6.5 million to 3 million by war's end, and 700,000 of the city's buildings were destroyed. American planes had dropped napalm-filled bombs, engulfing the city in chemically induced firestorms which generated temperatures of up to

25. Woodbridge, *UNRRA*, II, 371–372, 388, 412–445; Pendleton Hogan, "Shanghai After the Japs," *Virginia Quarterly Review*, XXII (January 1946), 91–108; Arthur Bryant, *Triumph in the West* (Garden City, N.Y., 1959), p. 506; Immanuel C. Y. Hsü, *The Rise of Modern China* (New York, 1975; 2nd ed.), p. 736.
26. In Davidman, *War Poems*, pp. 54–55.

1,800°F. The odor of burning flesh drifted upwards, sickening the pilots who delivered the horrible punishment. In one savage attack alone, on May 23, 1945, 83,000 people died in what observers described as a mass burning. The fifteen-mile stretch between Yokohama and Tokyo, said an American officer who accompanied American general Douglas MacArthur to Japan, had become a "wilderness of rubble."[27] A light dust hung in the air, staining visitors' clothing. Wood-and-paper houses had been reduced to powdered ashes, factories to twisted metal. A shanty town of rusted, corrugated sheets and other junk ringed the capital city, its inhabitants reminding some observers of the Okies who trekked to California during the Great Depression— except that the Japanese scene was more emotionally debilitating. Only the downtown commercial district was free from the mounds of debris. One of the first American naval officers to arrive in the humbled Japanese city wrote to a friend that "I feel like a tramp who has become used to sleeping in a graveyard."[28] A British visitor, Lord Alanbrooke, also visited Tokyo: "Everywhere the same desolation; it must be seen to be believed."[29]

Hiroshima and Nagasaki were special cases, sharing and suffering a special fate. Hiroshima had been Japan's eighth largest city. A residential, commercial center of 250,000 people, it was singled out by American officials because it also housed regional military headquarters. Until August 6, 1945, a cloudless, warm day, Hiroshima had not had to endure large-scale American

27. William J. Sebald, *With MacArthur in Japan* (New York, 1965), p. 39.
28. Otis Carey, ed., *War-Wasted Asia: Letters, 1945–46* (Tokyo, 1975), p. 61.
29. Quoted in Bryant, *Triumph*, p. 507. Other information on Japan is located in *New York Times*, September 1, 1945; Douglas MacArthur, *Reminiscences* (New York, 1964), p. 280; Robert J. Donovan, *Conflict and Crisis* (New York, 1977), p. 69; Sebald, *With MacArthur*, pp. 39–41; Paul H. Clyde and Burton F. Beers, *The Far East* (Englewood Cliffs, N.J., 1975), pp. 414–415; Alfred C. Oppler, *Land Reform in Occupied Japan: A Participant Looks Back* (Princeton, N.J., 1976), p. 17; Peter Calvocoressi and Guy Wint, *Total War* (New York, 1972), Chs. 20–21.

bombing raids. But at 8:15 AM the crew of the *Enola Gay*, a specially outfitted B-29, unleashed "Little Boy," an atomic device packing the power of 20,000 tons of TNT. The bomb fell for fifty seconds and exploded about 2,000 feet above ground. A blinding streak of light raced across the sky; a tremendous boom punctuated the air. A huge, purplish cloud of dust, smoke, and debris shot 40,000 feet into the atmosphere. At ground level the heat became suffocating, the winds violent. Buildings instantly disintegrated. Shadows were etched in stone. Trees were stripped of their leaves. Fires erupted everywhere, and the sky grew dark. Survivors staggered toward water to quench their intense thirst. Skin peeled from burned bodies. A maimed resident, Dr. Michihiko Hachiya, noted that "no one talked, and the ominous silence was relieved only by a subdued rustle among so many people, restless, in pain, anxious, and afraid, waiting for something else to happen."[30] The toll: seventy to eighty thousand dead, an equal number wounded, and 81 percent of the city's buildings destroyed. Three days later the nightmare was repeated in Nagasaki, where at least 35,000 died. Upon hearing of the success of the world's first nuclear destruction of a city, President Truman remarked, "this is the greatest thing in history."[31]

Whether this historical judgment was accurate or not, the tragedy at Hiroshima was but one chapter in the story of massive, war-induced destruction. This story, with all its horrid details, must be catalogued not for its shock value but for its illustration of how large were the problems of the postwar world, how shaky the scaffolding of the international order. Hitler once said about his warmongering pursuits that "we may be destroyed, but if we are, we shall drag a world with us—a world in flames."[32] He partially succeeded, and World War II,

30. Michihiko Hachiya, *Hiroshima Diary* (Chapel Hill, 1955; trans. by Warner Wells), p. 6.
31. Truman, *Memoirs*, I, 421. For accounts of Hiroshima, see John Hersey, *Hiroshima* (New York, 1946); John Tolland, *The Rising Sun* (New York, 1970); William L. Laurence, *Dawn Over Zero* (New York, 1946).
32. Quoted in Hermann Rauschning, *The Voice of Destruction* (New York, 1940), p. 5.

like any war of substantial duration, served as an agent of conspicuous change, of revolution. The conflagration of 1939–45 was so wrenching, so total, so profound, that a world was overturned—not simply a material world of crops, buildings, and rails, not simply a human world of healthy and productive laborers, farmers, businessmen, and intellectuals, not simply a secure world of close-knit families and communities, not simply a military world of Nazi stormtroopers and Japanese kamikazis, but all that and more. The war also unhinged the world of stable politics, inherited wisdom, traditions, institutions, alliances, loyalties, commerce, and classes. When Acting Secretary of State Dean Acheson surveyed the problems facing American foreign policy in the postwar era, he saw as uppermost "social *disintegration*, political *disintegration*, the loss of faith by people in leaders who have led them in the past, and a great deal of economic *disintegration*."[33]

Leaders of all political persuasions, as they witnessed the immensity of the destruction, spoke of a new age without knowing its dimensions. The normal way of doing things now seemed inappropriate, although as creatures of the past, the survivors remained attached to ideas and institutions which seemed to provide security through familiarity. They sensed the seriousness and the enormity of the tasks of cleaning up the rubble, of putting the broken world back together again, of shaping an orderly international system. Yet it was evident, too, that few nations or individuals had the material resources, talent, and desire—the sheer energy, guts, and money—to mold a brave new world out of the discredited and crumbled old. If the reconstruction tasks seemed herculean, however, the opportunities appeared boundless for the ambitious, the hearty, and the caring. One vigorous, optimistic, well-intentioned, competitive voice sounded above the rubble that constituted London, Berlin, Warsaw, Minsk, and Tokyo. That voice echoed with power from the United States, the wartime "arsenal of democracy."

33. Transcript of Proceedings, "American Foreign Policy," June 4, 1947, Box 93, Records of the U.S. Mission to the United Nations, National Archives, Washington, D.C. Emphasis added.

At war's end President Truman declared a two-day national holiday. Horns, bells, and makeshift noisemakers sounded across the nation. Paraders in Los Angeles played leapfrog on Hollywood Boulevard; farther north, jubilant sailors broke windows along San Francisco's Market Street. In New York City tons of litter were tossed from the windows of skyscrapers on cheering crowds below. Stock market prices shot up. A five-year-old boy recorded the August 1945 moment: "This is the best year. The war is over. Two wars are over. Everyone is happy. Tin cans are rolling. Everything is confused. And little pieces of paper."[34] It was truly a happy time. Not only was the dying over, but the United States had emerged from the global conflict in the unique position of an unscathed belligerent. No bombs fell on American cities. No armies ravaged the countryside. No American boundaries were redrawn. Factories stood in place, producing goods at an impressive rate. In August, at the General Motors plant in Moraine, Ohio, shiny new Frigidaire refrigerators and airplane propeller blades moved along parallel assembly lines. Farms were rich in crops, and full employment during the war years had buoyed family savings. "The American people," remarked the director of the Office of War Mobilization and Reconversion, "are in the pleasant predicament of having to learn to live 50 percent better than they have ever lived before."[35]

Whereas much of Europe and Asia faced the massive task of "reconstruction," the United States faced "reconversion"—adjusting the huge war machine to peacetime purposes. Automobile plants had to convert production from tanks to cars, a delightful prospect for auto manufacturers, who knew that Americans were eager to spend their wartime earnings on consumer goods once again. With great pride Americans applauded their good fortune. They were different. They had no rubble to

34. Quoted in "The Talk of the Town," *New Yorker*, XXI(September 1, 1945), 17.
35. Quoted in Eric Goldman, *The Crucial Decade—and After, 1945–1960* (New York, 1971), p. 14.

clear. The Russians knew, said Josef Stalin in a grand under-statement, that "things are not bad in the United States."[36]

Americans had worries. Some feared that the sparkling pros-perity of the war years would dissipate in a postwar economic disaster. They remembered that military production, not Roose-velt's New Deal reform program, had pulled the United States out of the Great Depression of the 1930s. Would there be enough jobs for the returning GIs? They also suffered temporary shortages of many goods, sugar and gasoline among them, and resented the rationing which limited their economic freedom. "Hey, don'tche know there's a war on?" said clerks to anxious consumers. There were not enough houses to meet the needs of an expanding and mobile American population, which grew from 131 million to 140 million during the war years. The national debt skyrocked from $37 billion to $269 billion. The war cost the federal government $664 billion. Inflation threat-ened economic stability. At least 10 million American families lived in poverty. Still, these national pains, although arousing grumbles, seemed bearable or were played down. As *Fortune* magazine commented two months after V-J Day: "August 14, 1945, marked not only the war's end but the beginning of the greatest peacetime industrial boom in the world's history."[37]

Cold data justified *Fortune's* enthusiasm. The Gross National Product of the United States expanded from $90.5 bil-lion (1939) to $211.9 billion (1945). Steel production jumped from 53 million tons in 1939 to 80 million tons at the close of the war. American businessmen, cut off from rubber imports from the Dutch East Indies during the war, developed synthetic rubber, launching a new industry. New aluminum plants went up, and the aircraft industry, in infancy when Germany attacked Poland, became a major new business as well. In 1939 only 5,856 military and civil airplanes were turned out; but in 1945 the figure reached 48,912, a decline from the peak of over

36. Quoted in Daniel Yergin, *Shattered Peace* (Boston, 1977), p. 298.
37. "It's Wonderful," *Fortune,* XXXII(October 1945), 125.

95,000 in 1944. All told, over 300,000 aircraft rolled from American factories during the war—a figure far surpassing that of any other nation, including Germany and Japan combined. Employment in the aircraft industry swelled 1,600 percent. With its numerous aircraft factories, Southern California bustled, becoming a mecca for dreamers of wealth and adventure. Four hundred forty-four thousand people moved to Los Angeles during the war.

Workers' wages kept up with inflation during the war years. Women took jobs once held by men who were called to military duty. Unable to spend their abundant incomes on the shrinking supply of consumer items during the war, many Americans visited their banks. Total personal savings increased from $6.85 billion to $36.41 billion. Americans continued to spend for pleasure as well. The World Series of baseball played on, and films whirred at local theaters. Beaches beckoned vacationers. In the summer of 1944, as Europe and Asia reeled from the blasts of war, Americans flocked to resorts and racetracks. Betting in horse racing totalled a record-breaking $1.4 billion in 1945, even though the tracks were closed from January to May. Farmers enjoyed some of their best years of the twentieth century. Whereas in 1939 they counted 66 million head of cattle, by 1945 that figure reached 83 million. Agricultural output increased 15 percent. American universities also enjoyed improvements. Government contracts for scientific research went to the California Institute for Technology for rocket studies; Princeton received grants for ballistics research. In mid-1945 the Massachusetts Institute for Technology held government contracts worth $117 million. The GI Bill, which offered money to veterans for their college educations, promised higher enrollments.[38] Despite uncertainties about the future, life

38. For the United States during and at the close of World War II, see Jack Goodman, ed., *While You Were Gone* (New York, 1946); Department of Commerce, Bureau of the Census, *Historical Statistics of the United States* (Washington, D.C., 1975); Richard Polenberg, *War and Society: The United States, 1941–1945* (Philadelphia, 1972); Goldman, *Crucial Decade*; Richard E. Lingerman, *Don't You Know There's a War On?* (New York, 1970); John M. Blum, *V Was for Victory* (New

looked good to Americans, and after the hardships and setbacks of the depression decade, "the old self-confident America was coming into its stride again."[39] Wartime musicials like *Carousel* and *Oklahoma* caught the optimistic mood, and sluggers Joe DiMaggio and Ted Williams were heading home to reclaim their baseball fame.

When foreign delegates journeyed to San Francisco for the United Nations Conference in April of 1945, many crossed the territorial United States and could not help but notice the stark contrast with war-torn Europe and Asia. Soviet Foreign Minister V. M. Molotov once referred to statistics in the *World Almanac* to remind Americans about their uniqueness as prosperous survivors of the Second World War.[40] During a conversation with Stalin in 1944, the President of the United States Chamber of Commerce, Eric A. Johnston, citing the American example, lectured the Soviet leader about the need for a better distribution of goods in Russia. Stalin replied, " . . . but in order to distribute, there must be something to distribute."[41] Months before, at the Teheran Conference, Stalin had toasted the United States as a "country of machines," applauding its great productive capacity for delivering victory to the Allies.[42] Truman's words also bear repeating: "I was thankful that the United States had been spared the unbelievable devastation of this war."[43] Even the death count for American servicemen, about 400,000, appeared merciful when compared to staggering figures elsewhere. Indeed, the *Saturday Evening Post* editorialized in 1945 that "we Ameri-

York, 1976); Geoffrey Perrett, *Days of Sadness, Years of Triumph: The American People, 1939–1945* (Baltimore, 1974); John B. Rae, *Climb to Greatness: The American Aircraft Industry, 1920–1960* (Cambridge, Mass., 1968); "Picture of the Week," *Life*, XIX(August 13, 1945), 26–27; "The Meaning of Victory," *Life*, XIX(August 27, 1945), 34.

    39. Allan Nevins, "How We Felt About the War," in Goodman. *While*, p. 23.

    40. V. M. Molotov, *Problems of Foreign Policy: Speeches and Statements, April 1945–November 1948* (Moscow, 1949), pp. 209–214.

    41. Quoted in Eric A. Johnston, "My Talk with Joseph Stalin," *Reader's Digest*, XLV(October 1944), 3.

    42. Quoted in Harriman and Abel, *Special Envoy*, p. 277.

    43. Truman, *Memoirs*, I, 341.

cans can boast that we are not as other men are."[44] The war had overturned a world, and many Americans believed that they were now on top of it. A new international system for the postwar era was in the making.

44. "Americans Hope for U.S. of Europe," *Saturday Evening Post*, CCXVII(April 7, 1945), 112.

2

Conflict: The Postwar International System

IN THE RUBBLE-STREWN POSTWAR WORLD, international relations changed markedly from prewar interactions. Any historical period, such as the Cold War, is identified by a particular structure of relationships among the world's leading nations —by, in short, the international "system." Thus, the Napoleonic era of the late eighteenth and early nineteenth centuries was characterized by bipolarism, wherein France and Britain vied for world mastery, established alliances with lesser powers, frequently clashed in war, and managed far-flung empires. The period between the Congress of Vienna in 1815 and the outbreak of World War I in 1914, often called the era of Pax Britannica, was multipolar, with a number of leading actors on the international stage who preferred diplomatic negotiations to military combat and who deliberately set about to create a balance of power for the maintenance of a conservative, imperial, anti-revolutionary world.

Any international system is conflict-ridden. "Peace," after all, is a very abstract term, difficult to employ as a description of any era. "Anarchy" probably more aptly approximates historical reality. The attempts nations make to reduce the anarchy constitute our diplomatic history. Conflict is inherent in any international system simply because countries seldom share common goals, interests, or ideologies. Some nations are more powerful or influential than others and flaunt their superiority. Others may resist. Some countries are dependent upon others. Some have what others want—territory, food, water, minerals, labor, and a multitude of things over which peoples have squabbled for centuries. Great nations are always looking for friends who will join them in formal or informal alliances to check the growth of those states they consider unfriendly or potentially so. Small nations have to be wary of the major actors, who may cast longing eyes on them and exploit their vulnerability. Nations which may wish to remain "neutral" or unaligned are wooed or cajoled.

The leading powers, whether aligned or at loggerheads, watch one another suspiciously, on the assumption that in international politics, as in business, one can supposedly trust friends seldom, enemies never. Slight shifts in the distribution of power—of resources—arouse concern. What one government considers "defense," another labels "offense." The construction of a military base, the testing of a new weapon, a request to alter a boundary, the signing of a treaty—all can be defined as both defensive or offensive, depending upon one's point of view. A rifle is a defensive weapon if seen from the butt, but it is a weapon of attack if one is staring into the muzzle. Suspicion and fear, those ancient diseases, undermine trust and prompt counter-measures. Leaders may assume evil intentions on the part of other nations and plan for the worst. Governments feel compelled to match the decisions of those whom they assume to be adversaries. Failure to develop a new weapon, for example, might entail extreme risk, for an enemy might gain advantage by producing it. Hence, leaders often escalate the level of conflict and chances for war through exaggerated perceptions of danger. In short, there is always an expanding nation, and there are countries reacting to that expansion. Differences in goals among the several parties of the international system feed instability. The degree of conflict may vary, but there is always conflict. "This is a lawless world," University of Chicago Professor Herman Finer told a radio audience in 1947, "because it is a world without a common morality or a common superior. Nationalisms and moralities collide."[1]

Higher degress of conflict are reached when the international system undergoes significant change, when it metamorphoses into a new or revised system. Such was the case after World War II. Change, by definition, is destabilizing. Some postwar leaders, even though immersed in day-to-day decisionmaking, pondered the general characteristics of the international system. They knew that significant changes had altered the configuration of power. As participants in and shapers of a new age, they were "present at the creation."[2] But the outline of the new system was only vaguely evident. With the historian's advantage of hindsight, however, we can delineate the peculiar properties of the postwar world and suggest that the process of creating a new system out of the ashes of the discredited prewar system intensified the conflict inherent in any international structure.

Yet this view of systemic conflict cannot serve as a comprehensive explanation for the origins of the Cold War. For if the Soviet–American confrontation was simply the inevitable product of the conflict-ridden international system, there would be little purpose in studying the leaders, ideas, policies, or needs of individual nations, because events would be largely beyond their control. Under this interpretation the system would dictate antagonistic relations. It would not matter whether different personalities or different national policies existed. Few scholars, however, subscribe to this restricted analysis of history. We know that leaders made choices, even if they only dimly understood their consequences. Harry S. Truman, Winston Churchill, and Josef Stalin helped to create the international system to which they had to react. A complete history of the beginnings of the Cold War, then, must include not only the traits of the international system but also the dynamics of particular nations and

1. Herman Finer, in "What Are the Implications of President Truman's Speech?" *University of Chicago Round Table*, No. 469 (March 16, 1947), p. 8.

2. Dean Acheson, *Present at the Creation* (New York, 1969).

individuals. In this chapter a macroanalytic view will enable us to identify the opportunities and constraints which faced the major actors. Or, as Professor Bruce M. Russett has suggested, this level of analysis outlines the "menu" of world affairs—the choices available, as well as the limits of choice. It sketches the "big picture," so that the disparate components of the postwar system can be examined in proper relationship.[3] It helps us to determine which nations held real or potential power and why, ultimately, they moved toward restrictive spheres of influence and away from a community of interest and international cooperation.

Conflict in the postwar years was accentuated by wrenching changes in the international system—a redistribution of power and a departure from a Europe-centered world. Two nations emerged from the rubble of World War II to claim first rank. The competitive interaction between the United States and the Soviet Union—"like two big dogs chewing on a bone," said Senator J. William Fulbright—contributed to the bipolarism of the immediate postwar years.[4] "Not since Rome and Carthage," Dean Acheson observed, "had there been such a polarization of power on this earth."[5] This new bipolar structure replaced the

3. For discussions of the workings of the international system and the behavior of nations, see Raymond F. Hopkins and Richard W. Mansbach, *Structure and Process in International Politics* (New York, 1973); Robert W. Tucker, "The United States," in Steven L. Spiegel and Kenneth N. Waltz, eds., *Conflict in World Politics* (Cambridge, Mass., 1971), pp. 15–37; Robert J. Art and Robert Jervis, eds., *International Politics: Anarchy, Force, Imperialism* (Boston, 1973); Alan Henrikson, "The Map as an 'Idea': The Role of Cartographic Imagery During the Second World War," *American Cartographer*, II(April 1975), 19–53; Arnold Wolfers, *Discord and Collaboration* (Baltimore, 1962); Marshall R. Singer, *Weak States in a World of Power* (New York, 1972); James Paul Warburg, "The United States and the World," address, April 3, 1948, Harry S. Truman Papers, Harry S. Truman Library; John H. Herz, *International Politics in the Atomic Age* (New York, 1959); Bruce M. Russett, *Power and Community in World Politics* (San Francisco, 1974); Hans J. Morgenthau, *In Defense of the National Interest* (New York, 1951) and *Politics Among Nations* (New York, 1967; 4th ed.).
4. Quoted in Yergin, *Shattered Peace*, p. 223.
5. Quoted in Joseph M. Jones, *The Fifteen Weeks* (New York, 1955), p. 141.

multipolar system of the 1930s, wherein at least six nations were active, influential participants. By the late 1940s, decisions made in Washington, D.C. and Moscow often determined whether people in other nations voted, where they lived, and how much they ate. The nations which had tried to wield such authority in the 1930s had fallen from their elevated status. Japan, Italy, and Germany were defeated and occupied; England, nearly bankrupt, dependent, and unable to police its empire, was reduced to a resentful second-rate power; France, much of whose territory had been held by the Germans during the war, was still suffering from unstable politics and no longer mustered international respect.

The abrupt removal of Germany and Japan from positions of high authority in international relations created power vacuums in Europe and Asia. The United States and Soviet Russia, eager to fulfill their visions of the postwar world and to seize opportunities for extending their respective influence, were attracted to these vacuums. With the old barriers to American and Soviet expansion gone, Russia and America clashed over occupation policies in Germany, Italy, Japan, Austria, and Korea. They squabbled over which political groups should replace the Nazi regimes in Eastern Europe. The filling of gaps or vacuums in any system is a natural process. In the postwar period the gaps were huge and worldwide, inviting a high degree of competition and conflict.[6]

Another change wrought by World War II was the destruction of the economic world. The war cut an ugly scar across Europe and Asia, but bypassed one major nation, the United States. "If Hitler succeeds in nothing else," mused OSS officer Allen Dulles, "like Samson, he may pull down the pillars of the temple and leave a long and hard road of reconstruction."[7] The postwar task was forbidding. Not only did cities have to be

6. For the dynamics of expansion, see Raymond Tanter and Richard H. Ullman, eds., *Theory and Policy in International Relations* (Princeton, 1972), pp. 80–122 and Robert W. Tucker, *The Radical Left and American Foreign Policy* (Baltimore, 1971), pp. 89–90.

7. Quoted in Lloyd C. Gardner, *Architects of Illusion* (Chicago, 1970), p. 54.

rebuilt, factories opened, people put back to work, rails repaired, rivers and roads made passable, and crop yields increased, but the flow of international commerce and finance had to be reestablished if nations were to raise through exports the revenue needed to buy the imports required for recovery. Many old commercial and financial patterns had been broken and, given the obstacle of economic wreckage, new exchanges were difficult to establish. Where would Germany's vital coal and steel go? Would industrial Western Europe and agricultural Eastern Europe recreate old commercial ties? Would the restrictive trade practices of the 1930s, especially the tariff barriers, continue into the 1940s? Would subservient colonies continue to serve as sources of rich raw materials? Could international agreements and organizations curb economic nationalism? Would trade be conducted on a multilateral, "open door" basis, as the United States preferred, or by bilateral or preferential methods, as many others, such as Britain and Russia, practiced? The answers helped to define the international system of the post-1945 era. These issues held more importance than simple economics, for leaders recognized that the economic disorders of the 1930s and the far-reaching impact of the Great Depression contributed to political chaos, aggression, and war. The new international system, it was hoped, would create stable economic conditions which would facilitate the development of pacific international relations. Yet the very efforts to realize these hopes engendered conflict.

World War II also bequeathed domestic political turmoil to its survivors. The regimes of the 1930s, now discredited, vied with insurgent groups for the governing power in many states. Socialists, Communists, and other varieties of the political left, many of whom had fought in the underground resistance movements and had thus earned some popular respect, challenged the more entrenched, conservative elites, many of whom had escaped into exile when the German armies rolled into their countries. In Poland, the Communist, Soviet-endorsed Lublin Poles challenged the political standing of the Poles who had fled to London. The conservative Dutch government-in-exile watched warily as leftist resistance groups gradually built a popular following. Political confusion in the Netherlands was heightened by the wartime loss of voting lists. In Greece a coalition of leftists in the National Liberation Front (EAM) vigorously resisted the return to power of a British-created government and the unpopular Greek monarchy of King George. In France Charles de Gaulle vied for power with the Communists. In China the civil war, which had raged for years between the Communists of Mao Tse-tung and the Nationalists of Chiang Kai-shek, flared up again at the close of the war. Yugoslavia was the scene of political battle between Josip Broz Tito's Partisans and a group headed by Dr. Ivan Subasic of the London emigré government, which in turn suffered strained ties with King Peter. Moreover, in the occupied nations of Germany, Austria, and Korea, the victors created competitive zones, postponing the creation of central governments. In the defeated countries of Japan and Italy, American officials decided who would rule, whereas in parts of Eastern Europe, Soviet officials placed Communists in positions of authority.

The major powers, in short, intervened abroad to exploit the political opportunities created by the destructive scythe of World War II. The stakes seemed high. A change in a nation's political orientation might presage a change in its international alignment. The great powers tended to ignore local conditions which might mitigate against alignment with an outside power. Americans feared that a leftist or Communist Greece would look to the East and permit menacing Soviet bases on Greek territory or open the door to a Soviet naval presence in the Mediterranean. The Russians dreaded a conservative anti-Soviet Polish government led by the London faction, for it might prove so weak and so hostile to Moscow as to permit a revived Germany to send stormtroopers once again through the Polish corridor into the heart of Russia. A Communist China, thought Americans, might align with Russia; a Nationalist China would remain in the American camp. All in all, the rearranging of political structures *within* nations drew the major powers into competition, accentuating the conflict inherent in the postwar international system.

If the war threw politics into chaos, it also hastened the disintegration of colonial and informal empires. The Japanese
movement into French Indochina and their drive for Dutch East
Indies oil had led to Pearl Harbor in 1941. The initially successful Japanese expansion had the effect of demonstrating to many
Asian nationalists that their white imperial masters could be
defeated. Some nationalists collaborated during the war with
their Asian brethren from Tokyo, and the Japanese, in need of
administrators to manage occupied areas, trained and armed
some native leaders. Japan granted Burma considerable auton-
omy in 1942, for example, and after the war the Burmese were
determined not to return to a position of subservience to Great
Britain. At the end of the war, the European powers, exhausted
and financially hobbled, had to struggle to reestablish mastery
over rebellious colonies. The appeal of the principle of self-determination, still echoing from the days of Woodrow Wilson and
given new emphasis by the Atlantic Charter of 1941, was far-
reaching.

No empire seemed immune to disintegration. The United
States granted the Philippines independence in 1946. The British, worn low by the war and by the challenges of nationalist
groups demanding independence, retreated from India (and
Pakistan) in 1947 and from Burma and Ceylon in 1948. Israel,
carved out of British-governed Palestine, became a new independent state in 1948. The British also found it difficult to maintain their sphere of influence in Iran, Greece, and Egypt and
began retreats from those politically unsteady states. The French
attempted to hold on to Indochina, where nationalist forces led
by Ho Chi Minh had declared an independent Vietnam. Bloody
battle ensued, leading ultimately to French withdrawal in 1954.
The Dutch also decided to fight, but after four debilitating years
of combat, they pulled out of Indonesia in 1949. The defeated
Japanese were forced to give up their claims to Formosa and
Korea, as well as Pacific island groups. Italy departed from
Ethiopia and lost its African colonies of Tripolitania (Libya)
and Eritrea. Lebanon, Syria, and Jordan, areas once managed by

Europeans, gained independence in 1943, 1944, and 1946, respectively.

The world map, as after World War I, was redrawn. The emergence of so many new states, and the instability associated with the transfer of authority, shook the very foundations of the international system. Power was being redistributed. In varying degrees, Russia and America competed for the allegiance of the new governments, meddled in colonial rebellions, and generally sought to exploit opportunities for an extension of their influence. Again, the stakes seemed high. The new nations could serve as strategic bases, markets for exports, sources of vital raw materials, sites for investments, and votes in international organizations. States such as India, which chose nonalignment in the developing Cold War, were wooed with foreign aid and ideological appeals. In the case of Indochina, the powers supported different sides: Washington backed the ruling French, and Moscow endorsed Ho and his insurgents.

As one United States government study noted, the disintegration of empires, especially the withdrawal of the British from their once vast domain, created an "over-all situation of near chaos" in the international system. In some areas, such as Southeast Asia, it meant a "new balance of power." The upheaval was fundamental: "Old values are being changed and new ones sought. New friendships are being formed."[8] The international system creaked and swayed under this unsettled burden.

Conflict also sprang from efforts to launch a new international organization to replace the defunct League of Nations. At

8. "Appraisal of U.S. National Interests in South Asia," SANACC 360/14, March 30, 1949, Box 65, State-War-Navy Coordinating Committee (SWNCC) Records, Records of Interdepartmental and Intradepartmental Committees, Diplomatic Branch, National Archives. For the disintegration of empires, see Stewart C. Easton, *The Rise and Fall of Western Colonialism* (New York, 1964); Rupert Emerson, *From Empire to Nation* (Cambridge, Mass., 1960); Lisle Rose, *Roots of Tragedy* (Westport, Conn., 1976); Gabriel Kolko, *The Politics of War* (New York, 1968); Rudolf von Albertini, *Decolonization* (Garden City, N.Y., 1971).

the Dumbarton Oaks Conference in 1944, the Allies initiated plans for a United Nations Organization. The United States, Britain, and Russia were its chief architects, and the institution they created at the San Francisco Conference from April to June of 1945 reflected their insistence on big-power domination. They agreed upon a veto power for the five "permanent members" of the Security Council (Britain, Russia, United States, France, and China) and assigned the General Assembly, the forum for smaller nations, a subordinate status. Nevertheless, because each of the Allies recognized that the new international body was potentially an instrument, through bloc voting, of one nation's foreign policy, they argued. Churchill crudely complained that China, hardly a "great" power, would be a "faggot vote on the side of the United States," and Russia protested that France would simply represent a British vote.[9] "China was a joke," remarked State Department veteran John Hickerson, "a FDR joke."[10] Because Britain could marshall the votes of several of its Commonwealth countries and the United States could count on most of the Latin American nations in the General Assembly, the conferees at the Yalta Conference of early 1945 granted Russia three votes, in order to alter somewhat the glaring imbalance.

Such compromise, however, broke down at the San Francisco Conference. Membership applications from Argentina and Poland produced heated differences. Against vehement Soviet objections Argentina, which had declared war against Germany at the last minute and which some critics considered a "fascist" nation, gained membership after the United States backed its application and the nations of the Western Hemisphere voted "yes" as a bloc. Yet when Lublin-led Poland, not yet reorganized according to the American interpretation of the Yalta accords, applied for entry, the United States voted "no," and the conference denied Poland a seat. Moscow railed at this, charging

9. Churchill is quoted in Diane Shaver Clemens, *Yalta* (New York, 1970), p. 48.
10. John D. Hickerson Oral History Interview, Harry S. Truman Library, Independence, Missouri.

a double standard. The United Nations Organization, which held its first session in January of 1946, thus began amidst controversy. Rather than serving as a stabilizing force in the postwar international system, the United Nations early became a source of conflict, a verbal battleground for the allegiance of world opinion, a vehicle for condemnatory resolutions, a largely United States–dominated institution, and a graveyard for idealistic hopes—in short, part of a "masquerade peace."[11]

The postwar international system suffered, too, from the destabilizing effect of the new atomic bomb. The "most terrible weapon ever known in human history," Secretary of War Henry L. Stimson quietly told the President, unsettled the world community, for it was an agent of massive human destruction, and "in a world atmosphere already extremely sensitive to power, the introduction of this weapon has profoundly affected political considerations in all sections of the globe."[12] Nations which possessed "the bomb" seemed to hold an advantage in international politics, for it could serve as a deterrent against an adversary as well as a means to annihilate an enemy. When combined with air power and a long-range delivery capability, it also hurdled geographical boundaries, rendering them useless as protective elements in a nation's security shield. With the perfecting of air war in World War II, "the roof blew off the territorial state."[13] As General Douglas MacArthur remarked after the atomic explosions: "Well, this changes warfare!"[14] The prospect of nuclear annihilation bothered everybody, but the United States was especially concerned about nuclear proliferation, which meant the loss of its atomic monopoly.

A question dogged the peacemakers: How were they to con-

11. For disputes over and in the United Nations, see Thomas M. Campbell, *Masquerade Peace: America's UN Policy, 1944–1945* (Tallahassee, 1973); Robert A. Divine, *Second Chance* (New York, 1967); Thomas M. Campbell and George C. Herring, eds., *The Diaries of Edward R. Stettinius, Jr., 1943–1946* (New York, 1975).
12. Henry L. Stimson and McGeorge Bundy, *On Active Service in Peace and War* (New York, 1947), pp. 634–643.
13. Herz, *International Politics*, p. 104.
14. Quoted in Yergin, *Shattered Peace*, p. 120.

trol the development, spread, and use of atomic energy? There had been arms races before, and ineffective disarmament conferences in the 1920s and 1930s, but the postwar nuclear race was conducted at a far different and more dangerous level. The atomic bomb was the "absolute weapon," not only more violent but also capable of speedy delivery, rapid retaliation, and immediate cataclysm.[15] Challenging the American monopoly, the Soviet Union successfully produced its own bomb in 1949. As the two bickering major powers groped for ways in which to deal with "the bomb" and undertook their atomic development programs, others held their breath. One observer suggested that a Soviet–American war "might not end with *one* Rome but with *two* Carthages."[16] The atomic bomb, uncontrolled, envied, copied, and brandished, became a major obstacle to a peaceful, orderly postwar international system.

The shrinkage of the world and the growth of a global outlook must be included in any estimation of the impact of World War II on the international system. Geography had not changed, but ways of moving across it and of thinking about it had. Improvements in transportation, especially in aviation, brought nations closer to one another. The world seemed more compact and accessible. People had to think now not only in traditional land miles but also in flying hours. In a popularization for school children, N. L. Englehardt, Jr. urged his young readers to think "air thoughts" and titled one of his chapters "How the World Has Shrunk."[17] Because the Atlantic Ocean could be traversed easily and quickly, that once-prominent barrier between the Old and New Worlds disappeared. As America was brought closer to Europe and the world, American strategic thinking expanded as well. In the world contracted by science, events in Greece or Iran or China held greater significance than ever before for American security. The Japanese attack upon Pearl Harbor, accomplished after crossing 3,500 miles of the Pacific Ocean,

15. Bernard Brodie, ed., *The Absolute Weapon* (New York, 1946).
16. Harold D. Lasswell, *Power and Personality* (New York, 1948), p. 180.
17. N. L. Englehardt, Jr., *Toward New Frontiers of Our Global World* (New York, 1943), p. 10.

had proved that great distances no longer served as protectors of security. "If you imagine two or three hundred Pearl Harbors occurring all over the United States," prophesied Assistant Secretary of State A. A. Berle, "you will have a rough picture of what the next war might look like. . . ."[18] Observers began to speak not only of an "atomic age," but of an "air age" and a "global age." The global war of 1939–45 had helped spawn a postwar globalism—an international interdependence. "The entire relations of the United States with the world," declared Dean Acheson, "are a seamless web. . . ."[19] Geographical isolation was gone with the past. Stimson perceived that the United States could never again "be an island to herself. No private program and no public policy, in any sector of our national life can now escape from the compelling fact that if it is not framed with reference to the world, it is framed with perfect futility."[20]

United States Chief of Staff General George C. Marshall typified strategic reconsiderations. "For probably the last time in the history of warfare those ocean distances were a vital factor in our defense. We may elect again to depend on others and the whim and error of potential enemies, but if we do we will be carrying the treasure and freedom of this great Nation in a paper bag." Because frontiers had been extended, because nations were brought nearer one another, and because the world had shrunk, the major powers coveted bases far from home, much as the United States had sought and acquired bases in the Caribbean in the early twentieth century to protect the Panama Canal. "We are now concerned with the peace of the entire world," said Marshall.[21] Two years later President Truman described a

18. Quoted in Joseph Jones, *A Modern Foreign Policy for the United States* (New York, 1944), p. 25.

19. Transcript of Proceedings, "American Foreign Policy," June 4, 1947, Box 93, Records of the U.S. Mission to the United Nations.

20. Stimson and Bundy, *On Active Service*, p. 652. For a very useful discussion of the global perspective, see Henrikson, "Map as an 'Idea.'" See also *Foreign Relations, 1946*, I, 1161, 1166; James Eayers, *In Defence of Canada: Peacemaking and Deterrence* (Toronto, 1972), pp. 322, 332; *Department of State Bulletin*, XIII(November 4, 1945), 709.

21. Quoted in Michael S. Sherry, *Preparing for the Next War: American Plans for Postwar Defense, 1941–45* (New Haven, 1977), pp. 200–202.

"much smaller earth—an earth whose broad oceans have shrunk and whose national protections have been taken away by new weapons of destruction."[22] In a similar vein, a Joint Chiefs of Staff report of late 1947 looked ten years into the future and predicted a "continuing shrinkage of the world from the accelerated pace of technological progress."[23] In short, a new aspect of the postwar international system was the interdependence or intertwining of events in all parts of the world, thereby drawing great powers into confrontations as never before. Globalism insured conflict.

Such was the postwar international system—with its opportunities and constraints, with its characteristics insuring conflict. The makers of the peace sought to reduce the conflict, but their decisions exacerbated it.

22. Department of State, *The Development of Foreign Reconstruction Policy* (Washington, D.C., 1947), p. 12.
23. "Estimate of Probable Development in the World Political Situation Up to 1957," Joint Strategic Plans Committee, JSPC 814/3, December 11, 1947, Box 11, Central Decimal File 092, Joint Chiefs of Staff Records, Modern Military Branch, National Archives.

3

Spheres: The Quest for Influence, 1944-50

PORTLY FOREIGN SECRETARY Ernest Bevin was irritated and contemplative. He complained to Secretary of State James F. Byrnes in a private meeting on December 16, 1945, that the Russians were attempting to undermine British interests in the Middle East. Even more, the Soviets were becoming entrenched in Eastern Europe. The emerging postwar international system, Bevin ruminated, was "drifting into the position of 'three Monroes.'" Like Britain in the Middle East and Russia in Eastern Europe, the United States had its "Monroe," or sphere of influence, in the Western Hemisphere and was now "extending it to the Pacific." Byrnes perked up, alert to any suggestion that his nation was behaving like other great powers in coveting a sphere of influence. The United States, retorted the American Secretary, "only wished to establish bases for security purposes in [Pacific] islands many of which were uninhabited."[1] That lame answer certainly did not separate the United States from other large nations; if anything, Byrnes demonstrated that the United States, for its own reasons, also sought to expand and secure its sphere of influence.

Yet Americans believed they were different—or at least they would not admit they behaved like Europeans. In 1823 the

1. *Foreign Relations, 1945*, II, 629; "A Conversation at the United States Ambassador's Residence, Moscow, on 17th December, 1945," CAB 133/82, Cabinet Records, Public Record Office, London, England.

Monroe Doctrine itself had striven to distinguish between the crass, monarchical Old World and the superior republicanism of the New, suggesting that the latter practiced a higher morality in international relations. Monroe's message held that the United States would not interfere in the affairs of Europe and that Europe must keep its hands off the Western Hemisphere. "The trouble with these people," Lord Halifax remarked about Americans in early 1945, "is that they are so much the victim of labels: 'Power Politics, Spheres of Influence, Balance of Power, etc.' As if there was ever such a sphere of influence agreement as the Monroe Doctrine!"[2] The point was well-taken: the Monroe Doctrine became invested with self-interest on behalf of a supreme United States position in the Western Hemisphere. Still, American diplomats in the first few postwar years seldom admitted the self-interest of their own sphere of influence; they spoke instead of an open international system characterized by the self-professed noble traits of the New World. By 1947, however, they had become more frank and more public about the existence of spheres and the importance of enlarging and protecting an American sphere of influence. In 1949, during the creation of the North Atlantic Treaty Organization, it was a common assumption that the United States was extending the Monroe Doctrine to Western Europe.

Indeed, as the two major antagonists of the postwar era, America and Russia, became caught up in the instability of the new international system and increasingly clashed over the making of the peace, they did what countries had done for centuries: They built competing spheres of influence. They sought friends; they built alliances; they put up fences; they drew lines; they charged each other with trying to foul the peace by meddling in the other's sphere. Gradually, beginning soon after V-E Day, nations gravitated toward or were pulled toward the American or Soviet spheres. Countries which did not choose sides felt the constant pressure of the superpowers. Thus, only three years after World War II, two camps dominated global

2. Quoted in Yergin, *Shattered Peace*, p. 61.

politics and the Cold War assumed "the character of position warfare."[3]

A "sphere of influence" refers to a grouping of states over which a major power wields authority or hegemony to such an extent that the influenced states usually give up some degree of their sovereignty to the influencing nation. The dominating state often acts unilaterally in its sphere, resisting or avoiding international sanctions. A large nation seeks to build and defend a "sphere of action," as Churchill called it, to provide security, to gain economic advantages through trade, investment, and raw materials exploitation, and to satisfy nationalist or ideological ambitions.[4] The hegemonic power exercises its authority through defense pacts, selection or imposition of local officials, positioning of troops, naval demonstrations, development of military bases, attachment of advisers to local institutions, commercial links, trade treaties, loans, and, finally, threats designed to force compliance. In short, influence may be exerted directly or indirectly. A sphere is in essence posted with a "keep out" sign, a warning to others that the major power has claimed special interests in the region. Spheres may be tightly closed or they may be porous, permitting other large nations to conduct reasonable, but not exploitative, relations within the sphere.[5]

Spheres of influence, of course, have had a long history. In the twentieth century, for example, the United States created a sphere in Latin America through continuation of the "hands-off"

3. Adam B. Ulam, *Expansion and Coexistence: Soviet Foreign Policy, 1917–73* (New York, 1974; 2nd ed.), p. 437.

4. Francis L. Lowenheim, Harold D. Langley, and Manfred Jonas, eds., *Roosevelt and Churchill: Their Secret Wartime Correspondence* (New York, 1975), p. 540.

5. For the traits of spheres of influence, see Geddes W. Rutherford, "Spheres of Influence: An Aspect of Semi-Suzerainty," *American Journal of International Law*, XX(April 1926), 300–325; Frederick L. Schuman, "Spheres of Influence," *Encyclopedia of the Social Sciences* (New York, 1944; 15 vols.), XIV, 297–299; Walter Lippmann, *U.S. War Aims* (Boston, 1944); "Sphere of Influence Arrangements Among the European Powers, 1871–1945," Office of Intelligence Research Report No. 4693, June 30, 1948, Box 8, Charles Bohlen Files, Department of State Records, National Archives.

principle of the Monroe Doctrine, political interferences like the Platt Amendment in Cuba and the Roosevelt Corollary in the Caribbean, military interventions in Haiti and Nicaragua, among others, lucrative trade and investment ties, and Pan-Americanism. The lecture that American Secretary of State Richard Olney delivered to the British during the Venezuelan controversy in 1895 typified great-power thinking: "Today the United States is practically sovereign on this continent, and its fiat is law upon the subjects to which it confines its interposition." The United States was "master of the situation and practically invulnerable as against any or all other powers."[6] The British themselves held sway over an elongated sphere of influence that stretched through the Mediterranean to the Persian Gulf and into Asia. In the 1930s Japan declared a "Greater East Asia Co-Prosperity Sphere" and cut a path through China into the East Indies and Indochina. Also during the depression decade, Hitler's Germany drew the Eastern European states—the "satellites"—into its orbit. The Nazi-Soviet pact of 1939, which partitioned Poland, also reflected the evident prewar politics of spheres.

During the Second World War, President Franklin D. Roosevelt seemed to be contemplating a postwar system of loose spheres, although his public rhetoric, laced with Wilsonian references, cast doubt on the practices of the past. The Atlantic Charter, which he and Churchill wrote in 1941, echoed Woodrow Wilson's lofty appeal for self-determination, the open door, and disarmament. Secretary of State Cordell Hull, who felt more deeply about these principles than did Roosevelt, stood foursquare against spheres of influence. Upon his return from the Moscow Conference in 1943, Hull told Congress that with a new postwar international organization "there will no longer be need for spheres of influence, for alliance, for balance of power, or any other of the special arrangements through which, in the unhappy past, the nations strove to safeguard their security or to promote their interests."[7]

Yet Roosevelt, at the same time, was envisioning a world of

6. *Foreign Relations, 1895*, Part I, p. 558.
7. Cordell Hull, *Memoirs* (New York, 1948; 2 vols.), II, 1314–1315.

"four policemen" (United States, Russia, Great Britain, and China) who would manage the international system on the basis of big-power politics.[8] After all, the Atlantic Charter, said Roosevelt, was just "a beautiful idea."[9] He thought more concretely, recognizing that spheres would in fact exist after the war. In February 1944, he informed Churchill that the United States would not "police" postwar France, because "France is your baby. . . ."[10] Several months later he wrote to Hull about Germany: "We have to remember that in their occupied territory [the Russians] will do more or less what they wish. We cannot afford to get into a position of merely recording protests on our part unless there is some chance of some of the protests being heeded."[11] The President wanted the Russians to hold elections in Eastern Europe, but he realized that the results would reflect the Russian desire for "friendly" governments. Roosevelt thus was paying deference in principle to Wilsonian democracy but in substance was endorsing spheres.

In the Spring of 1944, the British, surely sensing Roosevelt's proclivities but acting upon their own interests, asked the United States to approve a scheme wherein London would "take the lead" in Greece, and Moscow would do likewise in Rumania. Ambassador to the United States Lord Halifax saw no reason why the United States should object, he told Hull, for "we follow the lead of the United States in South America as far as possible."[12] Hull strongly dissented, but Roosevelt accepted a three-month trial. In October, Churchill journeyed to Moscow. Spheres of influence were very much on his mind. With Stalin he struck a bargain. In Rumania, they agreed, Russia would hold 90 percent predominance; in Greece, Britain would enjoy 90 percent influence; in Bulgaria, Russia would have 75 percent;

8. Robert A. Divine, *Roosevelt and World War II* (Baltimore, 1969), pp. 58–65; Herbert Feis, *Churchill, Roosevelt, Stalin* (Princeton, 1957), pp. 270–271.

9. Quoted in Gardner, *Architects of Illusion*, p. 52.

10. *Foreign Relations, 1944*, I, 166.

11. Quoted in Robert L. Messer, "Paths Not Taken: The United States Department of State and Alternatives to Containment, 1945–1946," *Diplomatic History*, I(Fall, 1977), 303n.

12. Quoted in Kolko, *Politics of War*, p. 142.

and in both Yugoslavia and Hungary, Britain and Russia would share authority on a 50–50 basis.[13] This frank if unenforceable division threw Hull into a funk, but Roosevelt did not protest. Churchill and Stalin had taken one precaution: They had deleted any mention of "dividing into spheres," because the Americans might be shocked.[14]

Similarly the phrase did not receive much currency at the Yalta Conference in February 1945, but the results bespoke it. With the spirit of compromise prevailing, the British, American, and Russian conferees, seeking to perpetuate their wartime cooperation, dismembered Germany into four zones, giving one to France. The Soviets received some Asian territory, partial control of Chinese railroads, and virtual recognition of its hand-picked Polish government headed by the Communists from Lublin. The United States earned a pledge from Russia that it would sign a treaty of friendship and alliance with America's client, Chiang Kai-shek. Furthermore, Churchill, Stalin, and Roosevelt agreed to establish a new world organization which also smacked of spheres of influence. The five "permanent" members of the Security Council alone were to have the veto, giving them supreme power in the institution. Frankly recognizing that Russia would be outvoted by two spheres, the United States–dominated Latin American nations and the British Commonwealth, the leaders at Yalta granted the Soviet Union three votes in the General Assembly. Under a provision for "territorial trusteeship," it was evident that former League of Nations mandates and areas detached from the losers of World War II would fall under the authority of the large-power victors. As created at San Francisco in April, the United Nations Organization reflected this trend toward spheres; indeed, Articles 51 and 52 permitted regional defense pacts.

Perhaps to blunt the conspicuous spheres of influence char-

13. Winston S. Churchill, *Triumph and Tragedy* (Boston, 1953), p. 227.
14. Quoted in Albert Resis, "The Churchill-Stalin 'Percentages' Agreement on the Balkans, Moscow, October 1944, *American Historical Review*, LXXXIII(April 1978), 372.

acter of the Yalta accords, the Big Three penned the "Declaration of Liberated Europe," a grand restatement of the Atlantic Charter for the "well-being of all mankind." The Allies pledged to assist European states to conduct "free elections."[15] Yet Churchill insisted that the reference to the Charter in the Declaration did not apply to the British Empire, and Roosevelt seems to have viewed the "free elections" pledge as more a sop to American public opinion than a hard and fast diplomatic position.[16] Two months after the conference, Ambassador to Russia W. Averell Harriman summed up Soviet views: "Stalin and Molotov considered at Yalta that by our willingness to accept a general wording on the declarations on Poland and liberated Europe, by our recognition of the need of the Red Army for security behind its lines, and of the predominant interest of Russia in Poland as a friendly neighbor and as a corridor to Germany, we understood and were ready to accept Soviet policies already known to us."[17] As for Asia, historian Akira Iriye has suggested that a new "Yalta system" emerged to replace "the long period of Anglo–Japanese domination, which had been followed by Japan's determination to establish a new order, with a situation in which the United States and the Soviet Union divided the region into spheres of predominance. . . ."[18]

Other wartime decisions fuelled the creation of spheres of influence. The armistice agreements in Eastern Europe placed Soviet officers in command of the Allied Control Commissions; British and American officials exercised authority in Italy; in Japan the United States took the leadership role. At the Potsdam Conference in July 1945, the great powers took another step toward distinctive spheres. Unable to agree on a reparations bill for defeated Germany, they decided that reparations would largely be taken from their respective zones. Would not the

15. *Foreign Relations, Yalta*, p. 972.
16. Clemens, *Yalta*, p. 263; John L. Gaddis, *The United States and the Origins of the Cold War, 1941–1947* (New York, 1972), pp. 163–164.
17. *Foreign Relations, 1945*, V, 821–822.
18. Akira Iriye, *The Cold War in Asia* (Englewood Cliffs, N.J., 1974), p. 96.

agreement "mean that each country would have a free hand in
their own zones and would act entirely independently of the
others?" asked Molotov. Byrnes answered that that was essentially true.[19] The chargé d'affaires in Moscow, George F.
Kennan, described the arrangement as "catch as catch can."[20]

Harry S. Truman, more so than Franklin D. Roosevelt,
scorned the Soviet sphere of influence budding in Eastern
Europe, for it was blatantly repressive, smacked of Old World
imperial machinations, and obstructed the instinctive American
view of an open postwar world. Although for most Americans,
including Truman Administration figures, "sphere of influence"
was an "unpopular term," as Harriman had noted earlier, some
prominent people argued that spheres of influence were a reality
of international politics that ought to be recognized.[21] "Spheres
of influence do in fact exist," concluded a State Department
report in mid-1945, "and will probably continue to do so for
some time to come."[22] To those who endorsed this minority
idea, spheres simply seemed inevitable. They embraced Robert
Frost's principle that good fences make good neighbors. So
thought Secretary of War Henry L. Stimson, who complained
that "some Americans are anxious to hang on to exaggerated
views of the Monroe Doctrine and at the same time butt into
every question that comes up in Central Europe." He counselled
that the United States should not try to challenge the Soviets in
the Balkans; peace was possible because "our respective orbits
did not clash."[23] Secretary of Commerce Henry A. Wallace
thought that "whether we like it or not, the Russians will try
to socialize their sphere of influence just as we try to democ-
ratize our sphere of influence. . . ." He favored "regional
internationalism."[24]

19. *Foreign Relations, Berlin*, II, 450.
20. George F. Kennan, *Memoirs, 1925–1950* (Boston, 1967), p. 260.
21. *Foreign Relations, 1944*, IV, 1009.
22. *Ibid., Berlin*, I, 262.
23. Quoted in Arthur Schlesinger, Jr., "Origins of the Cold War,"
Foreign Affairs, XLVI(October 1967), 28.
24. Quoted in Richard J. Walton, *Henry Wallace, Harry Truman,
and the Cold War* (New York, 1976), pp. 104, 107. See also Henry A.
Wallace, "The Path to Peace with Russia," *New Republic*, CXV(Septem-

Some State Department officers also foresaw and recommended a frank acceptance of a spheres-of-influence configuration to the international system. Cloyce K. Huston, Chief of the Division of Southern European Affairs, argued for a restrained American policy toward the Soviet sphere. American "barkings, growlings, snappings and occasional bitings," he concluded, only irritated the Soviets without dislodging them.[25] H. Stuart Hughes of the Division of Research for Europe reported later that the "spheres-of-influence concept survived in the State Department's bureaucratic underground." He recalled that "our contention had been that if each side would stay out of the other's sphere, then each could tolerate substantial dissent within the sphere." Thus, "one could find an intermediate course between armed antagonism and a cordial *modus vivendi*."[26] George F. Kennan, who like the others did not condone the repressive Soviet behavior in Eastern Europe, believed that the United States had insufficient power to roll back Soviet influence there. He urged that Europe be partitioned, that the United States build up a sphere of influence in Western Europe, and that we "keep ourselves out of the Russian sphere and keep the Russians out of ours."[27] Otherwise, the United States would be in "danger of losing, like the dog standing over the reflecting pool, the bone in our mouth without obtaining the one we saw in the water."[28]

A venerable and widely-respected American journalist, Walter Lippmann, also viewed the postwar world as a system of spheres. He predicted and advocated the growth of "regional constellations of states" with a great power presiding over

---

ber 30, 1946), 401–406; Ronald Radosh and Leonard P. Liggio, "Henry A. Wallace and the Open Door," in Thomas G. Paterson, ed., *Cold War Critics* (Chicago, 1971), pp. 76–113.

25. Quoted in Messer, "Paths Not Taken," p. 302.

26. H. Stuart Hughes, "The Second Year of the Cold War: A Memoir and an Anticipation," *Commentary*, XLVIII(August 1969), 29.

27. George F. Kennan to Charles Bohlen, January 26, 1945, Box 8, Bohlen Files.

28. Kennan, *Memoirs*, p. 256.

each.[29] Thus, the United States would be the most important partner in the "Atlantic Community," the Russians would dominate the "Russian Orbit," and China would oversee the "China Orbit." Within each "regional grouping" the major power's security would be insured, and global peace would be guaranteed if each power refrained from reaching into another's region for allies. A British diplomat who read Lippmann's exposition of these ideas in the columnist's *U.S. War Aims* told his Foreign Office colleagues that the book "runs directly counter to the trends of American popular mythology, which tends toward universalism and is sharply critical of anything remotely resembling a sphere of influence."[30]

Although most Americans did indeed tend toward "universalism"—a vague phrase meaning the American fulfillment of an open world, economically and politically—and did reject spheres of influence in principle, some observers made a distinction between what might be called "open" and "exclusive" spheres. An "open" sphere was one like Latin America under the Good Neighbor Policy, wherein, it was argued, the United States did not meddle in the internal affairs or undermine the sovereignty of the individual nations but wherein United States security was essentially guaranteed and Washington's leadership cued the foreign policies of the Western Hemispheric countries. An "exclusive" sphere, on the other hand, was anathema. It suggested deep intervention in the internal affairs of sovereign states by the dominating power, the direct control of policy, the suppression of civil liberties, and the exclusion of other nations, denying them normal diplomatic and economic relations.[31]

29. Lippmann, *U.S. War Aims*, p. 88. See also Walter Lippmann, "A Year of Peacemaking," *Atlantic Monthly*, CLXXVII(December 1946), 35–40.

30. J.C. Donnelly, Minutes, "Supplementary to Weekly Political Summary," July 16, 1944, AN 2829/20/45, Foreign Office Correspondence, Public Record Office.

31. For a discussion of the distinction between "open" and "exclusive" spheres, see Eduard M. Mark, "The Interpretation of Soviet Foreign Policy in the United States, 1928–1947" (Unpublished Ph.D. dissertation, University of Connecticut, 1978), pp. 135–137, 190–195, 205–206, 229–230, 267–269, 295.

Near the end of the Second World War, some American officials seemed inclined to grant the Soviets an "open" sphere in Eastern Europe. However, they balked at a sphere which might be used as a platform for expansionism, which excluded American influence, or which reassembled a Soviet imposition of totalitarian methods. Harriman complained in early 1945 that "Soviet control over any foreign country did not mean merely influence on their foreign relations but the extension of the Soviet system," including the secret police and the extinction of freedom of speech.[32] At the same time Joseph C. Grew feared that the Soviets were establishing more than a sphere of influence and were in fact "taking complete charge in satellite countries."[33] A year earlier, a State Department committee had distinguished between a "minimum" and "maximum" Soviet "pattern" in Eastern Europe. An American specialist on Soviet affairs, Charles E. Bohlen, commented during the committee's deliberations that a "minimum program," constituting an "assurance of friendly and independent governments in Eastern Europe for the purpose of guaranteeing Soviet security" but Soviet non-interference in internal affairs, would not constitute a threat to American interests; but should these states lose their independence through a "maximum" Soviet program, the United States would have to resist this apparent development of a "one-power aggregation" in Europe.[34] It did.

The Soviets probably did not have any blueprint or master plan for influencing or dominating their neighbors, but Americans watched with growing dismay as Moscow took unilateral and often ruthless steps to tie some of the Eastern European

32. *Foreign Relations, 1945*, V, 232.
33. *Ibid.*, p. 843.
34. "United States: Dominant Considerations in Judging a Soviet Regional Policy in Eastern Europe," March 15, 1944, Special Subcommittee on Problems of European Organization of the Advisory Committee on Postwar Foreign Policy, Box 85, Harley A. Notter Files, Department of State Records; Minutes, March 3, 1944, Box 84, *ibid.* (I thank Eduard M. Mark for drawing my attention to these documents.) For comments similar to those of Bohlen, see William T.R. Fox, *The Super-Powers* (New York, 1944), p. 97; Sumner Welles, *The Time for Decision* (New York, 1944), pp. 332–333.

states to the Red Star.[35] In Poland, which "had become a symbol of our ability to work out problems with the Soviet Union," the Russians brusquely installed the Communist Lublin Poles in office, arrested non-Communist officials, fixed voting lists to eliminate "fascists," postponed elections, suppressed civil liberties, imposed restrictions on travel, deported people, grabbed war booty, and annexed eastern portions of that much-abused country.[36] That same month Churchill complained privately that the Soviets were dropping an "iron screen" across Europe by setting up puppet governments.[37] In Rumania they abruptly forced King Michael to appoint Communist Petru Groza as prime minister and annexed Ruthenia and other districts from the former Axis satellite. The Baltic states of Estonia, Lithuania, and Latvia, part of the prewar *cordon sanitaire*, were completely absorbed. In Bulgaria Communists also came to power. Although Josip Broz Tito practiced an independent brand of Communism in Yugoslavia, most Western observers wrongly considered him to be a stooge of Moscow. Finland was defeated by the Soviets in the war and had to sign postwar agreements which signalled subservience to Moscow in foreign policy questions but freedom in internal matters. In Hungary Communists and non-Communists shared power. In Czechoslovakia the non-Communist government of Eduard Beneš tried to develop both cordial relations with Moscow and ties with the West but fell in 1948 to a political crisis which brought the Communists to power. Soviet trade treaties and joint stock companies also demonstrated the Soviet penetration of Eastern

35. For the suggestion that Stalin had no master plan for Eastern Europe, see Harriman and Abel, *Special Envoy*, p. 414; Isaac Deutscher, *Stalin: A Political Biography* (New York, 1966; 2nd ed.), pp. 536–537; Ulam, *Expansion and Coexistence*, pp. 345, 388–389; Marshall D. Shulman, *Beyond the Cold War* (New Haven, 1966), pp. 6–7.

36. The quotation is a statement Harry Hopkins made to Josef Stalin, from *Foreign Relations, Berlin*, I, 38.

37. "Note by Sir Archibald Clark Kerr on a discussion between the Prime Minister and the Soviet Ambassador at No. 10 Downing Street on May 18, 1945," Premier 3, 396/12, Prime Minister's Office Records, Public Record Office.

Europe. Russia, noted one American official, was creating a "Soviet Monroe Doctrine" for the area.[38]

Despite the checkerboard pattern of Soviet behavior in Eastern Europe—permitting free elections in Czechoslovakia but denying them in Poland, for example—the Truman Administration came to see the Soviet sphere of influence as an impenetrable bloc, an "exclusive" sphere, and vigorously protested the restrictive trade and political measures. What were the Soviets up to? Why would they not join Americans in an open world? Americans frequently asked these basic questions in their attempts to define the contours of the postwar era. They saw Soviet expansion and haughty unilateralism—"the old problem, really," remarked Bohlen, "of progressive aggression."[39] They attributed the evilest of intentions to the Soviets. Ambassador Harriman had suggested in the Fall of 1944 that Russia was becoming a "world bully."[40]

Soviet decisions and actions, of course, were hardly reassuring. Insensitive and inhumane, they proved uncooperative in repatriating American prisoners of war in Germany and Eastern Europe.[41] They paraded through Eastern Europe, manhandling and pushy, taking little notice of negative impressions abroad. Some Americans recalled the Nazi–Soviet Pact of 1939 and concluded that the Russians could not be trusted. Truman and many of his advisers believed in late Spring and early Summer 1945 that the United States had been "too easy" with Russia and that firmness might roll back Soviet influence from Eastern Europe and halt further advances.[42] Another worry dogged

38. Thomas Inglis of the Office of Naval Intelligence, quoted in Barton J. Bernstein, "American Foreign Policy and the Origins of the Cold War," in Barton J. Bernstein, ed., *Politics and Policies of the Truman Administration* (Chicago, 1970), p. 40.

39. Charles Bohlen lecture, April 28, 1948, Box 6, Bohlen Files.

40. *Foreign Relations, 1944*, IV, 989.

41. Russell D. Buhite, "Soviet-American Relations and the Repatriation of Prisoners of War, 1945," *The Historian*, XXXV(May 1973), 384–397.

42. Truman paraphrased by Edward Stettinius in Campbell and Herring, *Diaries of Stettinius*, p. 318.

them: Might the Soviets reach into other areas, not even respecting the traditional spheres of others?

Where does a large nation draw the line for its sphere? "If the policy is accepted that the Soviet Union has a right to penetrate her immediate neighbors for security," Harriman reasoned, "penetration of the next immediate neighbors becomes at a certain time equally logical."[43] The Russians "have gone imperialistic and are out to extend their spheres of influence in all directions and wherever possible," thought Byrnes.[44] The Deputy Director of the Office of European Affairs believed that even "to concede a limited Soviet sphere of influence" in Eastern Europe "might be to invite its extension to other areas. . . ."[45] Moreover, because the Soviets were seeking influence in such places as Libya, Manchuria, Turkey, and Iran, it appeared that the Soviet Union—even if acting out of a sincere desire for security—was probing and thrusting, taking advantage of the chaotic and fragile postwar international system. The trouble with a military frontier, said Bohlen, is that one hundred miles farther is always better.[46]

To the Soviets and the British, it appeared that the United States was doing much the same sort of thing. Washington continued to watch over the members of its traditional sphere of influence, drawing them closer in March of 1945 through a new defense pact—the Act of Chapultepec. Lend-Lease aid to Latin American countries during the war, United States naval bases, strong trade ties, large investments, support for particular political leaders, and the training of Latin American military officers permitted the United States to hang on to its vaunted position in the Western Hemisphere, despite noncompliant states like Argentina. During the 1930s and 1940s the United States self-consciously nudged out German and British interests.[47] "I think

43. *Foreign Relations, 1944*, IV, 993. See also *ibid., 1945*, V, 841.
44. Walter Brown Notes, July 22, 1945, Folder 602, James F. Byrnes Papers, Clemson University Library, Clemson, N.C.
45. John Hickerson in *Foreign Relations, 1945*, IV, 408.
46. Charles Bohlen lecture, July 10, 1947, Box 10, Bohlen Files.
47. See Gerald K. Haines, "Under the Eagle's Wing: The Franklin Roosevelt Administration Forges an American Hemisphere," *Diplomatic*

that it's not asking too much to have our little region over here which never has bothered anybody," Stimson said. Russia should not complain, because it "is going to take these steps . . . of building up friendly protectorates around her." His aide John McCloy agreed that "we ought to have our cake and eat it too; that we ought to be free to operate under this regional arrangement in South America, [and] at the same time intervene promptly in Europe . . . ," as the United States had been forced to do twice in this century in two world wars.[48] It was necessary for the United States to develop a "solid group in this hemisphere," Assistant Secretary of State Nelson Rockefeller believed, or Washington "could not do what we wanted to do on the world front."[49]

Elsewhere, too, the United States drove in stakes. In the Middle East the State Department backed American oil companies in their pursuit of lucrative and strategic concessions for exploting the black riches. By war's end American interests controlled nearly half of the proved oil reserves of the region. In Saudi Arabia, where American petroleum interests had been paramount since 1939, the United States built and operated the Dhahran Airport, "a vital link in U.S. round-the-world airplane operation." Technical assistance flowed to that Arab nation, so that, concluded a State Department report in 1946, it "is in a fair way to becoming an American frontier. . . ."[50] Earlier, Roosevelt had informed Churchill that the United States would

---

History, I(Fall, 1977), 373–388 and J. Fred Rippy, *Globe and Hemisphere* (Chicago, 1958).

48. Walter LaFeber, ed., *The Dynamics of World Power: Eastern Europe and the Soviet Union* (New York, 1973; 4 vols., edited by Arthur M. Schlesinger, Jr.), II, 84.

49. In 1946–47 one-quarter of United States exports flowed to Latin America; in 1950 direct United States investments in the area equalled over one-third of the world total of $12 billion, and about 40 percent of United States imports were drawn from its neighbors to the south. Department of Commerce, *Historical Statistics,* pp. 870, 903, 905. Rockefeller is quoted in David Green, "The Cold War Comes to Latin America," in Bernstein, *Politics and Policies,* p. 164.

50. Memorandum for the Use of the Mediterranean Fleet, "United States Policy Toward Saudi Arabia," November 8, 1946, Box 1812, Loy Henderson Files, Department of State Records.

respect traditional British interests in the Middle East. Churchill, always the realist about spheres of influence, replied: "Thank you very much for your assurances about no sheeps eyes at our oilfields in Iran and Iraq. Let me reciprocate by giving you fullest assurance that we have no thought of trying to horn in upon your interests or property in Saudi Arabia."[51]

In the Pacific the United States boldly took control of the former Japanese-dominated islands of the Carolines, Marshalls, and Marianas. Truman sought to answer criticism of American sphere-building when he said, ". . . though the United States wants no territory or profit or selfish advantage out of this war, we are going to maintain the military bases necessary for the complete protection of our interests and of world peace."[52] The Americans were trying to "get away with" the Pacific Islands, snarled British Colonial Secretary Oliver Stanley, but were wrapping up their case "in a rather diaphanous cover of the usual idealism."[53] Churchill always worried that the growing American sphere of influence would impinge upon his own. Let the Americans have their Pacific island outposts, he said. "But 'Hands Off the British Empire' is our maxim."[54]

In defeated Japan, the United States claimed supreme power for itself. A Far Eastern Commission of several nations existed, but its authority was negligible. The Allied Council of Japan, wherein the United States ostensibly shared power with Russia, Britain, and China, also became moribund quite early, leaving decisions in the hands of the strong-willed General Douglas MacArthur, who, Harriman noted, had the "last word." Harriman informed the Russians that the United States was "very firm on the matter of keeping the power in American hands,"

51. *Foreign Relations, 1944*, III, 103.

52. *Public Papers of the Presidents, Harry S. Truman, 1945*, p. 203 (hereafter *Public Papers, Truman*, date).

53. Quoted in Christopher Thorne, *Allies of a Kind: The United States, Britain and the War Against Japan, 1941–1945* (New York, 1978), p. 458.

54. Quoted in John W. Dower, "Occupied Japan and the American Lake, 1945–1950," in Edward Friedman and Mark Selden, eds., *America's Asia* (New York, 1971), p. 158.

and Truman told his Cabinet that the United States "would run this particular business."[55] Japan, concluded Edwin O. Reischauer, had the "sham facade of international control."[56] Stalin growled that the USSR was "treated like a piece of furniture" in Japan, and Byrnes admitted that "we were placed in an embarrassing position" because of analogies with the Soviet presence in Eastern Europe.[57] The United States gradually, although far less successfully, also attempted to draw China into the burgeoning American sphere.

Americans did not want to appear to be like other great powers and recoiled from popular comparisons between postwar Eastern Europe and Latin America, Poland and Mexico, or Rumania and Japan. Harry Howard of the Department of State once compared the Dardanelles, where the Russians were seeking authority, to the Panama Canal. His superior, Loy Henderson, "hit the ceiling" over the analogy and reminded Howard that he was "no mere academician now but an advocate" of American interests. Anyway, Henderson, concluded, the canal was built by the United States, but the Straits were an act of God.[58] As for Eastern Europe and Latin America, Americans distinguished between open and closed spheres. Byrnes recognized that large nations like Russia had special regional security interests, and that geographic propinquity dictated such special

---

55. Harriman and Abel, *Special Envoy*, p. 517. Truman is quoted in Thorne, *Allies of a Kind*, p. 659.

56. Edwin O. Reischauer, *The United States and Japan* (Cambridge, Mass., 1950), p. 45. Reischauer also wrote: "The Russians are right in believing that we seek to make Japan an ideological ally," and "our position there is not very different from that of Russia in the smaller countries of Eastern Europe, however dissimilar our motives may be." Pp. 40, 48. See also Lawrence S. Wittner, "MacArthur and the Missionaries: God and Man in Occupied Japan," *Pacific Historical Review*, XL(February 1971), 77–98; Howard Schonberger, "The Japan Lobby in American Diplomacy, 1947–1952," *ibid.*, XLVI(August 1977), 327–359.

57. Stalin quoted in Robert D. Warth, "Stalin and the Cold War: A Second Look," *South Atlantic Quarterly*, LIX(Winter 1960), 9; James F. Byrnes, *Speaking Frankly* (New York, 1947), p. 102. See also Truman, *Memoirs*, I, 430–432; Yergin, *Shattered Peace*, p. 146; Cordell Hull, *Memoirs* (New York, 1948; 2 vols.), II, 1466.

58. Harry Howard Oral History Interview, Truman Library.

interests, but "the good neighbor, unlike the institution of marriage, is not an exclusive arrangement. The best neighbors do not deny their neighbors the right to be friends with others." Byrnes stood emphatically, in a speech in October 1945, against "spheres of exclusive influence."[59]

To the Soviets, however, the distinction between "open" and "exclusive" spheres probably made no sense. They considered the United States' alleged "open" Good Neighbor sphere in Latin America virtually closed—evidence of capitalist imperialism. They perceived blatant United States intrusions in the internal affairs of the countries of the Western Hemisphere. And, from the Soviet perspective, the existence of an "open" sphere in Eastern Europe, with free elections, would likely mean that anti-Soviet groups would come to power which might invite outside powers into this area of prime importance to Soviet security. American trade with Eastern Europe might lead, furthermore, to economic, and hence political domination.

The Soviets also charged the United States and Britain with a double standard.[60] Accusations were flung back and forth; when Britain complained about Eastern Europe, Russia protested Anglo-American perfidy in Greece, Italy, and Japan.

59. *Department of State Bulletin*, XIII(November 4, 1945), 710. See also *ibid.*, XIV(March 10, 1946), 357–358 and Charles Bohlen to Walter Lippmann, February 17, 1948, Box 57, Walter Lippmann Papers, Yale University Library, New Haven, Conn. A British report made a similar distinction: "Our fundamental objection to Russian policy in Eastern Europe and up to the western border of the Soviet zone in Germany is that they are building up an exclusive sphere of influence and trying to communize it and exclude from it all 'Western' influence." "The Effect of Russian Influence in Western Europe on the European Economy," October 25, 1945, N15085/18/38, Foreign Office Correspondence.

60. Former Ambassador to Russia Joseph Davies wrote in his diary for September 22, 1945: "The Russians want to find out whether we will apply one rule for our security in the Pacific and refuse to apply the same rule in Europe where the Soviets similarly need it in their interest. . . . They also want to know whether, for reasons of security, the Panama Canal is to be controlled by the United States, while similar security against attack is to be denied them at their back door—the Dardanelles and the Straits." Diary, Box 22, Joseph Davies Papers, Library of Congress, Washington, D.C. See also Vera Micheles Dean, "Is Russia Alone to Blame?" *Foreign Policy Bulletin*, XXV(March 8, 1946), 1–2.

"The United Kingdom had India and her possessions in the Indian Ocean in her sphere of influence; the United States had China and Japan, but the Soviets had nothing," remarked Stalin. Bevin shot back that "the Russian sphere extended from Lubeck to Port Arthur."[61]

Surely, Stalin could not deny it; he played the spheres-of-influence game as well as any postwar leader. At Yalta, for example, Churchill appealed for French great-power status through the granting of a zone in Germany to France. In making his case, he said that France was to Britain what Poland was to Russia. Stalin, who had been trying futilely to gain Anglo-American recognition of the Soviet-backed Lublin government in Poland, seized the moment: "Why was more to be demanded of Poland than of France?" Who elected Charles de Gaulle, yet his French government was recognized?[62] At Potsdam Stalin sparred with Truman. The President asked for recognition of the Italian government. The Soviet Marshal complained that Rumania, Bulgaria, and Hungary were being treated like "leprous states." He would recognize Italy, where the "Russians had no rights," if Truman would recognize the governments of the Eastern European countries. Neither leader would budge.[63]

The Russians also thought that America's repeated call for the "open door" in the world economy was actually a cloak for expanding the United States' sphere of influence at the expense of others. When Moscow viewed the United States, it saw more than atomic bombs and foreign bases, more than superiority at the United Nations or a sphere in Latin America. It saw economic power.[64] Stalin apparently thought the "open door policy as dangerous to a nation as foreign military invasion."[65] The influx of American capital and trade into an economically weak area like Eastern Europe, as Molotov stated in 1946, might

61. Quoted in Yergin, *Shattered Peace*, p. 150.
62. Quoted in Clemens, *Yalta*, p. 152.
63. *Foreign Relations, Berlin*, II, 358–359, 362.
64. See Philip E. Mosely, "Soviet-American Relations Since the War," *Annals of the American Academy of Political and Social Science*, CCLXIII(May 1949), 202.
65. Quoted in Harriman and Abel, *Special Envoy*, p. 538.

make the United States "master." Furthermore, the principle should be applied "consistently." Molotov, as usual, was blunt in answering the Anglo-American call for international control of the Black Sea Straits: "Are the advocates of the principle of 'equal opportunity' willing to apply it to the Panama Canal as well?" And to the British Suez Canal?[66] At Potsdam Truman had in fact pressed for the internationalization of waterways but would not admit a double standard. When the Soviets rejected his scheme, the angry President thought the worst of Russia and indulged in exaggeration. "The Russians were planning world conquest," he concluded in his memoirs.[67]

In Iran, in early 1946, the United States and Russia clashed in a classic contest for spheres of influence. Both sought influence over Iranian political groups (the Russians in the northern province of Azerbaijan, and the Americans in the capital of Teheran). Both pursued oil concessions, which in themselves were avenues to influence—as the British learned from their large holdings in the Anglo-Iranian Oil Company. Both Russia and America maintained military personnel in the Middle Eastern nation. However, after the British and American forces withdrew, the Soviets stayed, violating a treaty deadline of early March 1946. The United States supported a United Nations investigation, whereupon Russia walked out of that body. "If the Russians get this [Iran]," snapped Henderson. "they'll try another."[68] Strong, angry words echoed across the globe, with the Americans charging that Russia was attempting to create a satellite in Iran, and the Soviets countering that the Anglo-Americans were subjugating a country which bordered the Soviet Union. Great Britain dominated Iranian oil, and advisers from an American military mission, under the leadership of Army Major General Robert W. Grow, counselled the Iranian army. The Russians undoubtedly felt a challenge close to home but believed that an agreement with Iran in early April, provid-

66. Molotov, *Problems of Foreign Policy*, pp. 210–216. See also *Soviet Press Translations*, I(November 1946), and III(January 15, 1947); *Foreign Relations, Berlin*, II, 303, 365.
    67. Truman, *Memoirs*, I, 412.
    68. Quoted in Yergin, *Shattered Peace*, p. 186.

ing for Soviet military withdrawal and the establishment of a joint Iranian–Soviet petroleum company, would help to counter the influence of the other powers. Yet American influence increased, with Ambassador George V. Allen "every day, in every way we can think of" urging the Iranian government to take a firm line against Russia throughout 1946. The agreement was never ratified by the Iranian parliament. Russia fumed and the United States claimed a Cold War victory. Iran entered the American sphere of influence.[69]

In early 1946, when the Iranian crisis began to smolder, Truman and other officials grew impatient with the Soviet Union. The list of irritants continued to swell: no elections in Eastern Europe; unilateral decisions; bombastic Communist language; Soviet atomic spies in Canada; and Russian vetoes in the first sessions of the United Nations. "I'm tired of babying the Russians," the president thought in January, after the meager results of the Moscow Foreign Ministers meeting in December. They had to be faced with an "iron fist."[70] In February Kennan wrote an influential telegram from Moscow: "We have here a political force committed fanatically to the belief that with the [US] there can be no permanent modus vivendi."[71] Speeches abounded at the same time; Byrnes and Senator Arthur Vandenberg of Michigan lectured the Soviets, especially after Stalin himself gave a disturbing speech in Russia. A British diplomat observed in mid-February that American "opinion against Russia had hardened. . . ."[72] Less than a month later, Churchill stung the Soviets with his speech on the "iron curtain." The question on American minds, Ambassador Walter Bedell Smith told Stalin in April, was "what does the Soviet Union want and how far is Russia going to go?"[73] Disputes over Manchuria,

69. For the Iranian crisis see Paterson, *Soviet-American Confrontation*, pp. 177–183.

70. Truman, *Memoirs*, I, 552.

71. *Foreign Relations, 1946*, VI, 706.

72. B. E. T. Gage, Minutes, "Political Situation in the United States," February 17, 1946, AN 423/1/45, Foreign Office Correspondence.

73. Walter Bedell Smith, *My Three Years in Moscow* (Philadelphia, 1950), p. 50.

Trieste, and the control of atomic energy (Baruch Plan) were blamed on the Russians. By May of 1946 Truman felt the need to "tell Russia where to get off. . . ."[74] It was time to "kick the Russians in the balls," a prominent lawyer blurted to a horrified Secretary of Commerce Henry A. Wallace.[75]

The United States decided to deny Russia a large reconstruction loan but offered $3.5 billion to Britain. The Americans, observed a British diplomat in May, had become "far tougher."[76] In April the battleship *Missouri* sailed to the Mediterranean, and in August the aircraft carrier *Franklin D. Roosevelt* cruised in those strategic waters. The Russians grew worried, but Admiral William Halsey bellowed that "it is nobody's damn business where we go. We will go anywhere we please."[77] American warships visited Plymouth, Malta, Gibraltar, Piraeus, Suda Bay, and elsewhere in the area, and American planes landed at Athens, Algiers, Marseilles, Naples, and Rome.[78]

In Germany in 1946 there was little movement toward economic unity because of both Soviet and French hesitancy to rebuild their former enemy. So in May, Military Governor Lucius Clay ended reparations shipments from the American zone. "After one year of occupation," he observed, "zones represent airtight territories with almost no free exchange of commodities, persons and ideas."[79] In April, at the Council of Foreign Ministers meeting in Paris, Secretary Byrnes formally launched what for him was a pet project and a test of Soviet

74. Quoted in Donovan, *Conflict and Crisis*, p. 213.

75. John M. Blum, *The Price of Vision: The Diary of Henry A. Wallace* (Boston, 1973), p. 536.

76. Piers Dixon, *Double Diploma* (London, 1968), p. 212.

77. For this quotation and the American awareness of the political impact of a fleet in the Mediterranean, see "Narrative of U.S. Naval Forces, Europe, 1 September 1945 to 1 October 1946," Command Files, Naval Historical Center, Old Navy Yard, Washington, D.C., and Memorandum of Conversation by James Riddleberger, September 7, 1946, Box 2, H. Freeman Matthews Files, Department of State Records.

78. "Quarterly Summary of U.S. Naval Forces Eastern Atlantic and Mediterranean," October 1, 1946–April 1, 1947, Command Files, Naval Historical Center.

79. Jean E. Smith, ed., *The Papers of Lucius D. Clay: Germany, 1945–1949* (Bloomington, Ind., 1974; 2 vols.), I, 213.

intentions. He proposed to Russia that it join the United States in signing a twenty-five-year treaty on German disarmament and demilitarization—in short, a security guarantee against a revived Germany. The Soviets would not consider such a treaty, Molotov replied in July. Byrnes grew angry, concluding that Russia was more interested in expansionism than security.[80]

A dispute over Turkey in the summer of 1946 spotlighted the acrimonious quest for spheres. In August the Soviets presented their position on the Straits to Ankara. They had long been insisting on a share in the governance of the Dardanelles, which, they crossly pointed out, had been used by German armed vessels during the war to ravage Black Sea Russia. Only the Black Sea nations, argued Moscow, should have a postwar role in controlling that strategic artery. Washington, reiterating the "open door" thesis, sought an international governing body, with Britain and the United States as members, and rejected an apparent Soviet bid for a naval base in Turkey. When Russia made its case in August, Washington read it as a set of demands prefacing a Soviet grab for Turkey. Exaggerated language filled Washington conference rooms. From Turkey, Ambassador Edwin Wilson cabled dire warnings of a Soviet thrust through Turkey into the Persian Gulf and Asia. On August 15, President Truman approved a memorandum which concluded that "the primary objective of the Soviet Union is to obtain control of Turkey." The United States would resist any Soviet "aggression," by "force of American arms" if necessary.[81] Turkey, it seemed, was a link in a global chain, and it was important not only to deny it to the Russian sphere but to secure it in the American sphere. Although, as in the earlier case of Iran,

80. The Russians may have rejected the proposed treaty because they would not entrust their security to Americans or to a paper document, because they did not want an American presence in Europe, or because they believed that the treaty was a ruse to permit termination of reparations shipments to Russia. See *Department of State Bulletin*, XV (July 28, 1946), 170; John Gimbel, "Die Vereinigten Staaten, Frankreich und der Amerikanische Vertragsentwurf zur Entmilitarisierung Deutschlands," *Vierteljahrshefte für Zeitgeschichte* (1974), pp. 258–286; Yergin, *Shattered Peace*, pp. 225–230.

81. *Foreign Relations, 1946*, VII, 840–841.

Russia made no military move against its neighbor, and although there was no direct evidence of Soviet intentions of world conquest, Americans again thought the worst. Turkey gravitated toward the American sphere of influence, and an infuriated Russia once again licked its wounds, charging a double standard. But where would the Soviet "predatory character" expose itself next, asked Truman's "get-tough" staffers?[82]

As the United States "got tough" in the first half of 1946, so did the Russians. They accelerated verbal thrusts against a perceived Anglo-American alliance. The Soviet line hardened after Churchill's "iron curtain" speech of March 5, 1946, in Fulton, Missouri. Truman was on the platform with Churchill—a sign to Moscow that the president approved the message. Stalin reacted angrily to the former prime minister's stern, critical words about the Soviet sphere of influence and his call for an Anglo-American partnership against Russia. "Russia was not attacking," cried Stalin, "she was being attacked." He told the British ambassador in Moscow that he "knew it was said that Mr. Churchill was not a member of the British Government, but he held an important position in England and his speech had not been repudiated."[83] In April a conspicuous anti-American bias, heretofore muted or nonexistent, marked Soviet editorials. Increasingly, the United States, the practitioner of "atomic diplomacy," was highlighted as the leader of an Anglo-American coalition seeking world hegemony. They were "ganging up" against Russia, spoiling the once flourishing wartime cooperation evident at Yalta. For the remaining months of 1946, the heated rhetoric became hotter. An "Anglo-American bloc," concluded a Soviet editorial which reviewed the year, was attempting to substitute an "imperialist trust for a democratic peace."[84]

82. The phrase was used by the Moscow Embassy. White House Daily Summary, August 6, 1946, Department of State Records.
83. Paraphrase by Sir Maurice Peterson, "Interview between His Majesty's Ambassador and Stalin," May 28, 1946, N6984/140/38, Foreign Office Correspondence.
84. *New Times* (Moscow), January 1, 1947. For evidence of the harsher Soviet tone which became noticeable in April 1946, see "Interpretive Report on Soviet Policy based on the Press for April 1 to 28, 1946," by American Embassy in Moscow, April 30, 1946, Box 1384,

By the Fall of 1946, then, both major powers were glaring at one another from their respective spheres of influence, often using shrill language, and each convinced that the other was hell bent on expansion. Most Americans attributed international troubles to Russia. From France, for example, Ambassador Jefferson Caffery gloomily reported the growing appeal of the French Communist Party, "the advance of the 'Soviet Trojan Horse.' "[85] Secretary of Commerce Henry A. Wallace did not agree with the tendency to blame all on Russia, and in a Madison Square Garden speech in September of 1946 he publicly criticized his own government for its hard-line policy. Truman fired him from the Cabinet. The next month, renowned religious philosopher Reinhold Niebuhr captured in a few taut words in *Life* magazine what he and many other Americans were thinking: "Russian truculence cannot be mitigated by further concessions. Russia hopes to conquer the whole of Europe strategically and ideologically."[86]

To head off just such an eventuality, the United States had been employing its vast wealth through a variety of reconstruction loans and relief programs to assist other nations to recover from the war's devastation and to draw them into its sphere of influence. In September of 1946 Byrnes recognized the relationship between foreign aid and spheres: "We must help our friends in every way and refrain from assisting those who either through helplessness or for other reasons are opposing the principles for which we stand."[87]

Moscow Post Files, Department of State Records; Maurice Peterson to Ernest Bevin, July 22, 1946, copy in 861.00/7-2246, Department of State Records; British Embassy, Moscow, "Soviet Union Quarterly Report, July–September, 1946," October 22, 1946, Box 1384, Moscow Post Files, Department of State Records; *New Times*, March 15, May 1, May 15, June 1, August 1, 1946; White House Daily Summary, May 21 and August 16, 1946, Department of State Records; "Interpretive Report on Soviet Policy Based on the Press for May, 1946," June 13, 1946, Box 1384, Moscow Post Files, *ibid.*

85. White House Daily Summary, November 21, 1946, Department of State Records.

86. Reinhold Niebuhr, "The Fight for Germany," *Life* XXI(October 1946), 65.

87. *Foreign Relations, 1946*, VII, 223.

In March of the following year, the president gravely addressed a joint session of Congress and issued his "Truman Doctrine." He said it "must be the policy of the United States to support free peoples who are resisitng attempted subjugation by armed minorities or by outside pressures." The world, he stated, was now divided between two "alternative ways of life."[88] The immediate setting for this dramatic announcement was the civil war in Greece, where Communist-led rebels battled the British-backed conservative government in Athens. The insurgents received sanctuary and aid from Yugoslavia, and because Yugoslavia was thought to be merely a Moscow puppet, Americans assumed that Russia itself was directing the rebellion. American officials regarded Greece as a strategic spot and before 1947 had criticized (although increasingly more in private than in public) the sometimes brutal and usually ineffective British efforts to defeat the Greek leftists. When economically-hobbled Britain could no longer maintain the Mediterranean nation in its sphere, the United States decided to intervene and to draw the fabled but now enfeebled birthplace of "democracy" into the expanding American sphere of influence. "If Greece should fall under the control of an armed minority," Truman concluded in an early version of the "domino theory," "the effect upon its neighbor, Turkey, would be immediate and serious. Confusion and disorder might well spread throughout the entire Middle East." Western Europe might also succumb.[89] To halt this perceived Soviet probe of a "soft spot," the president successfully requested in his Truman Doctrine address that Congress approve $400 million for aid to Greece and Turkey.[90]

"Containment" became the American byword, especially after George F. Kennan, writing as Mr. "X," published an article in the July 1947 issue of *Foreign Affairs* that recommended a "policy of firm containment, designed to confront the Russians

88. *Public Papers, Truman, 1947*, p. 178.
89. *Ibid.*, p. 179.
90. Ambassador to Turkey Edwin C. Wilson in Senate, Committee on Foreign Relations, *Legislative Origins of the Truman Doctrine* (executive session hearings; historical series; Washington, D.C., 1973), p. 52.

with unalterable counter-force at every point where they show signs of encroaching upon the interests of a peaceful and stable world."[91] As Acheson similarly put it, the United States had to resist a Soviet "pincher movement" threatening Iran, Greece, Turkey, Germany, France, and Italy. The stakes were large. "You weren't going to have a strong Turkey if Greece went to pieces. And furthermore, each country to the west, which might be penetrated, would automatically bring about the collapse of countries to the east of that."[92]

The trend toward spheres in Europe was also boosted by the Marshall Plan. Although by 1947 the United States had spent some $9 billion since V-E Day to help Western Europe recover from the staggering impact of the war, that area still desperately needed outside help. To Americans who believed that the Soviets were prowling about, looking for chaotic environments to exploit, there seemed to be an urgent need for a major American counteroffensive. Americans thought that political extremism flowed from economic instability and that the large Communist parties in France and Italy, in particular, would come to power unless the United States sponsored a new, massive, and coordinated American aid program. "It is important," concluded an interdepartmental committee report,

to maintain in friendly hands areas which contain or protect sources of metals, oil and other national [sic] resources, which contain strategic objectives, or areas strategically located, which contain a substantial industrial potential, which possess manpower and organized military forces in important quantities, or which for political or psychological reasons enable the U.S. to exert a greater influence for world stability, security and peace.[93]

Western Europe was defined as part of the American sphere of influence—the "keystone in the arch which supports the kind of

91. "X," "The Sources of Soviet Conduct," *Foreign Affairs*, XXV (July 1947), 581.
92. Princeton Seminar Transcript, July 8–9, 1953, Box · 64, Dean Acheson Papers, Truman Library.
93. "Report on the Special Ad Hoc Committee," SWNCC-360, April 21, 1947, Box 65, SWNCC Records.

a world which we have to have in order to conduct our lives . . . ,"
as Acheson later noted.[94] On June 5, 1947, Secretary of State
George C. Marshall told a Harvard commencement audi-
ence that the United States would help Europe rebuild itself.
He did not specifically exclude Eastern Europe and Russia from
his offer, but few American officials expected participation by
members of the Soviet sphere. The European Recovery Program
(ERP) was an American-directed project for "friends" of the
United States, to recall Byrnes's 1946 comment. *"The United
States must run this show,"* insisted Under-Secretay of State Will
Clayton.[95]

American diplomats not only saw the ERP as a way of shor-
ing up Western Europe; they also hoped that success there
would undermine the Soviet sphere. One of the tenets of the
containment doctrine was that holding the line against the Soviets would eventually throw them on the defensive. "If we can get
the grass to grow a little greener" in Western Europe, said Harriman, "that success will roll back behind the iron curtain. . . ."[96]
Truman was over-optimistic in early 1948: "If that European recovery program works, we will raise the Iron Curtain by
peaceable means," because people would be attracted to the
higher standard of "personal welfare" in Western Europe.[97]
That did not happen. The Marshall Plan and the Soviet reaction
to it divided Europe even more.

In July 1947 V. M. Molotov led a large Soviet delegation to
Paris to discuss a Europe-wide program. He gruffly departed
after a few days, charging that the United States was attempting
to undermine the sovereignty of individual nations. It was a
"clean break," concluded Bevin, with "no doors left open."[98]

94. House of Representatives, Committee on International Relations,
Foreign Economic Assistance Programs (executive session hearings; historical series; Washington, D.C., 1976), Part 2, vol. IV, p. 38.
95. *Foreign Relations,* 1947, III, 232.
96. House of Representives, Committee on Foreign Affairs, *Emer-
gency Foreign Aid* (hearings; Washington, D.C., 1947), p. 122.
97. *Public Papers, Truman, 1948,* p. 234.
98. White House Summary, July 3, 1947, Department of State
Records.

Both sides shoved aside the fledgling Economic Commission for Europe, a continent-wide agency. Russia did not join the ERP; Moscow's pressure on Eastern Europe kept that region out; and East Germany also did not participate. The Department of State explained why: "If the USSR chose to participate in the recovery program, it would have been obliged to sacrifice the exclusive economic controls established in Eastern Europe since the war and to permit a western reorientation of satellite economies into the broader European economy envisaged by the program. Such a course, which would jeopardize Soviet hegemony in Eastern Europe, was unacceptable."[99] In short, it was a question of spheres of influence, and the Soviets chose not to have theirs diminished.

American leaders knew that there was something to Molotov's charge that the United States would be intervening in the domestic affairs of other nations. "In the end," concluded Kennan, "we would not *ask* them, we would just *tell* them what they would get."[100] Senator Henry Cabot Lodge of Massachusetts concluded that "this Marshall plan is going to be the biggest damned interference in internal affairs that there has ever been in history. We are being responsible for the people who stay in power as a result of our efforts." Indeed, "it doesn't do any good to say we are not going to interfere when the people in power stay there because of us."[101] The Russians feared American power in Eastern Europe, so they boycotted the program, and the United States reaped the propaganda advantage of claiming that the Soviet Union had divided Europe. Exaggerated Soviet verbiage, spread through the Cominform, the Soviet propaganda agency created in September of 1947, further aggravated the division. The Marshall Plan, which ultimately expended $13 billion, was, according to Communists, an "American design to

99. Secretary's Weekly Summary, July 14, 1947, *ibid.*
100. Quoted in John Gimbel, *The Origins of the Marshall Plan* (Stanford, 1976), p. 263.
101. Senate, Committee on Foreign Relations, *Foreign Relief Aid: 1947* (executive session hearings; historical series; Washington, D.C., 1973), p. 153.

enslave Europe."[102] Thus the war of words continued and the lines separating the spheres were cut more deeply.

Through 1947 and 1948 the two superpowers growled and snapped at one another. Trust was gone. Each, it appeared to the other in mirror image, was intent upon world conquest. American officials thought that the Soviets were tactically flexible and would attempt to expand their sphere of influence by measures short of war, by political subversion through "stooges," and by hostile propaganda designed to split Westerners.[103] The Soviet Union, concluded the National Security Council in March of 1948, was engaging the United States in a "struggle for power, or 'cold war,' in which our national security is at stake and from which we cannot withdraw short of eventual national suicide." The United States, to meet this global threat, needed to undertake "a world-wide counteroffensive against Soviet-directed world communism."[104]

The United States became active on a global scale. This activity took varied forms: An "information program" beamed at Eastern Europe; food shipments to Italy just before national elections there; support for the reestablishment of French rule in Indochina; pressure on the Dutch to recognize the moderate Indonesian national group and to grant the East Indies or Indonesia independence, so as to head off the Communist appeal there; continued aid to the faltering Chiang Kai-shek in China; the 1947 inter-American military alliance known as the Rio Pact; military missions to fourteen Latin American countries, as

102. Margaret Carlyle, ed., *Documents on International Affairs, 1947–1948* (London, 1952), pp. 129–130. For the Marshall Plan, see Paterson, *Soviet-American Confrontation*, ch. 10.

103. See, for example, Secretary's Weekly Summary, May 19, 1947, Department of State Records; "Guidance on Military Aspects of United States Policy . . . International Control of Atomic Energy," by Joint Strategic Survey Committee for Joint Chiefs of Staff, JCS 1764/1, July 14, 1947, Box 166, Central Decimal File 471.6, Joint Chiefs of Staff Records; Secretary's Weekly Summary, December 15, 1947, Department of State Records; *Foreign Relations, 1948*, V, Part 1, 119–120.

104. "The Position of the United States with Respect to Soviet-Directed World Communism," NSC-7, March 30, 1948, National Security Council Records, Modern Military Branch, National Archives.

well as to Greece, Turkey, Iran, the Philippines, China, and
Saudi Arabia; occupation forces in Germany, Austria, Trieste,
Japan, and (until 1949) Korea; "military understandings" with
Brazil, Canada, and Mexico; and support for the British "strategic position" in the Middle East.[105] American planners
assumed that if Russia did the unlikely and risked war with the
United States, the American monopoly of the atomic bomb
would eventually turn back the Soviet thrust. The overwhelming
atomic destruction of the Soviet Union, it was believed in late
1947, would force an early Russian capitulation. The atomic
bomb gave the United States a "tremendous strategic advantage," for "it is a weapon which can be used to destroy both the
will and the ability of the enemy to wage war."[106]

Scares marked early 1948. In February Communists took
command of the Czech government, confirming for Kremlin-
watchers that the Soviet Union was continuing its expansionism.
The Czech coup "scared the living bejesus out of everybody,"
recalled the State Department's John Hickerson.[107] Acheson
remembered that events in Czechoslovakia sent "a very considerable chill" through American diplomats who entertained the
thought of a "quick [Soviet] overrunning of Europe."[108]

105. Secretary's Weekly Summary, July 7, 1947, Department of
State Records; Clinton P. Anderson, *Outsider in the Senate* (New York,
1970), pp. 70–71; George C. Herring, "The Truman Administration and
the Restoration of French Sovereignty in Indochina," *Diplomatic History*, I(Spring 1977), 97–117; Clark M. Clifford, "A Viet Nam Reappraisal," *Foreign Affairs*, XCVII(July 1969), 603; Robert J. Mc-
Mahon, "The United States and Decolonization in Southeast Asia: The
Case of Indonesia, 1945–1949" (Unpublished doctoral dissertation, University of Connecticut, 1977); "Military Aid Priorities," SANACC
360/11, Subcommittee for Rearmament, August 18, 1948, SWNCC
Records; *Foreign Relations, 1948*, V, 655–656.

106. "Guidance for the Preparation of a Joint Outline War Plan,"
Joint Staff Planners to Joint War Plans Committee, August 29, 1947,
381-USSR, Box 37B, Joint Chiefs of Staff Records; "Broiler," by Joint
Strategic Plans Group, JSPG 496/1, November 8, 1947, *ibid*. The plan-
ners code-named their various "war plans," 1946–1948, "Pincher,"
"Broiler," "Bushwacker," and "Grabber."

107. John D. Hickerson Oral History Interview, Truman Library.

108. Quoted in Princeton Seminar transcript, October 10–11, 1953,
Box 65, Acheson Papers.

Rumors shot around Washington in March that war might be imminent. "We are faced with exactly the same situation with which Britain and France were faced in 1938–39 with Hitler," Truman told his daughter.[109] A leaked March 5 cable from General Clay suggested his feeling that Russia might take some abrupt military action. Truman went before a special joint session of Congress and denounced the Soviets for spoiling the postwar peace and subjugating Eastern Europe. He also called for congressional passage of Marshall Plan legislation, the restoration of Selective Service, and universal military training. The conclusions reached by a study group of prominent citizens at the Council on Foreign Relations in New York reflected the impact of the early 1948 "war scare:"

When the group first assembled [in October 1947], many of its members were inclined to believe that our major difficulties in dealing with the Soviet Union were caused by its suspicion and fear of the Western powers and that this suspicion might be removed by a reasonable policy on our part, a policy which other members of the group believed to border on appeasement. . . . At the present time [April 1948], almost no member of the group continues to feel that it is worth while to attempt to lessen Soviet suspicion by concessions on our part. . . . The emphasis is now definitely on firmness.[110]

Embittering disputes in Germany also demonstrated that the two major powers, basically abandoning diplomacy, were intent upon building spheres of influence. In December of 1946 British and American officers had fused their German zones, creating "Bizonia." After years of hesitation because of their own fears of a reconstructed Germany, the French attached their zone to "Bizonia" in 1949 to form the Federal Republic of Germany, or West Germany, which participated in the Marshall Plan. The Soviets in turn erected the People's Republic of Germany, or East Germany. Deep in East Germany Berlin also remained divided. The Berlin crisis of 1948–49 exposed the great postwar schism even more starkly. The Soviets boldly attempted to absorb the city into its zone by sealing it off. The United States

109. Margaret Truman, *Harry S. Truman* (New York, 1973), p. 359.
110. "American-Russian Relations," Records of Groups, vol. XIV, Council on Foreign Relations Files, New York.

responded with a heroic airlift of food and supplies.[111] The crisis was eventually defused, but the tension had been electric. Stalin's comment in early 1948 that "the West will make Western Germany their own, and we shall turn Eastern Germany into our own state" aptly captured the development of spheres in Central Europe and the world as a whole.[112]

Even the dramatic break between Josip Tito's Yugoslavia and Russia in mid-1948 bespoke the development: Moscow tried unsuccessfully to discipline this independent-minded member of its sphere as Washington warily edged toward closer commercial relations with the Balkan country, extending loans in 1949 and military aid two years later. Still, Tito would not leave one sphere to join another. "We have never given anybody reason to hope that we would join the Western bloc or any other bloc for that matter," he noted.[113]

The superpowers also built their military spheres in Europe. "England is so weak she must follow our leadership," Harriman concluded with exaggeration in 1946. "She will do anything that we insist and she won't go out on a limb alone."[114] Britons, of course, resented their junior-partner status vis-à-vis the United States, but they struck a loose postwar alliance with the upstarts of 1776, in part in order to salvage what they could of their faltering empire, especially in the Middle East. The "Anglo-Ameri-

111. Secretary Marshall told a Cabinet meeting that the "present tension in Berlin is brought about by loss of Russian face in our successes in Italy, France, Finland, and added to this is the Tito defection from Russia. It is caused by Russian desperation in face of success of the European Recovery Program." Cabinet Meeting, July 23, 1948, Notes on Cabinet Meetings, Matthew Connelly Papers, Truman Library. For Germany, see Paterson, *Soviet-American Confrontation*, ch. 11; Bruce Kuklick, *American Policy and the Division of Germany* (Ithaca, 1972); John H. Backer, *Priming the German Economy: American Occupational Policies, 1945–1948* (Durham, N.C., 1971); John Gimbel, *The American Occupation of Germany* (Stanford, 1968); Manuel Gottlieb, *The German Peace Settlement and the Berlin Crisis* (New York, 1960).

112. Quoted in Milovan Djilas, *Conversations with Stalin* (New York, 1962), p. 153.

113. Josip Broz Tito, "On Certain International Questions," *Foreign Affairs*, XXXVI(October 1957), 77. See also Paterson, *Soviet-American Confrontation*, pp. 139–142.

114. Harriman and Abel, *Special Envoy*, p. 531.

can alignment," as Ambassador Walter Bedell Smith called it in 1946, eventually blossomed into the North Atlantic Treaty Organization of 1949, wherein the United States, Britain, Canada, and nine European nations created a formal security pact.[115] A year earlier, with American encouragement, Britain, France, Belgium, Luxembourg, and the Netherlands had formed the Brussels Pact for collective defense. In NATO, the United States became the key member, providing a security shield and the dollars and military equipment to make the regional association viable.

Although NATO was designed to serve as a deterrent, with the atomic bomb the conspicuous weapon, few leaders were anticipating a Soviet military thrust. NATO was as much as anything else designed to lift Western European spirits, to thwart internal subversives or Communists, to rearm West Germany, and to tie the NATO countries more closely to the American sphere, lest they be attracted to neutralism or appeasement. Harriman said that the United States wanted to avoid a "neutral third group" in Europe. "Appeasement psychology, like isolationism in the US, is not deeply buried," he believed.[116] Europeans had to be given a "will to resist," as Dean Acheson phrased it, or a "general stiffening of morale," as Hickerson remarked.[117] American leaders thought that the European Recovery Program would fail unless there was a "sense of security" to accompany it.[118] "If everyone believes that the next year or next month all his efforts may be wiped out," Acheson told a Senate committee, "they are not going to make that type of effort which is necessary for recovery. So there is this very

115. Great Britain, France, Belgium, Luxembourg, Netherlands, Denmark, Ireland, Italy, Norway, Portugal, Canada, and the United States were the original members. Greece and Turkey joined in 1952; West Germany entered NATO in 1954.

116. House, *Foreign Economic Assistance Program*, Part 2, vol. IV, p. 25; *Foreign Relations, 1948*, III, 183.

117. Senate, Committee on Foreign Relations, *North Atlantic Treaty* (hearings; Washington, D.C., 1949), p. 213; *Foreign Relations, 1948*, III, 40.

118. Acheson in Princeton Seminar transcript, October 10–11, 1953, Box 65, Acheson Papers.

close link between recovery and confidence."[119] NATO, then, would shore up the American sphere and draw a line which the Soviets were warned not to cross. "The Atlantic Pact," Senator Tom Connally reasoned, "is but the logical extension of the principle of the Monroe Doctrine."[120] The Soviets reacted angrily to this strengthening of its adversaries, sensing "a new, sharper phase" of the postwar struggle and condemning the pact for "trying to kindle the flames of a new war. . . ."[121] Moscow eventually tried to match NATO with its own military scheme, the Warsaw Pact.

In 1949 the contest for spheres also took a decisive turn in Asia. After years of ultimately futile American aid, Chiang Kai-shek's corrupt and inefficient regime collapsed, leaving Mao Tse-tung's Communists in control of that huge country. The United States had sought to contain Mao but found Chiang an ineffective instrument. Always fearing that the Chinese Communists were "willing to lend" themselves to "Soviet purposes," as Kennan wrote in his Long Telegram of 1946, American leaders played down Sino-Soviet differences and the intensity of Chinese nationalism and concluded by mid-1949 that Mao's emerging government did not serve Chinese interests, but those of Russia.[122] China, it appeared to American analysts, had turned toward the Soviet sphere. American critics and stalwarts of the "China lobby," such as publisher Henry Luce and Congressman Walter Judd of Minnesota, castigated the Truman Administration for having "lost" China, for having "lost" a member of the American sphere. Truman and Acheson could agree that China was "lost," but they blamed Chiang, not themselves, for this setback. In either case, events in China by the end of 1949 demonstrated once again that the world that the Americans and Soviets had come to dominate was profoundly splintered.

Why did the leaders of the great powers not behave in such

119. Senate, *North Atlantic Treaty*, pp. 213–214.
120. Quoted in Walter LaFeber, *America, Russia, and the Cold War, 1945–1975* (New York, 1976; 3rd ed.), p. 85.
121. Cominform Bulletin quoted in Marshall D. Schulman, *Stalin's Foreign Policy Reappraised* (New York, 1966), p. 94.
122. *Foreign Relations, 1946*, VI, 704.

a way as to minimize the inherent and war-induced conflict of the international system? Why did they perceive each other as threatening aggressors with whom compromise seemed impossible? And why did they develop opposing spheres of influence? Foreign policy is devised by individuals who must react not only to the external stimuli of the international environment but also to their peculiar domestic stimuli—strategic needs, economic necessities, ideological tenets, political pressures, interest groups, or powerful individuals. To determine why the United States and the Soviet Union behaved as they did after the Second World War, a study of the internal characteristics of the antagonists, the fundamental and tactical elements of their diplomacy, is in order.

4

Abundance: The "Fundamentals" of the United States

THE POSTWAR INTERNATIONAL SYSTEM, lacking stability and rife with tension, provided its two most prominent members with numerous opportunities to clash and to build spheres of influence. The United States and the Soviet Union, groping toward their different definitions of the new world order, did just that. "Something new had to be created," recalled Dean Acheson, and the role for the United States "was one of fashioning, trying to help fashion what would come after the destruction of the old world."[1]

Clearly, systemic conditions drew the major powers into conflict, yet the United States and Russia themselves, for their own reasons, had to decide whether or not to exploit opportunities, struggle against the profound problems bequeathed by the Second World War, and undertake an activist, inevitably globalist, foreign policy. Nations do not simply react to the international environment or to the foreign policies of other countries. They also act purposefully to expand and protect what in general they consider to be their national well-being or, in the case of the United States, to shape an "environment in which the Amer-

1. Transcript, Eric Sevareid's "A Conversation with Dean Acheson," CBS Television Network, September 28, 1969.

ican experiment of life can prosper."[2] Internal stimuli, then, helped to prompt the American and Soviet governments to "fashion" a new postwar international system of spheres of influence.

The focus in this chapter is on the internal factors that propelled the United States to center stage. What American "fundamentals"—ideas, economic and strategic needs, power—explain why the United States wanted to and had to become a central participant in the making of the postwar world. The fundamentals transcended personalities or changes in administration; both Franklin D. Roosevelt and Harry S. Truman were guided by them. Foreign policy, diplomat Charles Bohlen reminded Americans, was not rooted in particular leaders but "in our American traditions and in the requirements of the national interest."[3] The *fundamentals* or *whys* of American foreign relations, therefore, were distinct from the *tactics* or *hows* of diplomacy. Policymakers, as chapters 5 and 6 demonstrate, determined not the fundamental factors themselves, but how they were to be satisfied and exercised.

Ideology, economic-strategic needs, and elements of national power comprised America's fundamentals, generating an activist, expansionist diplomacy. Among the components of the American ideology, we can discover American dreams about the new world order—what they wanted to avoid, sought to create, and hoped to enjoy. American economic and political ideals and principles from the past pointed the way: an "open door" world of equal trade and investment opportunity; private enterprise, as opposed to government ownership of the means of production; multilateralism or cooperation in foreign commerce; freedom of the seas; the right of self-determination and self-government; democratic, constitutional procedures; the limitation of force in international relations; "good neighborism"; and freedom of religion and speech. Woodrow Wilson immortalized many of these ideas in his famous Fourteen Points, Roosevelt implanted

2. Dean Acheson in House, *Foreign Economic Assistance Programs*, vol. IV, Part 2, p. 38.
3. *Department of State Bulletin*, XX(February 6, 1949), 157.

some of them in the Atlantic Charter, and Truman listed many of them as the "fundamentals" of American foreign policy in his Navy Day speech of October, 1945.[4] All in all, Americans believed in an "open world," free from barriers to political democracy and economic opportunity.

Americans in the postwar years, remembering the tragedies wrought by economic depression, aggression, and war in the 1930s, constantly spoke of the interlocking connection between peace and prosperity. Just before his death, President Roosevelt told Congress that "we cannot succeed in building a peaceful world unless we build an economically healthy world."[5] Congressman Carl T. Durham of North Carolina informed columnist Marquis Childs in 1945 that "starvation, illness, and the coming cold winter are foregone conclusions in many countries, and we are all aware of what this will breed."[6] Indeed, "hungry people are not reasonable people," concluded a State Department official.[7] Americans believed that economic instability and povery bred political chaos, revolutionary behavior, totalitarianism, violence, aggression, and war. It was assumed that these conditions were attractive to political extremists like Communists who always preyed on weaknesses and dislocations. George F. Kennan expressed the prevailing sentiment starkly: "World communism is like a malignant parasite which feeds only on diseased tissue."[8] Economic reconstruction and the revival of free-flowing world trade and finance offered one route to prosperity and, in turn, peace. "Nations which act as enemies in the market-place," Under-Secretary of State Will Clayton mused, "cannot long be friends at the council table."[9] President Truman stated that "in fact the three—peace, freedom, and world trade—are inseparable."[10]

4. *Public Papers, Truman, 1945*, pp. 433–434.
5. Samuel Rosenman, ed., *Public Papers of Franklin D. Roosevelt* (New York, 1938–1950; 13 vols.), XIII, 595.
6. Carl T. Durham to Marquis Childs, September 18, 1945, Folder 576, Durham Papers, University of North Carolina Library, Chapel Hill.
7. *Department of State Bulletin*, XIV(May 19, 1946), 831.
8. *Foreign Relations, 1946*, VI, 708.
9. *Department of State Bulletin*, XII(May 27, 1945), 979.
10. *Public Papers, Truman, 1947*, p. 167.

Because the postwar world economy was interdependent, Americans understood that economic catastrophes did not respect national boundaries. Secretary of the Interior Julius Krug remarked that "depressions are as catching as the common cold," and W. Averell Harriman, describing the United States as the "financial and economic pivot of the world," feared that "economic stagnation in the United States would drag the rest of the world down with us."[11] To prevent contagious depressions, to insure that the world did not plummet again into the depths of depression, the United States had to restore and maintain its primacy in the international economy. In 1947 the United States accounted for one-third of the world's total exports and about half of the world's industrial output. Secretary of State George C. Marshall told a Harvard University audience, in advocating the "plan" for economic recovery that eventually bore his name, that "it is logical that the United States should do whatever it is able to do to assist in the return of normal economic health in the world, without which there can be no political stability and no assured peace."[12] Acheson summarized the question earlier when he explained that the "great difference in our second attempt to establish a peaceful world is the wide recognition that peace is possible only if countries work together and prosper together. That is why the economic aspects are no less important than the political aspects of peace."[13]

The political world Americans envisioned was very much like their own. They rightfully prided themselves on their Bill of Rights, their enduring Constitution, and their stable, representative form of government. What is more, they assumed that other peoples would want the same and should be shown the way. Roosevelt's special aide Harry Hopkins said in 1945:

I have often been asked what interests we have in Poland, Greece,

11. Quoted in Paterson, *Soviet-American Confrontation*, p. 5.
12. *Department of State Bulletin*, XVI(June 15, 1947), 1160.
13. *Ibid.*, XXII(April 22, 1945), 738. For a fuller explication of the "peace and prosperity" concept, see Thomas G. Paterson, "The Quest for Peace and Prosperity: International Trade, Communism, and the Marshall Plan," in Bernstein, *Politics and Policies*, pp. 78–112.

Iran, or Korea. Well I think we have the most important business in the world—and indeed, the only business worthy of our traditions. And that is this—to do everything within our diplomatic power to foster and encourage democratic government throughout the world. We should not be timid about blazoning to the world our desire for the right of all peoples to have a genuine civil liberty. We believe our dynamic democracy is the best in the world. . . .[14]

As Hopkins's impassioned words attest, embedded in the American ideology was the belief that the United States was blessed with superior principles and institutions which others should adopt. Call it missionary zeal, a sense of manifest destiny, conceit, arrogance, or chauvinism, Americans had it: a self-image which obscured blatant violations (such as racial segregation at home)—a self-satisfaction that Americans were an exceptional people. The Puritan fathers thought so when they delivered their lofty sermons against the perfidies of the Old World; American rebels in 1776 echoed the belief in casting off the British yoke; President James Monroe espoused his "doctrine" in 1823 to emphasize the uniqueness of the Western Hemisphere; Woodrow Wilson had insisted in the era of World War I that America was a beacon of sanity for mankind; and during the Second World War, the United States became the "arsenal of democracy." "All nations succumb to fantasies of innate superiority," historian Arthur M. Schlesinger, Jr., has written. "When they act on these fantasies, as the Spanish did in the sixteenth century, the French in the seventeenth, the English in the eighteenth, the Germans and Japanese and Russians and Americans in the twentieth, they tend to become international menaces."[15] Certainly postwar Americans never classified themselves as such. Rather, they were benefactors, celebrants of the

14. Quoted in Henry H. Adams, *Harry Hopkins: A Biography* (New York, 1977), p. 398.
15. Arthur Schlesinger, Jr., "America: Experiment or Destiny?" *American Historical Review*, LXXXII(June 1977), 518. Denis Brogan wrote in 1952 that "probably the only people in the world who now have the historical sense of inevitable victory are the Americans." Denis W. Brogan, "Illusions of American Omnipotence," *Harper's*, CCV(December, 1952), 21–28.

American success story, spreading their economic and political riches to the less fortunate through world leadership.[16]

Lessons from the past also held a place in the American ideology. Biographer Gaddis Smith has noted that Dean Acheson believed that "only the United States had the power to grab hold of history and make it conform."[17] What history? The history of depression, political extremism, aggression, and war in the twentieth century. Americans recalled that they had jilted the League of Nations and had courted isolationism and an appeasement policy in the dreadful 1930s. Many Americans blamed themselves for permitting Japanese militarists, German stormtroopers, and Italian fascists to march and plunder. "History has bestowed on us a solemn responsibility," Truman remarked in 1944. "We shall, we must, be a mighty force at the peace conference. We failed before to give a genuine peace—we dare not fail this time."[18] It was America's second chance—the opportunity to throw off the mistakes of the past and claim its rightful first ranking among nations. The United States would permit no more Munichs, no more appeasement, no more compromise with aggressive totalitarianism, no more depression, and no more Pearl Harbors.[19] The new bywords were leadership and

16. Jonathan Daniels talked with President Roosevelt in mid-1944: "All throughout his conversation he indicated an almost boyish interest in geography, and I got the strange impression that in planning the future of the world he was like a boy playing trains with the world, setting up cities, planning free towns." Jonathan Daniels, *White House Witness* (Garden City, N.Y., 1975), p. 222. For the missionary, expansionist character of the American self-image, see Stephen E. Ambrose, *Rise to Globalism: American Foreign Policy, 1938–1976* (Baltimore, 1976; rev. ed.), p. 118; O. Edmund Clubb, *The Witness and I* (New York, 1974), p. 16; Walton, *Henry Wallace, Harry Truman, and the Cold War*, pp. 37–38; Tucker, *Radical Left*, pp. 69, 74; J. William Fulbright, "Reflections: In Thrall to Fear," *New Yorker*, XLVII(January 8, 1972), 41–62; William A. Williams, *The Tragedy of American Diplomacy* (New York, 1962), pp. 9–10.

17. Gaddis Smith, *Dean Acheson* (New York, 1972), p. 416.

18. *Congressional Record*, XC(1944), Appendix, p. 265. See also *Public Papers, Truman*, 1948, p. 292.

19. For discussion of the historical imperative, see Ernest R. May, *"Lessons of the Past* (New York, 1973), and Michael Roskin, "From Pearl Harbor to Vietnam: Shifting Generational Paradigms and Foreign Policy," *Political Science Quarterly*, LXXXIX(Fall 1974), 563–588.

preparedness. "We must continue to be a military nation if we are to maintain leadership among other nations," Truman told his Cabinet in his worry about the dangers of demobilizing too rapidly. Secretary Byrnes added that "we must not make the mistake made after the last war."[20]

As an avid reader of historical works, President Truman believed that history "has some extremely valuable lessons to teach." Indeed, he wrote, "we must know how to apply the lessons of history in a practical way."[21] The lessons he drew from history often reached as far back as the days of ancient Greece, but his immediate instruction came from the tumultuous events of the decade of the Great Depression. He and other Americans feared that the 1940s would be an ugly replay of the 1930s, and they came to believe that the Soviets were seizing the staff of aggressive totalitarianism wrested from the Nazis in World War II. NBC news analyst Clifton Utley expressed a popular postwar assumption: "If we run out again we will create a vacuum."[22] The experience of pre-1945 American–Russian relations helped to conjure up the image of a self-interested, recalcitrant, revolutionary, untrustworthy nation bent on destroying Western capitalism—a burly, bewiskered, Bolshevik whacking away at the foundations of world order. The iconoclastic Bolshevik Revolution, the seizure of foreign-owned property, the refusal to honor Czarist debt obligations, antagonism between Americans and Communists during the Allied intervention in the Russian civil war, anticapitalist propaganda, the ineffectiveness of American diplomatic recognition in 1933 in smoothing relations, and the gruesome Stalinist purges all served to sear this image on the American mind. The Nazi-Soviet pact of 1939, furthermore, convinced Americans that Nazi Germany and Soviet Russia were really two of a kind, that, as the *Wall Street Journal* put it,

20. Cabinet Meeting, August 31, 1945, Notes on Cabinet Meetings, Connelly Papers. See Byrnes in *Department of State Bulletin*, XIV (March 24, 1946), 482, and Truman in Blum, *Price of Vision*, p. 602.
21. Truman, *Memoirs*, I, 119, 121.
22. Minutes, April 30–May 1, 2, 1946, 34th Annual Meeting of the Chamber of Commerce, Chamber of Commerce Library, Washington, D.C.

"the principal difference between Mr. Hitler and Mr. Stalin is the size of their respective mustaches."[23]

FBI Director J. Edgar Hoover, among others coined a phrase for this simple Communist/Nazi analogy: "Red Fascism."[24] "There isn't any difference in totalitarian states," asserted Truman. "I don't care what you call them, Nazi, Communist or Fascist. . . ."[25] As Moscow spread its influence over Eastern Europe after the war, Americans warned against another system of "satellites." "It looks like the same pattern that Hitler adopted in 1936 when he began to take over the small countries around him," brooded one Congressman.[26] General John R. Deane, head of the American military mission to Russia during the war, wrote in his 1947 memoir that even the marching style of Russian soldiers "closely resembled the [German] goose-step, with arms rigid and legs kicked stiffly to the front. . . ."[27] New Deal "Brain Truster" A. A. Berle also drew heavily on the stereotyped "Red-Fascist" analogy when he recorded the following comments in his 1945 diary: "Same tactics are used: violent propaganda, smear accusations, portrayal of other people's patriotism as criminal or reactionary, financing of fifth columns, stimulated disorders, street terrorism, ultimately direct territorial and occupation demands."[28] Thus, thought Americans, aggressive Nazism cloaked as aggressive Communism (or vice-versa) linked the 1930s and 1940s, and menacing totalitarianism was once again roaming—this time as a Russian bear—far beyond its own habitat. "The image of a

23. *Wall Street Journal*, June 25, 1941.

24. See Les K. Adler and Thomas G. Paterson, "Red Fascism: The Merger of Nazi Germany and Soviet Russia in the American Image of Totalitarianism, 1930's–1950's," *American Historical Review*, LXXV (April 1970), 1046–1064.

25. *Public Papers, Truman, 1947*, p. 238. For other allusions to "Red Fascism," see Truman, *Truman*, pp. 323, 359, 360.

26. Carl T. Durham to John A. Buchanan, March 25, 1947, Folder 773, Durham Papers.

27. Deane, *The Strange Alliance*, p. 4.

28. Adolf A. Berle, *Navigating the Rapids, 1918–1971* (New York, 1973), p. 541.

Stalinist Russia," Kennan argued a decade after popularization of the analogy," "poised and yearning to attack the West, and deterred only by our possession of atomic weapons, was largely a creation of the Western imagination."[29] Imagination or not, distortion or not, Americans imbibed and nourished this component of their postwar ideology, one of the fundamental forces making an activist American foreign policy seem imperative.

Another well-spring of American foreign policy was the fundamental factor of economic-strategic needs—those requirements of the domestic economy and national security which had to be met in order to maintain American well-being. Throughout their history Americans had been a proud, successful trading people. Foreign commerce had always constituted a profitable segment of their economy, and in the War of 1812 and World War I, the United States was willing to fight to uphold the principle of freedom of the seas for its merchants. In the 1930s Secretary of State Cordell Hull, through the Reciprocal Trade Agreements Program and the Export-Import Bank, had attempted to maintain America's prominent position in the global economy. Foreign trade was more than a pocketbook issue; from the American perspective foreign trade contributed to economic health which permitted them, and other countries as well, to enjoy stable, democratic government. As David Potter illustrated in his book *People of Plenty*, Americans had long considered themselves democratic because they were prosperous and prosperous because they were democratic.[30] Foreign trade was significant in strategic terms too, helping the United States to acquire vital raw materials essential to the production of defense goods. Moreover, it was assumed in the peace and prosperity idiom, that foreign trade created bonds of understanding among nations, reducing chances for breaches of peace.

In the postwar era, the United States was the largest supplier

29. George F. Kennan, "Overdue Changes in Our Foreign Policy," *Harper's,* CCXIII(August 1956), 28.
30. David M. Potter, *People of Plenty: Economic Abundance and the American Character* (Chicago, 1954).

of goods to world markets, with exports valued at $10 billion in both 1945 and 1946 and $14 billion a year later.[31] "Any serious failure to maintain this flow," declared an assistant secretary of state, "would put millions of American businessmen, farmers, and workers out of business."[32] American leaders, fearing a postwar recession, believed that successful and expanding foreign trade spelled the difference between depression and prosperity. Statistics buttressed such an assumption. Although the value of exports seldom climbed above 10 percent of the Gross National Product, that seemingly low figure could be misleading. Key industries such as automobiles, trucks, coal, machine tools, and steel relied upon foreign outlets for their economic health. One-eighth of Monsanto Chemical's sales were to customers abroad, and General Motors shipped about 10 percent of its products overseas. Nearly 20 percent of American steel workers owed their jobs to steel exports; the figure for coal miners was 18 percent. In 1947 about half of America's wheat was shipped abroad, and surpluses of citrus fruits, eggs, cotton, rice, and tobacco also needed foreign markets. Secretary of the Treasury John Snyder persuasively pointed up the significance of foreign trade: "The importance of U.S. exports to the American economy is evidenced by the fact that they exceed in volume such important single elements of the national product as expenditures on producers' durable equipment, consumers' expenditures on durable goods, the net changes in business inventories, the total expenditures by State and local governments or even private construction."[33]

Dire consequences were predicted should economic dislocations abroad, especially in Europe, make it difficult for foreign buyers to purchase American products. The Committee for Economic Development, a group of businessmen running America's

31. For these figures and other data cited below, see Paterson, *Soviet-American Confrontation*, ch. 1.

32. Willard L. Thorp in Department of State, *Problems of United States Foreign Economic Policy* (Washington, D.C., 1947), p. 3.

33. John Snyder to the President, "Comments on Draft of the Economic Report of the President," [n.d.], OF 396, Truman Papers.

largest corporations, anticipated "great readjustment, much inefficient production and a lower standard of living," and the president of the Chamber of Commerce, Eric Johnston, warned that a sharp drop in foreign trade "would mean vast population shifts, and . . . new ways of subsistence would have to be found for entire geographic regions."[34] Truman himself joined the "peace and prosperity" ideology with economic-strategic needs in a 1946 statement: "A large volume of soundly based international trade is essential if we are to achieve prosperity in the United States, build a durable structure of world economy and attain our goal of world peace and prosperity."[35]

American leaders also emphasized that exports paid for imports that were vital to American industry and to the military establishment. In many categories of raw materials, the United States was a "have-not" nation. The director of the Bureau of Mines reported domestic deficiencies in zinc, tin, mercury, manganese, lead, cobalt, tungsten, chromite, industrial diamonds, nickel, bauxite, and copper—or a total of more than fifty materials.[36] Imported materials from fifty-seven different countries were necessary to American steel production. Truman noted that strategic raw materials from abroad contributed to a major new weapon in the American arsenal: "Without foreign trade . . . it would be difficult, if not impossible, for us to develop atomic energy."[37] Oil also held both economic and strategic importance. A Senate committee concluded that "the United States, accounting for about two-thirds of the entire world's petroleum consumption, is compelled to control an adequate share of foreign oil production and reserves to insure high living standards in its domestic economy," and Petroleum

34. Committee for Economic Development, *International Trade, Foreign Investment, and Domestic Employment* (New York, 1945), p. 10; Johnston in B. C. Forbes, ed., *America's Fifty Foremost Business Leaders* (New York, 1948), p. 226.
35. *Public Papers, Truman, 1946*, p. 354.
36. Senate, Committee on Foreign Relations, *European Recovery Program* (hearings; Washington, D.C., 1948), p. 369.
37. *Department of State Bulletin*, XXI(September 12, 1949), 401.

Administrator for War Harold Ickes worried whether the United States would be able to "oil another war in the future."[38] Petroleum, as World Wars I and II demonstrated and as the Japanese knew before Pearl Harbor, moved tanks, ships, and airplanes alike. American leaders feared that the Second World War, in its insatiable thirst for oil, had depleted American resources and that postwar consumption would outstrip supply. "Oil, enough oil, within our certain grasp seemed ardently necessary to greatness and independence in the twentieth century" was Herbert Feis' summary of American thinking, although he considered the fears exaggerated.[39]

America's security needs demanded not only economic expansion in order to satisfy raw-materials requirements but also a global military watch. With the two vast oceans no longer providing natural defensive barriers, with the advent of atomic weapons, the air age, and wide-ranging naval fleets, Americans believed it necessary to secure outlying bases to protect approaches to the United States and to permit the American military to police or deter disorders far from home. "Experience in the recent war demonstrated conclusively," a Joint Chiefs of Staff (JCS) report noted in 1946, "that the defense of a nation, if it is to be effective, must begin beyond its frontiers."[40] In early 1946 the JCS approved a list of twenty foreign locations where American military air transit rights were desired. Sites as

38. "Report of the Group on American Interests in Foreign Countries," October 15, 1945, vol. VIII, Special Committee Investigating Petroleum Resources, U.S. Senate Records, National Archives; Petroleum Administrator Harold Ickes quoted in Herbert Feis, *Three International Episodes: Seen from E.A.* (New York, 1966 [c. 1947]), p. 99. See also *Department of State Bulletin*, XIII (August 5, 1945), 175.

39. Feis, *Three International Episodes,* p. 97. See also Herbert Feis, *Petroleum and American Foreign Policy* (Stanford, 1944; Ford Research Institute, Stanford University Commodity Policy Studies No. 3); David A. Rosenberg, "The U.S. Navy and the Problem of Oil in a Future War: The Outline of a Strategic Dilemma, 1945–1950," *Naval War College Review* XXIX(Summer 1976), 53–64; Bernard Brodie, *Foreign Oil and American Security* (New Haven, 1947), p. 1.

40. "Statement of the Effect of Atomic Weapons on National Security and Military Organization," JCS 1477/10, March 31, 1946, Box 166, Central Decimal File 471.6, Joint Chiefs of Staff Records.

far-flung as Algiers (Algeria), Cairo (Egypt), Dhahran (Saudi Arabia), Karachi (India), Saigon (French Indochina), Acapulco (Mexico), San Jose (Guatemala), and the Cook Islands (New Zealand) came within JCS's definition of needs.[41] The State Department itself formulated an extensive list of foreign bases considered "essential" or "required" for national security. Burma, Canada, the Fiji Islands, New Zealand, Cuba, Greenland, Ecuador, French Morocco, Senegal, Iceland, Liberia, Panama, Peru, and the Azores, among others, earned spots in this impressive example of the postwar American global perspective.[42] Many of these areas in fact became sites for the American military. Admiral Chester W. Nimitz reasoned that "the ultimate security of the United States depends in major part on our ability to control the Pacific Ocean," and he joined Truman Administration officials in a policy of retaining under American control the Pacific islands (Carolines, Marshalls, and Marianas) captured from the Japanese.[43] "You mean to put them [American naval forces] everywhere?" Senator Claude Pepper of Florida asked Navy Secretary Forrestal on the telephone. "Wherever there is a sea," Forrestal crisply replied.[44]

Nations seek to fulfill their ideological preferences and to realize their economic-strategic needs. They also strive to enlarge and protect their national power, another fundamental of American foreign policy. "International politics, like all politics," Hans J. Morgenthau has written, "is a struggle for power."[45] Power is the facilitator, the enforcer, the symbol of greatness, and the ability to modify the conduct of other states or to prevent them from influencing you. Power, of course, is not absolute, and it never reaches as far as the nation possessing it would like it to reach because of obstacles thrown up by the

41. *Foreign Relations, 1946,* I, 1144 (with maps).
42. *Ibid.,* pp. 1180–1182.
43. Quoted in Robert G. Albion and Robert H. Connery, *Forrestal and the Navy* (New York, 1962), p. 170.
44. Telephone Conversation, Senator Claude Pepper and James Forrestal, March 24, 1947, Box 91, James Forrestal Papers, Princeton University Library, Princeton, N.J.
45. Morgenthau, *Politics Among Nations,* p. 25.

international system and the hostility of other nations. No nation possessing power is willing to give it up. The very existence of power thrusts a nation into the maelstrom of world politics. "Evasion of major international issues is a real possibility for Costa Rica," concluded a National Security Council paper. "For the U.S. it is an illusion. Our silence is as loud as our words."[46]

Foreign commentators sensed America's flush of power and wondered how it would be used. *The Economist* (London) editorialized in 1947 that World War II "has enormously increased the scale upon which the United States now towers above its fellows. Like mice in the cage of an elephant, they follow with apprehension the movements of the mammoth. What chance would they stand if it were to begin to throw its weight about, they who are in danger even if it only decides to sit down?"[47] From the perspective of official London, historian Christopher Thorne has written, the United States' quest for strategic predominance "began to take on some of the less endearing characteristics of a runaway rhinoceros."[48] Indeed, the British ambassador to Washington drew London's attention to "America's consciousness of superior power, or as one columnist puts it, 'her capacity for Promethean rule,' " and remarked, with a touch of ridicule, that Americans were "accustomed enough at home to the idea of bigger and better elephants. . . ."[49]

Because they seemed uneasy about wielding their power too conspicuously, Americans, quipped an Asian diplomat, were like the "virgin who wanted to do it, but didn't know how."[50] Churchill was more frank, annoyed with American criticism of British practice of "power politics": "Is having a Navy twice as strong as any other 'power politics'? Is having an overwhelming Air Force, with bases all over the world, 'power politics'? Is having all the gold in the world buried in a cavern 'power

46. NSC-51 (March 29, 1949), quoted in McMahon, "The United States and Decolonization in Southeast Asia," p. 266.
47. *The Economist*, CLII(May 24, 1947), 785.
48. Thorne, *Allies of a Kind*, p. 502.
49. Earl of Halifax to Ernest Bevin, August 9, 1945, AN 2560/22/45, Foreign Office Correspondence.
50. Quoted in Diary, November 2, 1946, Box 24, Davies Papers.

politics'?"[51] Actually, Americans had always known how to exercise power, their self-effacing confessions to the contrary notwithstanding, and their expansionist record in the nineteenth and twentieth centuries stood as salient testimony. In the postwar world, the foundations of their national power insured that they would want to and had to advance that record.

Economic power, political power, and military power were the elements of national strength for Americans. Their vast economic power gave them a heady place in the world economy and influence over war-torn nations eager for relief and reconstruction funds. Harriman assumed in 1944 that "economic assistance is one of the most effective weapons" with which the United States could affect events in Russia's developing sphere in Eastern Europe.[52] British Prime Minister Clement Attlee recognized the impact of this economic power when his government asked Washington for a postwar loan. "We weren't in a position to bargain," he said. "We had to have the loan."[53] Soviet official Andrei Zhdanov summarized an assumption common to both Communists and non-Communists: "Of all the capitalist powers, only one—the United States—emerged from the war not only unweakened, but even considerably stronger economically and militarily."[54] America was the "workshop of the world."[55] This prominent economic status carried responsibility. "The United States is the only country in the world today," Secretary Marshall announced in 1948, "which has the economic power and productivity to furnish the needed assistance."[56] President Truman minced no words: "We are the giant of the economic world."[57]

51. Quoted in Thorne, *Allies of a Kind*, p. 515.
52. *Foreign Relations, 1944*, IV, 931.
53. Francis Williams, *Twilight of Empire: Memoirs of Prime Minister Clement Attlee* (New York, 1962), p. 134.
54. Andrei Zhdanov, *The International Situation* (Moscow, 1947), pp. 11–12.
55. M.J. Brown, "The Foreign Policy of the United States," *Yearbook of World Affairs, 1948* (London, 1948), p. 39.
56. Senate, *European Recovery Program*, p. 2.
57. Department of State, *Peace, Freedom, and World Trade* (Washington, D.C., 1947), p. 5.

Americans were proud that they had more airplanes, more automobiles, more refrigerators, and more bathtubs than anybody else. They produced and used more coal and steel than any other people. Their corporations controlled 42 percent of the proved oil reserves in the Middle East. By 1948 Americans produced about 41 percent of the world's goods and services. Their abundant fields yielded an agricultural surplus to feed a hungry world. The president boasted that the United States had "fifty percent of the world's industrial machine and produces two-thirds of the world's combined industrial output. We are richly endowed with natural resources. We possess the mobility, the friends, and the good-will . . . that enable us to supplement our supply of raw materials with purchases throughout the world." In short, Truman asserted in 1947, "we have it in our power today either to make the world economy work or, simply by failing to take the proper action, to allow it to collapse."[58]

The United States also enjoyed enviable international political power. As Truman said, America possessed "friends." The members of the American sphere of influence, in Asia, Latin America, the Middle East, and Europe, voted with the United States within international organizations. In the Security Council of the United Nations, the United States did not have to exercise its veto power until 1970. Its friends and clients in the Council provided American positions with majority votes, therein bestowing a "hidden veto" power upon the United States. Russia, on the other hand, had to resort conspicuously to the veto—105 times between 1946 and 1969. As it was, a large percentage of the Soviet vetoes were rendered impotent by American political power exerted somewhere else in the United Nations.[59] For example, with the help of the usually loyal votes of some twenty Latin American governments, the United States commanded results in the General Assembly. In the period

58. "Remarks by the President to the Group Meeting at the White House," draft, October 27, 1947, OF 426, Truman Papers.
59. See John G. Stoessinger, *The United Nations and the Superpowers* (New York, 1970; 2nd ed.), p. 10; Harlan Cleveland, "U.S. Learns the Politics of the Veto," *New York Times*, January 18, 1976.

1945–66, the United States repeatedly received a two-thirds majority vote for its positions on Cold War issues.[60]

The United States also occupied a prominent position in the United Nations Relief and Rehabilitation Administration, the agency launched by forty-four nations in 1943 to help feed, clothe, and dispense medicine to the hundreds of thousands of people uprooted by the war in Europe and Asia. The United States provided three-quarters of UNRRA's $4-billion expenditure before the organization was disbanded in 1947. Yet although the United States carried weight in high echelons, it did not control distribution in the field. UNRRA existed only so long as the United States was willing to fund the body. The Truman administration killed UNRRA because it decided that the United States should unilaterally distribute the benefits of its economic power to maximize political influence, rather than suffer the dissipation of that power in an international association. Acheson explained in 1947 that henceforth the United States would extend relief aid "in accordance with our judgment and supervised with American personnel."[61]

In both the International Bank for Reconstruction and Development (World Bank) and the International Monetary Fund, the United States flexed its political (and economic) muscle. Created in 1944 at the Bretton Woods Conference, these institutions were nominally "international." Actually they became instruments of American diplomacy, because the Bank and Fund were located in Washington, D.C., Americans sat as key officials (the president of the World Bank has always been an American), the dollar was in great demand and all dollar loans from these organizations had to be approved by the United States, and especially because the United States, as the largest subscriber, held one-third of the votes. In the early years of the World Bank, loans went to American friends like France and

60. Edward T. Rowe, "The United States, the United Nations, and the Cold War," *International Organization*, XXV(Winter 1971), 59–78; Frederick H. Gareau, *The Cold War, 1947 to 1967* (Denver, 1969); Kolko, *Politics of War*, pp. 467–479.

61. Senate, Committee on Foreign Relations, *Assistance to Greece and Turkey* (hearings; Washington, D.C., 1947), p. 37.

Denmark and were denied to countries closely linked to the Soviet Union such as Poland and Czechoslovakia. A Bretton Woods negotiator recognized that the Bank and Fund came to resemble "the operation of power politics rather than of international cooperation—except that the power employed is financial instead of military and political."[62] As the piper, the United States called the tune.

"The surest guaranty that no nation will dare again to attack us," Truman stated shortly after World War II, "is to remain strong in the only kind of strength an aggressor can understand —military power." Military power, he knew, meant more than soldiers and armaments. He pointed to the productive power of American farms, mines, and factories and the abundance of natural resources as important parts of the totality of American military power. Indeed, the "United States now has a fighting strength greater than at any time in our history. It is greater than that of any other nation in the world."[63] The administration suffered public pressure to "bring the boys home" hurriedly after the war, but despite demobilization, the United States still maintained the world's largest navy, an unmatched air force of long-range capabilities, a peacetime army far larger than ever before, and a monopoly of the deadliest weapon of all, the atomic bomb.[64] National security was insured and America's adversaries were at bay. Still, Americans sometimes felt insecure, uncertain as they were about Soviet intentions, usually believing the worst could happen and on occasion underestimating their own military might.

With its two-ocean navy, America was the postwar mistress

62. For American participation in the World Bank and International Monetary Fund, see Paterson, *Soviet-American Confrontation,* ch. 7, and Alfred E. Eckes, Jr., *A Search for Solvency: Bretton Woods and the International Monetary System, 1941–1947* (Austin, 1975). Harry White quoted in Lloyd C. Gardner, *Economic Aspects of New Deal Diplomacy* (Madison, Wis., 1964), p. 290.

63. *Public Papers, Truman, 1945,* pp. 404–406.

64. See, for example, Thomas B. Inglis, "Basic Factors in World Relations," February, 1947, Office of Naval Intelligence, Strategic Plans Division Records, Office of Chief of Naval Operations, Box 110 (A-14), Naval Historical Center.

of the seas. As Secretary Forrestal, who had enthusiastically read Alfred T. Mahan's *The Influence of Sea Power Upon History,* observed, "no enemy can reach us without crossing the sea. We cannot reach an aggressor without crossing the sea."[65] The President waxed proud in October, 1945, when he detailed American naval superiority at the end of the war: "The fleet, on V-J Day, consisted of twelve hundred warships, more than fifty thousand supporting and landing craft, and over forty thousand navy planes. By that day, ours was a seapower never before equalled in the history of the world." Even after demobilization, he went on, "the United States will still be the greatest naval power on earth."[66]

Truman also applauded America's air force. In the "air age," Americans flew supreme, able to defend American skies, to deliver destruction to others, and to frighten would-be aggressors. In 1943 Hollywood producer Walt Disney released a film, *Victory Through Air Power,* which helped herald the new era and to popularize the crippling capabilities of air power. According to one film critic, Disney impressed the "lay mind with the seemingly limitless potential of the airplane as an offensive instrument of war." Viewers of the dramatic film—including Roosevelt and Churchill, who viewed it one evening at the 1944 Quebec Conference—saw in "a roaring blaze of technicolor" the leveling of Japan by tons of air-delivered bombs.[67] Aware of their air superiority, American officials could agree with Harriman's statement in 1947 that American air power served to deter the Soviet military, because "there is only one thing which the leaders of the Soviet Union fear, and that is the American air force."[68]

American armed forces joined naval and air power to enhance the impressive military standing of the United States. Total

65. Quoted in Albion and Connery, *Forrestal and the Navy,* p. 186.
66. *Public Papers, Truman,* 1945, p. 432.
67. Review by T.M.P. in *New York Times Film Reviews, 1913–1968* (New York, 1970; 6 vols.), III, 1947. See also Bob Thomas, *Walt Disney: An American Original* (New York, 1976), pp. 183–186.
68. "Statement by W. A. Harriman," September 8, 1947, Folder C2-1, President's Air Policy Commission Records, Truman Library.

American military personnel numbered 3 million in 1946 (down from the wartime peak of 12 million), 1.6 million in 1947, 1.4 million in 1948, and 1.6 million in 1949. The Army, which had major occupation responsibilities in Germany and Japan, accounted for much of this total.[69] Civilian and military officials often complained that the Army was undersized and unready for combat, but an annoyed President trimmed the budget requests of all three armed services and lectured them that they exaggerated their needs.[70] Even so, the federal budget reflected the new sense of military preparedness. In fiscal year 1947 defense expenditures represented one-third of the budget, "fabulously large compared to the prewar defense budgets."[71] Secretary Forrestal was one who repeatedly warned about military inadequacies but, at the same time, boasted of American sea and atomic supremacy. Like Truman he knew that America's industrial strength also counted in judgments of military power, and he believed that large foreign aid programs—even though they might divert funds from the military—should receive priority. "As long as we can outproduce the world, can control the sea and can strike inland with the atomic bomb," Forrestal reasoned, "we can assume certain risks [spending less than the desired military appropriations so that funds could be spent instead in foreign aid programs] otherwise unacceptable in an effort to restore world trade, to restore the balance of power— military power—and to eliminate some of the conditions which breed war."[72] Military strength, then, lay not just in arms and men but in an economically healthy, politically stable world.

The atomic bomb: Everyone mentioned it and stood in awe of it. This novel weapon had proven its deadly power over Hiroshima and Nagasaki, but it appears that in the postwar era its

69. Department of Commerce, *Historical Statistics*, p. 1141.

70. See Richard F. Haynes, *The Awesome Power: Harry S. Truman as Commander-in-Chief* (Baton Rouge, La. 1973), pp. 120–125 and Yergin, *Shattered Peace*, pp. 270–271.

71. Warner R. Schilling, "The Politics of Defense: Fiscal 1950," in Warner R. Schilling, Paul Y. Hammond, and Glenn H. Snyder, *Strategy, Politics, and Defense Budgets* (New York, 1962), p. 30.

72. Walter Millis, ed., *The Forrestal Diaries* (New York, 1951), pp. 350–351.

power was more symbolic than real, more diplomatic than military. Truman was not sure that "it can ever be used," and, of course, it never was used again in combat.[73] Still, American leaders thought their monopoly of the atomic device, which prevailed until the Soviets exploded their own in 1949, bestowed advantages on the United States. The bomb, they hoped, would serve to restrain the Soviets and might prompt them to make diplomatic concessions, especially over Eastern Europe. The Joint Chiefs of Staff and General Dwight D. Eisenhower agreed that the "existence of the atomic bomb in our hands is a deterrent, in fact, to aggression in the world."[74] Harriman reported from Moscow in the Fall of 1945 that the Soviets themselves "recognized it was an offset to the power of the Red Army. This must have revived their old feeling of insecurity."[75]

Secretary Byrnes articulated more fully than most the potential diplomatic power of the atomic bomb. He "looks to having the presence of the bomb in his pocket" as an "implied threat" at the London Foreign Ministers Conference (1945), Secretary of War Henry L. Stimson grimly recorded in his diary.[76] At that stormy conference itself, V. M. Molotov, as if he had been reading Stimson's private diary, asked Byrnes if he had an atomic bomb in his side pocket. Byrnes quipped that Southerners "carry our artillery in our hip pocket. If you don't cut out all this stalling and let us get down to work, I am going to pull an atomic bomb out of my hip pocket and let you have it."[77] This apparently light moment carried diplomatic meaning: The

73. Diary, October 5, 1945, Harold Smith Papers, Franklin D. Roosevelt Library.

74. Dwight D. Eisenhower to Bernard Baruch, June 14, 1946, Box 166. Central Decimal File 471.6, Joint Chiefs of Staff Records. See also William Leahy to Bernard Baruch, June 11, 1946, Bernard Baruch Papers, Princeton University Library; Admiral C. W. Nimitz to Bernard Baruch, *ibid.*

75. *Foreign Relations, 1945*, V, 923.

76. Quoted in Barton J. Bernstein, "The Quest for Security: American Foreign Policy and International Control of Atomic Energy, 1942–1946," *Journal of American History*, LX(March 1974), 1015. See also Bernstein, "Roosevelt, Truman, and the Atomic Bomb, 1941–1945: A Reinterpretation," *Political Science Quarterly*, XC(Spring 1975), 23–69.

77. Quoted in Lisle Rose, *After Yalta* (New York, 1973), p. 124.

United States was thinking about the marvels of its atomic power, a point that had to put other nations on edge.

The atomic bomb, then, was an implied threat. By the Spring of 1946, however, it appears that Byrnes had learned that atomic power, rather than bearing diplomatic fruit, actually interfered with his attempt to negotiate peace treaties with Hitler's defeated satellites in Eastern Europe. At the March 22, 1946, Cabinet meeting, Byrnes said he believed that the forthcoming Bikini atomic test was "ill-advised" and should be postponed—or abandoned altogether. The reason: The dramatic explosion in the Pacific would disrupt the Paris Peace Conference. He remarked further that the operation had "developed into a big show on the strength of the atomic dictator"—the United States.[78] Holstered or unholstered, the atomic bomb had become a spectacular symbol of American technological ingenuity and supremacy—of American power. The United States understandably would not turn the weapon over to an international control authority. "When we get down to cases," Truman remarked, "is any one of the Big Powers—are we?—going to give up these locks and bolts which are necessary to protect our house . . . against possible outlaw attack . . . until the community is sufficiently stable? Clearly we are not. Nor are the Soviets."[79]

Americans celebrated the elements of their national power and were cognizant of the weight they carried in international affairs, but not necessarily of the reactions that power might trigger.[80] They believed themselves to be exceptional, and foreign observers frequently reminded them of their rare status.

78. Byrnes seemed to worry, too, that the Soviets would want to be present at the test site. Cabinet Meeting, March 22, 1946, Notes on Cabinet Meetings, Connelly Papers.

79. Quoted in Donovan, *Conflict and Crisis*, p. 130.

80. For an interpretation to the contrary, see Professor Adam Ulam's statement that "I don't think we realized how strong we were," in House of Representatives, Committee on Foreign Affairs, *The Cold War: Origins and Development* (hearings; Washington, D.C., 1971), p. 20, and his *The Rivals* (New York, 1971), which finds an "era of American omnipotence" but also argues that Americans did not attempt to use their power, especially their atomic power.

American diplomats knew, too, that the prominent and activist international position of the United States spawned the envy and resentment of others. Byrnes mentioned that Americans appeared to others to "hog leadership," and John Foster Dulles came back from Europe in mid-1947 to report that "even in countries like Britain and France there is rising apprehension at our alleged 'aggressive imperialism.' "[81] Americans were generally and genuinely surprised that their power and intentions evoked hostility and suspicion in others.

In the Fall of 1945, Truman's Cabinet discussed the need for universal military training. One of the participants questioned why the United States had to "police the world." The President declared emphatically that it must, for "in order to carry out a just decision the courts must have marshals" and "in order to collect monies for county governments it has been found necessary to employ a sheriff."[82] Joseph Jones, who later helped write the momentous Truman Doctrine, captured the popular, postwar American mood: "The moment is ours."[83] Exuberant, self-confident, proud of their heritage and ideals, instructed by lessons from the past, needing foreign trade, having a global strategic outlook, and flushed with power, Americans wanted to, and felt they had to, seize the moment—"to grab hold of history and make it conform." They ultimately failed to do so because their power was not omnipotent but relative—with its effectiveness dependent upon local and international conditions—and because a bold and hostile Soviet Russia, with another vision of history, arose as a challenger.

81. Cabinet Meeting, October 12, 1945, Notes on Cabinet Meetings, Connelly Papers (Byrnes's comment was in reference specifically to the United Nations Food and Agriculture Organization); John Foster Dulles to Geoffrey Parsons, June 16, 1947, John Foster Dulles Papers, Princeton University Library. See also Howard K. Smith, *The State of Europe* (New York, 1949), pp. 70, 92–94. Arnold Toynbee referred to the " 'invisible empire' which the United States has built up through its commerce, the size of which we sometimes might not appreciate," in "British Foreign Policy," Discussion Meeting Report, March 13, 1947, Records of Groups, vol. XIV, Council on Foreign Relations Files.

82. Cabinet Meeting, September 7, 1945, Notes on Cabinet Meetings, Connelly Papers.

83. Jones, *A Modern Foreign Policy*, p. 33.

5

Toughness: The Tactics of Truman's Diplomacy

WHEN THE Soviet commissar for foreign affairs heard about the death of Franklin D. Roosevelt, he rushed in the dark of the early morning hours to Spaso House, the American ambassador's residence in Moscow. V. M. Molotov was visibly shaken and pensive, wondering about the new man in the White House to whom the powers of government now belonged.[1] The British ambassador to Russia also worried. Archibald Clark-Kerr told Ambassador Harriman on April 13, 1945, the day after the president's death, that he was deeply troubled about the future of world affairs, because "so much that matters was gathered in the hands and heart of that man."[2]

The president of the United States in the 1940s, and after, was correctly recognized as the supreme decisionmaker and chief diplomat in the creation and conduct of American foreign policy. Roosevelt's successor, Truman, put it bluntly: "I make American foreign policy."[3] His assistant, Clark M. Clifford, once observed that the American government is a chameleon which takes its color from the character and personality of the

1. Harriman and Abel, *Special Envoy*, p. 440.
2. Archibald Clark-Kerr to W. Averell Harriman, April 13, 1945, Box 1372-B, Moscow Post Files, Department of State Records.
3. Quoted in Clinton Rossiter, *The American Presidency* (New York, 1956), p. 10.

president.[4] As Franz Schurmann has written, the president transforms "ideological beliefs into structures of organizational power."[5] Not only as the principal diplomat but also as the commander-in-chief of the military establishment, leader of his political party, chief executive of a huge bureaucracy, and initiator or vetoer of legislation, the president sits at the pinnacle of authority and influence, not only in the nation but also in the world. By negotiating executive agreements instead of treaties (which require the Senate's approval), the president also enjoys discretionary authority and an aggrandizement of his powers in the making of foreign policy. Whether the president exercises all of the powers at his command and whether he is able to persuade others to follow his preferences depends upon the particular individual and the prevailing milieu.

To emphasize presidential mastery of the American foreign policy process is to beg significant questions. Does it really matter who is president—a Roosevelt or a Truman? This question springs from one that humanists and social scientists have been grappling with for centuries: In the great scheme of things, do individuals count? If we accept the proposition, which was spelled out in the last chapter, that certain fundamentals stand at the core of American foreign policy, we could argue that any president is bound, even dictated to, by those basic beliefs and needs. In other words, he has little freedom to make choices wherein his distinctive style, personality, experience, and intellect shape America's role and position in international relations in a way that is uniquely his. It might be suggested that a person's behavior is a function not of his individual traits but rather of the office that he holds and that the office is circumscribed by the larger demands of the national interest, rendering individuality inconsequential. It might be said, moreover, that to attribute importance to individuals in international diplomacy, the scholar

4. Arthur M. Schlesinger, Jr., *The Imperial Presidency* (Boston, 1973), p. 381.
5. Franz Schurmann, *The Logic of World Power* (New York, 1974), p. 17.

must prove that other officials in similar posts would have acted differently. These are formidable points, and they deserve consideration.

By whom and how diplomacy is made and conducted constitute part of a comprehensive view of the Cold War. Conduct, or tactics, directly influence foreign leaders and hence help to shape the chances for success or failure in negotiations. Harriman believed that "personal relationships could influence—even if they could not determine—the affairs of nations. . . ." In the last days of the 1944 presidential campaign, Harriman, as a Democrat and ambassador to the Soviet Union, blended his political and diplomatic preferences when he publicly told the American people that Roosevelt had earned the confidence of foreign leaders, "an invaluable asset in obtaining decisions which will further our interests and build the kind of world in which we want to live. This confidence we can ill afford to lose at this critical and formative time."[6] No doubt, Harriman had in mind the working relationship between Roosevelt and Stalin and Stalin's own earnest hope that the president would be reelected.[7]

Harriman's essential point, and the premise of this chapter, is that how we behave affects how others react to us and hence influences the outcome of negotiations. If we shout or lecture, we may not be listened to. If we are rude, others may take offense. If we do not explain ourselves well, we may be misunderstood. If we dress in a particular way, we may be stereotyped. If we take off a shoe and pound it on the table, we may be considered emotionally unstable and unreliable. If we stalk out of a meeting in protest, we may be thought intemperate or lacking interest in serious talks. If we strut in a haughty manner, others may be put off. If we are self-righteously rigid, others may decide not to talk with us. How we express ourselves—the words we use—may determine how persuasive we are. For example, when a government report on United States relations with nations rich in raw materials used the expression "exploit" rather than "develop" to describe American purposes, a State

6. Harriman and Abel, *Special Envoy*, pp. 94, 367.
7. Lowenheim, Langley, and Jonas, *Roosevelt and Churchill*, p. 587.

Department official objected, for "the flavor of a word can make a great deal of difference in the effect of the document on sensitive readers in other countries."[8] George F. Kennan, who probably exaggerated the significance of diplomatic style but who nevertheless knew its place, has written in his memoirs that "it is axiomatic in the world of diplomacy that methodology and tactics assume an importance by no means inferior to concept and strategy."[9] How something is done, and who does it, matters. Many diplomatic leaders, who like others nurture their personal likes and dislikes, have thought so themselves.

Throughout the Cold War American and Soviet leaders have frequently disparaged the style and personnel of the other, bemoaning the apparent negative impact upon negotiations. "If Roosevelt lived," Molotov mused in late April of 1945, there would be much less chance of "complications" arising in Soviet-American relations.[10] Several months later he complained that Truman, unlike Roosevelt, did not hold a "friendly" attitude toward the Soviet Union.[11] In May, to allay such Soviet wariness about his administration, Truman sent the ailing Harry Hopkins—Roosevelt's trusted adviser and close friend—rather than Harriman to meet with Premier Josef Stalin. Stalin held Hopkins in high esteem because the American had made an exhausting trip to Russia in 1941 to demonstrate United States support for Russia after Germany's military attack of that June. The Soviet leader remembered that gesture, and as a result the Hopkins-Stalin talks of 1945 proceeded in an amiable and constructive manner, providing one of the few positive moments in the emerging Cold War.[12] The American assumption had been

8. Memorandum, W. B. Brown to Mr. Coombs, April 11, 1952, Box 25, President's Materials Policy Committee Records, Truman Library.

9. Kennan, *Memoirs*, p. 290.

10. Quoted in Yergin, *Shattered Peace*, p. 82. See also Andrei Vyshinsky's comment: "The death of Roosevelt had disturbed Soviet leaders. They knew ROOSEVELT, and knew what to expect. They did not know TRUMAN or what his attitude would be." Diary-Journal, July 15, 1945, Box 18, Davies Papers.

11. *Foreign Relations, 1945*, II, 247.

12. Harriman and Abel, *Special Envoy*, p. 268.

that the outcome of this special assignment might be affected by whom the president chose to be his emissary.

Two years later Dean Acheson revealed how much he himself was affected by style. This polished, aristocratic public servant found the Soviets insulting, coarse, and offensive. "Senator," he remarked at a Congressional hearing, "I think it is a mistake to believe that you can, at any time, sit down with the Russians and solve questions." He pressed the point: "You cannot sit down with them."[13] Out of office he was more outspoken: "I got along with everybody who was housebroken. But I was never very close to the Russians. They were abusive; they were rude. I just didn't like them."[14] It is not surprising, then, that Acheson was one among a growing number of top American officials who presided over a gradual abandonment of diplomacy itself in the Cold War.

Acheson's contemporaries thought that tactics were important, and they spent considerable energy in scrutinizing the personalities, methods, and styles of their adversaries and commenting at length about personal likes and dislikes. The international system was inherently conflict-ridden, and the fundamental characteristics of the United States and the Soviet Union determined basic interests and policies, but had different individuals and styles been present, perhaps the sharper edges of the Soviet-American confrontation might have been blunted. At least we know that both Americans and Russians thought so. Systemic disorders and fundamental needs and beliefs foment profound diplomatic crises, but key individuals, operating with their particular traits, interpret the crises and determine whether they are kept manageable and defused quickly or are prolonged and escalated to the brink of war. Top diplomats decide whether negotiations are to serve as an avenue to tension-reducing solutions.

Decisionmaking in both the Roosevelt and Truman administrations was concentrated in the hands of the president and a small circle of advisers around him. Roosevelt was a devoted practitioner of personal diplomacy, often neglecting to inform

13. Senate, *Legislative Origins of the Truman Doctrine*, p. 95.
14. *New York Times*, October 13, 1971.

the Department of State about his plans and decisions. Roosevelt believed that through his magnetic personality and contagious charm he could establish, as Harriman recalled, "a close personal relationship with Stalin in wartime, to build confidence among the Kremlin leaders that Russia, now an acknowledged major power, could trust the West."[15] As Roosevelt told Churchill, "I think I can personally handle Stalin better than either your Foreign Office or my State Department."[16] Roosevelt may not have been wrong. Stalin often deferred to Roosevelt but did not hesitate to "stick a knife into Churchill whenever he had the chance."[17] Roosevelt's death in 1945 denies us a true testing of his firm belief in the magic of his personalized diplomacy, but we do know that the Soviets sensed a serious change in style and attitude with the entrance of Harry S. Truman into the White House.[18]

V. M. Molotov witnessed the difference between the two presidents first-hand and early. On April 23, 1945, just over a week after FDR's death, Truman held a momentous meeting with the Soviet commissar. The new president sharply scolded the Soviet diplomat and demanded compliance with the Yalta agreement providing for the reorganization of the Polish government. Molotov insisted that the Soviets were working toward that goal. Truman pressed again, charging Moscow with failing to honor its side of the bargain. The usually blunt and irascible Molotov turned "a little ashy."[19] According to Truman, the

15. Harriman and Abel, *Special Envoy*, p. 170. See also p. 390.
16. Quoted in Yergin, *Shattered Peace*, p. 65.
17. Harriman and Abel, *Special Envoy*, p. 228. Also p. 362.
18. Historians often cite a Roosevelt letter to Churchill of April 6, 1945 to argue that FDR himself was moving toward a "tougher" stance vis-à-vis Russia just before he died. But, as Warren F. Kimball has pointed out, that letter was written by hard-liner Admiral William D. Leahy, not FDR. The president himself wrote a letter on April 10, two days before his death, in which he told Churchill that problems with the Soviets usually straightened out and that he and Churchill should "minimize the general Soviet problems as much as possible. . . ." Warren F. Kimball, "Churchill and Roosevelt: The Personal Equation," *Prologue*, VI(Fall 1974), 173–174.
19. Charles E. Bohlen, *Witness to History, 1929–69* (New York, 1973, p. 213.

Soviet diplomat said, "I have never been talked to like that in my life." Truman shot back in Dutch-uncle style: "Carry out your agreements and you won't get talked to like that."[20] Molotov stormed out of the White House. Harriman regretted that the President had gone "at it so hard," and Henry L. Stimson commented on Truman's "rather brutal frankness," but Truman himself gloated over what he called his "tough method": "I gave it to him straight 'one-two to the jaw.' I let him have it straight."[21] Truman's dressing-down of Russia's foreign secretary suggested to officials in both Washington and Moscow that the new president was his own man, with his own ideas and ways of conducting diplomacy—certainly not a replica of Franklin D. Roosevelt. A British diplomat at the Potsdam Conference noted a difference. "Roosevelt's death changed everything," Lord Moran recorded in his diary. "Truman is very blunt; he means business" and "can hand out the rough stuff."[22]

Truman was, of course, strikingly different from Roosevelt in background, personality, and style. Whereas the latter was a compromiser, the former usually made up his mind quickly, or at least gave this impression, and stuck steadfastly to his convictions. Blacks and whites, with few gray areas, characterized his thinking. Whereas Roosevelt was ingratiating, patient, and evasive, using a variety of techniques from jokes, to rambling storytelling, to "discursive flashes," to hard-nosed politicking to win his point, Truman was brash, abrupt, decisive, impatient, and quick-tempered—characterized by "promptness and snappiness," said Stimson.[23] A man of simple dignity and personal integrity, Truman prided himself on blunt, tart, unadorned language; Roosevelt was a master of dissembling and used disarm-

20. Truman, *Memoirs*, 81–82.
21. Harriman and Abel, *Special Envoy*, pp. 452, 454; Truman quoted in Gaddis, *United States and the Origins of the Cold War*, p. 205.
22. Moran, *Churchill*, p. 306.
23. "Discursive flashes" is a phrase coined by Anthony Eden in Thorne, *Allies of a Kind*, p. 245; Stimson is quoted in Donovan, *Conflict and Crisis*, p. 20. Privately, Truman exploded against the French over their lack of cooperation in Germany and Lebanon: "Those French ought to be taken out and castrated." As for Charles de Gaulle: "I don't like the son of a bitch." *Ibid.*, pp. 58–59.

ing, vague phrases. "The buck stops here," read a sign on Truman's desk. "Give 'em hell, Harry" his political aids recommended, and the President usually did.[24] Truman was "best when he's been mad," noted one of his assistants.[25] Churchill, long an unabashed commentator on human behavior, remarked favorably after meeting Truman at Potsdam that the Missourian was "a man of exceptional character and ability . . . , simple and direct methods of speech, and a great deal of self-confidence and resolution." Indeed, he "takes no notice of delicate ground, he just plants his foot down firmly on it."[26] Truman himself wrote to his mother about his chairmanship at Potsdam: "They all say I took 'em for a ride when I got down to presiding."[27] Indeed, he usually demonstrated simplicity, bravado, and verbal sparring but little low-key patience or understanding of subtleties that are usually essential to constructive diplomatic talks. A self-conscious, bumptious style of toughness came to stand as a trademark of the Truman administration and ultimately became an impediment to diplomacy.

Secretary of Commerce Henry A. Wallace, who would later break with the president, noted in his diary that Truman "seemed as though he was eager to decide in advance of thinking."[28] Truman took enormous pride in his decisiveness.

24. For comments on Truman's "tough" style and its importance, see John L. Gaddis, "Harry S. Truman and the Origins of Containment," in Frank J. Merli and Theodore A. Wilson, eds., *Makers of American Diplomacy* (New York, 1974), pp. 493–520; Yergin, *Shattered Peace*, pp. 72–73; Bert Cochran, *Harry S. Truman and the Crisis Presidency* (New York, 1973); William A. Williams in House, *The Cold War*, p. 44; Athan Theoharis, "The Origins of the Cold War: A Revisionist Interpretation," *Peace and Change*, IV(Fall 1976), 3–11.

25. Handwritten notes by George Elsey, March 2, 1948, Box 20, George Elsey Papers, Truman Library. Elsey also remembered that Truman "did have something of a quick temper and snapped back, sometimes too fast, in press conferences on domestic as well as foreign matters." George Elsey Oral History Interview, Truman Library.

26. "Note of the Prime Minister's Conversation with President Truman at Luncheon, July 18, 1945," by Winston Churchill, Premier 3, 430/8 Prime Minister's Office Records; Churchill ("takes no") quoted in Charles L. Mee Jr., *Meeting at Potsdam* (New York, 1975), p. 75.

27. Quoted in Truman, *Truman*, p. 269.

28. Quoted in Walton, *Henry Wallace, Harry Truman, and the Cold War*, p. 36.

At the same time, he once admitted that "he was not a deep thinker."[29] He said he was "not up on all details" and had "to catch the intricacies of our foreign affairs."[30] On April 21, 1945, just two days before his confrontation with Molotov, Truman told Secretary of State Edward M. Stettinius, Jr., that he, the president, "was very hazy about the Yalta matters" and was "amazed" that the agreement on Poland "wasn't more clear cut."[31]

Although an apt pupil, the new President had much to learn, for as vice-president he had not been included in high-level foreign policy discussions. FDR guarded "his" diplomacy, permitting only a handful of chosen advisers to become privy to "his" foreign policy. During the entire 1944 presidential campaign, Truman had met personally with Roosevelt only five times; he met with the chief executive only three times between the inauguration and FDR's death. Roosevelt, Truman remarked with chagrin in 1948, "never did talk to me confidentially about the war, or about foreign affairs or what he had in mind for the peace after the war."[32] As a senator from 1934 to 1944, Truman did not pay particular attention to foreign affairs; he did not sit, for example, on the Foreign Relations Committee. This distance from important decisions meant that Truman probably did not understand, and certainly did not respect, Roosevelt's personally-crafted wartime agreements with Russia.[33] Thus, the new president was not sensitive to Stalin's protests that he, Truman, was not fulfilling the intent of those accords or continuing Roosevelt's policies. Then, too, because Roosevelt conducted a personal diplomacy that deliberately bypassed the foreign affairs bureaucracy—especially the State Department—his

29. Wallace paraphrase in Blum, *Price of Vision*, p. 373.
30. Quoted in Yergin, *Shattered Peace*, p. 72.
31. Campbell and Herring, *Diaries of Stettinius*, p. 325.
32. Quoted in Truman, *Truman*, p. 358.
33. It was also Truman who said in 1941: "If we see that Germany is winning the war we ought to help Russia, and if Russia is winning we ought to help Germany, and in that way let them kill as many as possible, although I don't want to see Hitler victorious under any circumstances. Neither of them think anything of their pledged word." *New York Times*, June 24, 1941.

death gave long-ignored, disaffected officials an opportunity to reassert their policymaking roles and to gain the new president's ear and support for their counsel. Many of them were not saying the same things that Roosevelt had said, nor were they saying them the way he did.

Henry A. Wallace wondered whether Truman "has enough information behind his decisiveness to enable his decisions to stand up."[34] The question, however, was not whether Truman had a fount of information but the kinds and sources of the information. First, the president used stored information or memory; he recalled the past frequently, drawing lessons which served as guides for policymaking. Truman and many other Americans, as we have already noted, saw the 1940s as a potential replay of the 1930s—with depression, totalitarianism, aggression, and war. Second, Truman used intelligence gathered by his advisers at home and by American diplomats abroad.

As a novice president who had had little contact with high-level diplomacy or the major decisions of World War II, Truman looked in particular to his immediate circle of advisers for information and guidance. They reinforced and encouraged the president's propensity to read simple lessons from history, to see the Soviets as Nazis reincarnate, to distrust negotiations with unregenerate Moscow, and to put his tough, decisive style to work in diplomacy. Secretary of State Edward R. Stettinius, Jr., Admiral William Leahy, Undersecretary of State Joseph Grew, Ambassador W. Averell Harriman, Secretary of the Navy James V. Forrestal, White House assistant Clark M. Clifford, and Secretary of State James F. Byrnes, among others, were listened to by the president not simply because they held positions of authority but because they tended to share Truman's ideas and his diplomatic style. In other words, not only did they go to him; he sought advice from them and drew comfort from the fact that the elite of the foreign affairs establishment thought and wanted to act much like him. Officials who disagreed with him, who regretted his "get-tough" foreign policy, found themselves increasingly isolated. Secretary of War Henry L. Stimson, Secre-

34. Blum, *Price of Vision*, pp. 440–441.

tary of Commerce Henry A. Wallace, and Secretary of the Treasury Henry Morgenthau, Jr., for example, all tried to persuade the president to be more tolerant of the Soviet Union; each resigned or was forced out in 1945–46. The president preferred to surround himself with like-minded people. Secretary of State Byrnes's view was that "the only way to negotiate with the Russians is to hit them hard, and then negotiate."[35] Stalin once quipped that Byrnes was the "most honest horse thief he had ever met."[36] J. Edgar Hoover, longtime director of the Federal Bureau of Investigation, fed into other government agencies information and rumors picked up from a variety of reliable and not-so-reliable sources which suggested a Soviet quest for "world domination."[37] Harriman, who was one of the first diplomats to discuss Soviet-American relations with the new president after Roosevelt's death, also suspected aggressive Soviet intentions and believed in pressing Moscow to adopt American principles in organizing and governing the postwar world. "When it comes to matters of greater importance," Harriman believed as early as September, 1944, "we should make it plain that their failure to *conform to our concepts* will affect our willingness to cooperate with them. . . ." Moreover, on "vital" questions, the United States should inform Moscow that Washington would stand firm, and, he maintained; "I am satistified that in the last analysis Stalin will back down."[38] The deputy administrator of the Foreign Economic Administration, Oscar Cox, spoke with Harriman in April of 1945 and "was disturbed by the undertones of what he said. He seems to be trending towards an anti-Soviet position."[39] Truman told Harriman, surely knowing that the Ambassador shared his opinion, that the president was not afraid of the Russians, because "they needed us more than we

35. Quoted in Thomas G. Paterson, "Potsdam, the Atomic Bomb, and the Cold War: A Discussion with James F. Byrnes," *Pacific Historical Review*, XLI(May 1972), 228.

36. Blum, *Price of Vision*, p. 475.

37. See, for example, Director of the FBI to the Attorney General, October 2, 1946, Box 130, Correspondence of James Forrestal, Department of Navy Records, National Archives.

38. *Foreign Relations, 1944*, IV, 997. Italics added.

39. Diary, April 26, 1945, Oscar Cox Papers, Roosevelt Library.

needed them." He did not expect to win 100 percent of the American case, Truman added, but "we should be able to get 85 percent."[40] Truman and his advisers agreed that "plain talk" would help to achieve this high percentage of victories.[41] Even Stimson, who futilely advised the president not to challenge the Soviets in their own backyard of Eastern Europe, believed that Stalin "can only understand rough talk."[42] The former ambassador to Russia, Joseph Davies, travelled with Truman to the Potsdam Conference and concluded that the president "was surrounded by powerful elements, many of whom were hostile to the Soviets, and did not wish to further good relations with them."[43]

From abroad also came encouragement for a frank expression of American determination in the face of perceived Soviet expansionism. Ambassador to Greece Lincoln MacVeagh exaggerated a Soviet threat and distorted the realities of the civil war, depicting it as the handiwork of Moscow. Ambassador Laurence A. Steinhardt misread Czech politics and undermined non-Communists by successfully urging upon Byrnes an abrupt severance of American aid to Prague; and Ambassador Arthur Bliss Lane repeatedly reported with embellishment Soviet machinations and brutalities in Poland, helping to set in the American mind the belief that what happened in Poland would happen elsewhere in the world.[44] Burton Y. Berry and Maynard B. Barnes, the

40. Quoted in Gaddis, "Harry S. Truman," p. 500.

41. For the expression "plain talk," see "Memorandum on Secretary of State Byrnes' Diplomacy with Regard to the Soviet Union," by C. M. Richardson Dougall, September 1946, RP 4, Foreign Policy Studies Branch, Division of Policy Research, Department of State Records.

42. Quoted in Sherry, *Preparing for the Next War*, p. 174.

43. Journal, July 16, 1945, Box 18, Davies Papers. Henry Wallace's diary, published in Blum, *Price of Vision*, is replete with similar observations.

44. For the roles of these ambassadors, see Paterson, *Soviet-American Confrontation*, pp. 120–136; Martin Weil, *A Pretty Good Club: The Founding Fathers of the U.S. Foreign Service* (New York, 1978), pp. 194–197. Also see their cables in the appropriate *Foreign Relations* volumes. Steinhardt's papers are housed at the Library of Congress; Lane's are in the Yale University Library. Lane has also written *I Saw Poland Betrayed.*

American ambassadors to Rumania and Bulgaria, respectively, reported that it was impossible to deal with the Russians, for, as Barnes put it, they had a "record for double dealing."[45] Kennan advised in 1946 that a "Russian is never more agreeable than after his knuckles have been sharply rapped. He takes well to rough play and rarely holds grudges over it."[46] Right or wrong, this sort of suggestion accorded with Truman's instinctive toughness.

Thus, as historian Ernest R. May has written, "on the whole, the bureaucracy presented to Truman and his advisers a picture of a powerful, ambitious, ruthless, deceitful Soviet Union. . . . Some of them used black and white to portray issues that might have been sketched more faithfully in grays."[47] As May has pointed out, these diplomats in the field witnessed at first hand numerous ugly events stemming from Soviet or Communist activities. What they saw hardened their already tough cynicism toward the Soviet Union and their preference for a flexing of the American diplomatic muscle. Whether their reports and advice were hyperbolic or not, Truman was receptive to such reporting in the first years of the Cold War. It was not, then, so much that Truman was influencing the bureaucrats, or that they were shaping him, but rather that they were thinking along parallel lines. In September of 1946, when the United States was engaged at the Paris Peace Conference in friction-ridden attempts to write treaties for Hitler's former Eastern European satellites of Rumania and Hungary, President Truman cabled Byrnes to "do everything you can to continue but in the final analysis do whatever you think is right and tell [the Russians] to go to hell if you have to."[48] Although Byrnes and the American delegation were more polite than this, the thrust of the president's message was something that they already understood and endorsed, because they had helped shape it. In 1947, former Secretary of State Cordell Hull thought that relations with the USSR were

45. Quoted in May, *"Lessons" of the Past,* pp. 27, 29.
46. Kennan, *Memoirs,* p. 564.
47. May, *"Lessons" of the Past*, pp. 30–31.
48. Harry S. Truman to James F. Byrnes, September 24, 1946, Folder 52, Byrnes Papers.

being mishandled. "It isn't any use kicking a tough hound around," he complained to Acheson, "because a tough hound will kick back."[49]

Unanimity of opinion, of course, was not always present in the foreign affairs establishment, although the president usually demanded and received compliance with his desires. When, in late 1945, Secretary of State Byrnes made compromises with Russia at the Moscow Foreign Ministers Conference on Eastern Europe issues, Truman exploded in disapproval. Byrnes had always been a political rival of Truman's (Byrnes had wanted to be the Democratic vice-presidential candidate in 1944), and that may have exacerbated the matter. Also, Truman thought that Byrnes had failed to keep the president adequately informed about decisions made during the conference. "I'm tired of babying the Soviets," read a memorandum that Truman prepared for a meeting with Byrnes.[50] Three years later he recalled that "Byrnes lost his nerve in Moscow." Indeed, Truman lectured Byrnes that "his appeasement policy was not mine."[51] Byrnes, who continued through 1946 to negotiate with the Soviets in search of peace treaties, soon fell into line behind the president, moved in part by this display of presidential prerogative and power in the making of American foreign policy.

Although Byrnes was willing to accommodate Truman, his colleague in the Cabinet, Commerce Secretary Henry A. Wallace, would not bow to presidential dictate. In 1945–46 he urged Truman, to no avail, to chart a more conciliatory course toward the Soviets. Then, in September of 1946, the independent-minded Wallace told an audience at Madison Square Garden that " 'getting tough' never brought anything real and lasting— whether for schoolyard bullies or businessmen or world powers. The tougher we get, the tougher the Russians will get."[52] For

49. Diary, October 17, 1947, Box 2, Felix Frankfurter Papers, Library of Congress.

50. Truman, *Memoirs*, I, 552.

51. Notes from interview with Harry S. Truman, August 30, 1949, Notebooks, Box 85, Jonathan Daniels Papers, University of North Carolina Library.

52. *Vital Speeches*, XII(October 1, 1946), 739.

his renegade views Wallace was fired. Truman privately recorded his thoughts: "The Reds, phonies and the 'parlor pinks'
seem to be banded together and are becoming a national danger.
I am afraid they are a sabotage front for Uncle Joe Stalin."[53]
At the press conference announcing Wallace's departure,
Truman stated that "the government of the United States *must
stand as a unit* in its relations with the rest of the world."[54]

Divisions within the administration and the ultimate presidential mastery of the foreign affairs bureaucracy were illustrated again in early 1948, when the White House staff was
drafting a major address to Congress for March 17. Although
some advisers thought that Truman should "scare" the country
about the foreign danger, Secretary of State George C. Marshall,
who replaced Byrnes in January of 1947 and who had in March
of that year expressed mild criticism of the president's strong
rhetoric in the "Truman Doctrine" speech, opposed an alarmist
message. Marshall was "nervous," according to a Truman aide,
because the world was a "keg of dynamite" which the president
should not ignite. Assistants Clark Clifford and George Elsey,
on the other hand, thought that the President "*must*, for his
prestige, come up with [a] strong foreign speech—to demonstrate his *leadership*." They were annoyed that Marshall and
Senator Arthur Vandenberg, bipartisan chairman of the Foreign
Relations Committee, were getting credit for foreign policy
triumphs like the Marshall Plan, whereas the president's prestige
had slumped because of his troubles with Palestine and China.
Marshall also thought that the final text of Truman's St.
Patrick's Day speech of March 17, to be delivered later that day,
was "too tough." In this speech, Truman depicted the postwar
international conflict as a simple morality play of "tyranny
against freedom."[55] For the message to Congress, Marshall
favored temperate, nondenunciatory language, whereas Clifford
urged a "blunt" style, finding Marshall's approach too "timid."
The president agreed with Clifford and said that Marshall's draft

53. Quoted in Truman, *Truman*, pp. 317–318.
54. *Public Papers, Truman, 1946*, p. 431. Emphasis added.
55. *Ibid., Truman, 1948*, p. 189.

"stank."[56] Rejecting his secretary of state's advice, Truman sounded a bell of alarm in a message which helped produce a war scare.[57]

The president commanded the results of another squabble with the State Department in mid-1948—this time over the Arab-Jewish fight in Palestine. The State Department, concerned about maintaining Arab states as economic and political friends, sought mediation, a trusteeship plan, or partition, but the White House, sensitive to the large Jewish vote in the forthcoming presidential election, backed the creation of the new state of Israel. Marshall bluntly told Truman that he would vote against him in the election if the president recognized the new nation of Israel for "domestic political considerations."[58] The American delegation to the United Nations almost resigned en masse when the president abruptly recognized Israel on May 14. State Department officials also grew restless, but Clark Clifford informed them that the president demanded conformity. Truman in fact instructed State Department officials to avoid commenting on Palestine questions "until after [the] elections."[59] Once the president had announced his policy toward Israel, the foreign affairs bureaucracy knew that it could no longer debate it —at least not in public. As Clifford told Undersecretary of State Robert A. Lovett after the president named his first ambassador to the new Middle Eastern nation, Truman "had made up his mind" and "there was obviously no room for argument."[60]

Bureaucracies and their members can sometimes moderate the president's orders; they can both impede and facilitate the execution of policy, even though the White House holds the power of formulation. The Point Four Program provides a case in point. In late 1948, after Truman's stunning victory over Governor Thomas Dewey in the presidential election, White House aides were looking for a "dramatic topic" to use in the

56. Handwritten notes by George Elsey, [n.d. but March, 1948], Box 20, Elsey Papers.

57. *Public Papers, Truman, 1948*, pp. 182–186.

58. *Foreign Relations, 1948*, V, Part 2, 975.

59. *Ibid.*, p. 1490.

60. *Ibid.*, p. 1131.

inaugural address.[61] Ben Hardy, a lower-echelon officer of the State Department, had an idea: the use of technical assistance as a means to uplifting developing nations and drawing them into the American sphere. He timidly carried his scheme to the White House, knowing that his departmental superiors had no enthusiasim for such a program. Truman advisers Clark Clifford and George Elsey warmly received Hardy's pet project and gave it standing as "point four" in the president's January 1949 speech. The Department of State was plainly angry with Truman's call for a "bold new program," for it had no plans whatsoever for such a venture.[62] Asked by the White House to come up with a program, State officers procrastinated; moreover, they only made lukewarm attempts to marshall public opinion and congressional support. The State Department, complained a Truman aide, was "deferring it as a major effort."[63] Finally, in May of 1950, the authorization for Point Four emerged from a Congress which matched the hesitancy of the State Department. Hardly "bold," the program was launched with meager appropriations and scant enthusiasm.[64]

Usually, however, the president can make bureaucrats responsive and subordinate to his wishes. "Presidential *power* is the power to persuade," Richard Neustadt has written.[65] As chief

61. Clark Clifford to Herbert Feis, July 16, 1953, Box 36, Elsey Papers.

62. Acheson later noted in his memoirs that "my first knowledge of the famous Point Four Program, which I was to carry out, came on the platform in front of the Capitol listening to the President expound it in his inaugural address." Asked to comment on this, White House adviser George Elsey explained that Acheson "had not known very long he was going to be Secretary of State; he had an awful lot of other matters to attend to. There was no particular reason for the President to have 'cleared', if you will, the text of the inaugural address with all his current or prospective Cabinet members." Acheson, *Present at the Creation*, p. 254; Elsey Oral History Interview.

63. Memorandum for Files by David D. Lloyd, December 3, 1949, Chronological File, David D. Lloyd Papers, Truman Library.

64. Thomas G. Paterson, "Foreign Aid Under Wraps: The Point Four Program," *Wisconsin Magazine of History* LVI(Winter 1972–73), 119–126.

65. Richard E. Neustadt, *Presidential Power: The Politics of Leadership* (New York, 1960), p. 10. Italics in original.

executive the President can hire and dismiss—a telling power. As one observer has put it, "no man can *argue* on his knees."[66] The president chooses his key advisers, who in turn select bureaucrats who are expected to share the president's basic predilections. Thus, the president determines who will whisper in his ear, a Harriman, Clifford, Wallace, or Marshall. Several months after entering the White House, Truman remarked that he, like Roosevelt, was surrounded by "prima donnas." He did not humor them, he said, as Roosevelt had: "I fire one occasionally and it has a salutary effect."[67] When Truman dramatically fired General Douglas MacArthur from his command in Korea in 1951, he demonstrated that power. "I could no longer tolerate his insubordination," Truman later wrote.[68]

Because of the prestige of his office, the president can also command publicity for his policies and arouse public support in the form of pressure on the bureaucracy. At his call, newspapermen, radio microphones, and television cameras will be in place for public announcements. His speeches gain national media coverage. The president largely decides which issues are worth the bureaucracy's attention, and over which it is worth fighting. If he feels intensely about an issue, that feeling of commitment is conveyed to his subordinates. He can also decide not to do something—not to recognize a new government, not to negotiate, not to intervene, not to send foreign aid. Furthermore, the president's ideology, his fundamental beliefs and ideals, permeate the consensus-prone bureaucracy.[69] An official in the foreign

66. Walter Bagehot quoted in *ibid.*, p. 34. Italics in original.
67. Quoted in Truman, *Truman*, p. 290.
68. Truman, *Memoirs*, II, 442.
69. See the instructive essays by Stephen D. Krasner, "Art Bureaucracies Important? (Or Allison Wonderland)," *Foreign Policy*, No. 7 (Summer 1972), pp. 159–179; Robert J. Art, "Bureaucratic Politics and American Foreign Policy: A Critique," *Policy Sciences*, IV(1973), 467–490; and James Nathan, "The Roots of the Imperial Presidency: Public Opinion, Domestic Institutions, and Global Interests," *Presidential Studies Quarterly*, V(Winter 1975), 63–74. For the contrary view that bureaucracies can shape or even dominate policymaking, see Graham T. Allison, "Conceptual Models and the Cuban Missile Crisis," *American Political Science Review*, LXII(September 1969), 689–718 and his *Essence of Decision* (Boston, 1971).

affairs establishment soon learns that he enjoys influence only so long as he has the president's encouragement and backing. "The State Department doesn't have a policy unless I support it," snapped Truman during a press conference.[70]

The "national security managers," to use Richard Barnet's phrase, fall in line with presidential preference or leave government.[71] Bureaucrats tend to tell the president what he wants to hear. Sometimes, they are reluctant to express opinions which might be looked upon with disfavor by superiors. Many foreign service officers who watched the "China hands" fall victim to ill-placed right-wing charges that they undermined Chiang in order to help Mao, and who watched the State Department's loyalty board harrass and dismiss talented diplomats, were intimidated into silence or learned to "play it safe."[72] Large bureaucracies tend by nature to become lethargic and unimaginative, thereby leaving the initiative to the president and his close advisers.[73] Professor Irving L. Janis has described a phenomenon he calls "groupthink." That is, members of a policymaking group tend to fall victim to group pressures for unanimity or consensus and to suppress their desires to express alternative policies which might disrupt or divide the group. The dynamics of working for concurrence, for consensus, for like-mindedness, can thus reduce disagreement and the consideration of policy options.[74] Even when dissent or irreconcilable conflict do arise within the bureaucratic network, a governmental tradition usually asserts itself: An official who wants to stay at his post or who decides to leave government, must not speak out,

70. *Public Papers, Truman, 1946*, p. 102.

71. Richard A. Barnet, *Intervention and Revolution* (New York, 1968), p. 23.

72. See James C. Thomson, Jr., "On the Making of U.S. China Policy, 1961–9: A Study in Bureaucractic Politics," *China Quarterly*, No. 50 (April–June 1972), p. 222, and Thomson's review of Clubb's *Witness and I* in *New York Times Book Review*, February 23, 1975, pp. 1–2.

73. See Leslie H. Gelb and Morton H. Halperin, "Diplomatic Notes: The Ten Commandments of the Foreign Affairs Bureaucracy," *Harper's Magazine*, CCXLIV(June 1972) 28–37.

74. Irving L. Janis, *Victims of Groupthink* (Boston, 1972).

must not air his differences or grievances publicly.[75] Henry A. Wallace was a conspicuous exception. He took his case against the "get-tough" policy to the electorate in the form of an unsuccessful 1948 presidential candidacy under the banner of the Progressive Party.

The president, in short, was and is the master of American foreign policy. When the Soviets insisted that they would not be "intimidated" by American and British "methods"—which they thought were designed to "impose their will upon other countries, and on the Soviet Union particularly"—they meant the activities of Truman and his subordinates, who, the Soviets believed, had deviated from both the style and policy of the Roosevelt administration.[76] Roosevelt had been "a farsighted statesman of the first rank," and his death "was a veritable gift to the gods" of American reaction and expansion, concluded one Soviet analyst.[77] Whereas Roosevelt and Stalin had "clicked," Truman and the Russian leader never warmed to one another.[78] Stalin was "an S.O.B.," concluded Truman after Potsdam. "I guess he thinks I'm one too."[79]

Stalin may have privately commented on Truman's parent-

---

75. Two illustrations: In early 1946, Chester Bowles, then the head of the Office of Price Administration, privately applauded Joseph Davies for his critique of the "get-tough" policy. Then Bowles added: "As a member of the Administration I do not want to be in the position of criticizing the Administration even by remote implication and for that reason I am writing you this personal letter rather than endorsing your statement in public as I would prefer to do." (Chester Bowles to Joseph Davies, February 22, 1946, Box 5, Chester Bowles Papers, Yale University Library.) "I was always quite happy to do what the Under Secretary or Secretary [of State] decided should be done—even if I lost," recalled veteran diplomat George McGhee. "Issues worth resigning over are few and far between," he concluded. (George McGhee Oral History Interview, Truman Library.) For a general discussion of this tradition, see James C. Thomson, Jr., "Getting Out and Speaking Out," *Foreign Policy*, No. 13 (Winter 1973–74), pp. 49–69.

76. *New Times* (Moscow), June 1, 1946.

77. *Ibid.*, June 6, 1947.

78. Memorandum, December 10, 1943, Box 39, Isador Lubin Papers, Roosevelt Library.

79. Quoted in Gaddis, *United States and the Origins of the Cold War*, p. 243.

age, but we do not know. In any case, it seems reasonable to
suggest that the Soviet leader exaggerated the difference between
Truman and Roosevelt by contrasting the two Presidents' starkly
different styles and personalities. As different as Roosevelt and
Truman were as individuals, it does not appear that their basic
policies clashed to the extreme extent that Henry A. Wallace
and the Soviets thought. FDR had to deal with the problems of
war, of course, whereas Truman grappled with the issues of
peace, so the question cannot be dealt with conclusively. Nevertheless, both presidents saw diplomatic bargaining power in the
American monopoly of the atomic bomb; both sought to use
America's economic power as leverage in diplomacy; both held
to the essential tenets of the American ideology, with its emphasis
on political and economic democracy; both wanted a United
Nations Organization that would be dominated by the big
powers, and especially the United States; both envisioned a
strong United States as the major actor in the postwar world.
John D. Hickerson, director of the Office of European Affairs,
recalled that FDR's death did not alter ongoing negotiations and
programs conducted by the State Department: "We went right
ahead; really we weren't conscious of any change."[80]

Still, the two presidents went about the business of diplomacy differently. Roosevelt was more patient with the Russians,
more willing to settle issues at the conference table, more tame
and less abusive in his language, less abrupt in his decisions, and
more solicitous of Soviet opinion and fears than was Truman.
Postwar conflict would have been present no matter which man
was president. The characteristics of the international system
and the clashing fundamental needs and ideas of the United
States and the Soviet Union insured tension; but because the
tactics and mechanics of policymaking in their administrations
differed, the two men impressed the Soviets and others quite differently, as the record makes evident. Tactics joined system and
fundamentals to cause the Cold War.

80. Hickerson Oral History Interview, Truman Library.

6

Consent: American Public Opinion and Congress

〰〰〰〰〰〰〰〰〰〰〰〰〰〰〰〰〰〰〰〰〰〰〰〰〰

"THE PRESIDENT'S JOB is to *lead* public opinion, not to be a blind follower," stated George Elsey, one of Harry S. Truman's chief advisers and speechwriters. "You can't sit around and wait for public opinion to tell you what to do." He grew more emphatic: "In the first place, there isn't any public opinion. The public doesn't know anything about it; they haven't heard about it. You must decide what you're going to do and do it, and attempt to educate the public to the reasons for your action."[1] This unabashed stress on the president's inititative in foreign policy and the self-conscious notion that the "public" must be coaxed or "educated" into supporting what the chief executive has already decided, underscores the point that the president enjoyed considerable freedom in the making of a foreign policy designed to satisfy America's fundamental needs and ideas. One student of the topic has graphically described the president as a "kind of magnificent lion who can roam widely and do great deeds so long as he does not try to break loose from his broad reservation." The "restraints" of his domain are "designed to keep him from going out of bounds, not to paralyze him in the field that has been reserved for his use."[2] Few presidents, springing as they do themselves from the American mind and

1. Elsey Oral History Interview, Truman Library.
2. Clinton Rossiter, *The American Presidency* (New York, 1956), p. 52.

spirit, have strayed "out of bounds" and few have ever been par-
alyzed in efforts to achieve their self-defined "great deeds."
Harry S. Truman was no exception when he attempted to meet
the perceived Soviet threat and to arouse public support for his
containment policies and the shaping of an American sphere of
influence.[3]

In the early years of the Cold War, public opinion and the
Congress set very broad and imprecise limits on presidential
activity in international affairs. Foreign policy initiative lay with
the executive branch. The administration's diplomacy was not
determined by the buffeting winds of public sentiment or by an
obstructionist Congress. Seldom did Truman have to do what he
did not want to do; seldom did he have serious trouble overcoming
the obstacles of a parsimonious Congress or interest groups in
order to pilot his foreign programs through either a Democratic or
Republican-controlled Capitol Hill. Congress was generally compliant, and the American people were "yea-sayers." Although
Truman officials occasionally suggested that they were sensitive
to or influenced by public attitudes, a search of the minutes and
records of such high-level policy-making groups as the Cabinet,

3. This chapter has been informed by the following studies of the re-
lationship between public opinion and foreign policy: Blair Bolles, "Who
Makes Our Foreign Policy," Foreign Policy Association *Headline Series*,
No. 62 (March–April 1947), pp. 5–86; Lester Markel, *et. al., Public
Opinion and Foreign Policy* (New York, 1949); Bernard C. Cohen, *The
Influence of Non-Governmental Groups on Foreign Policy Making* (Bos-
ton, 1959); Bernard C. Cohen, *The Public's Impact on Foreign Policy*
(Boston, 1973); Walter LaFeber, "American Policy-Makers, Public
Opinion, and the Outbreak of the Cold War, 1945–50," in Yōnosuke
Nagai and Akira Iriye, eds., *The Origins of the Cold War in Asia* (New
York and Tokyo, 1977), pp. 43–65; Gabriel A. Almond, *The American
People and Foreign Policy* (New York, 1950); James N. Rosenau,
National Leadership and Foreign Policy (Princeton, N.J. 1963); James
N. Rosenau, *Public Opinion and Foreign Policy* (New York, 1961);
William R. Caspary, "U.S. Public Opinion during the Onset of the Cold
War," *Peace Research Society (International) Papers*, IX(1968), 25–46;
Bernard C. Cohen, "The Relationship Between Public Opinion and
Foreign Policy Maker," in Melvin Small, ed., *Public Opinion and His-
torians: Interdisciplinary Perspectives* (Detroit, 1970), pp. 65–80; Doris
A. Graber, *Public Opinion, the President, and Foreign Policy* (New
York, 1968).

the Committee of Three (Secretaries of State, War, and Navy), and the Secretary of State's Staff Committee, as well as official diplomatic correspondence, does not reveal that American leaders paid much attention to American public opinion or that they were swayed by it to do something they did not wish to do.[4] President Truman charted his own foreign policy course and successfully persuaded the reluctant to walk his path.

Some scholars, without precise evidence as to how public opinion has actually affected policy, have attributed more importance to public opinion than Truman did. On the other hand, others have been skeptical of an interpretation which stresses the public's power over leaders.[5] Bernard C. Cohen, for one, has written that "even though foreign policy leaders have widely underestimated their freedom of maneuver in foreign policy, they still perceive that freedom more accurately than many scholars have, and more accurately even than they themselves usually admit openly."[6] Clinton Rossiter has marvelled at Truman's "spacious understanding" of presidental power, despite the president's often humble, folksy explanation of his role. Truman once said, for example, that although the Constitution gave him many powers, "the principal power that the President has is to bring people in and try to persuade them to do what they ought to do without persuasion. That's what I spend most of my time doing. That's what the powers of the President amount to."[7] This self-deprecating and disingenuous statement

4. The Cabinet meeting minutes are located in the Connelly Papers, Truman Library. The records of the Secretary's Staff Committee and the Committee of Three are found in the National Archives.

5. For scholars who attribute influence to public opinion, see, for example, Thomas A. Bailey, *Man in the Street* (New York, 1948) and Gaddis, *United States and the Origins of the Cold War*. See the works by Cohen above and Ralph B. Levering, *American Opinion and the Russian-American Alliance, 1939–1945* (Chapel Hill, N.C., 1976) for doubts about the impact of public opinion on leaders.

6. Cohen, "Relationship," p. 79.

7. Rossiter, *American Presidency*, p. 122. On another occasion Truman wrote that "all the President is, is a glorified public relations man who spends his time flattering, kissing and kicking people to get them to do what they are supposed to do anyway." Quoted in Truman, *Truman*, p. 356.

did not accord with the facts. In fact, Truman was a maestro in drawing full tones from his constitutional strings and from his public chorus.

Certainly, Truman and his advisers worried about public opinion. They read the polls. They courted the ethnic vote. They buttonholed congressmen. They warned against the dangers that could come from negative opinion. In 1947, Clark Clifford urged his boss to name the new European Recovery Program the "Truman Plan." "Are you crazy," Truman interjected. "If we sent it up to that Republican Congress with my name on it, they'd tear it apart. We're going to call it the Marshall Plan."[8] Thus, Truman officials were sensitive to the public pulse, but they believed that public opinion and Congress could be persuaded and cultivated on most issues—that they were permissive rather than restrictive. The president's power to create and to lead public opinion was studiously exercised. Any president can preempt the airwaves to make his case. Reporters flocked to Truman's press conferences, and as James Reston of the *New York Times* witnessed, "when the press conference ends, the scramble of reporters for the telephones is a menace to life and limb. . . ."[9] The president grabbed headlines; even his daily walks, colds, and piano-playing became news.

The president exploited frightening world events in order to garner support for his foreign policy. Truman once remarked that without Moscow's "crazy" actions, "we never would have had our foreign policy . . . we never could have got a thing from Congress."[10] He exaggerated, but what he meant is illustrative: He exploited Cold War tensions through a frequently alarmist, hyperbolic, anti-Communist rhetoric which he thought necessary to insure favorable legislative votes, to disarm his critics, and to nudge budget-conscious Congressmen to appropriate funds for

8. Quoted in Truman, *Truman*, p. 353. Clark Clifford corroborates this vignette in Clark M. Clifford, "The Presidency As I Have Seen It," in Emmet John Hughes, *The Living Presidency* (New York, 1973), p. 318.

9. James Reston, "The Number One Voice," in Markel, *Public Opinion and Foreign Policy*, p. 66.

10. Quoted in Neustadt, *Presidential Power*, p. 50.

Truman programs such as the Marshall Plan. Truman molded public opinion behind America's Cold War effort in a sometimes excitable manner, thereby intensifying Soviet-American conflict. His heated rhetoric also built up a momentum; extreme anti-Communist language used in the early Cold War would be recalled by Truman's critics later when they demanded that he confront the Soviet/Communist threat on all fronts at the same time with equal commitment—that, in other words, he fulfill the apparent pledge of his own tough words.

American leaders complained during and after the war about lingering American "isolationism" and bemoaned the work needed to convert it to "internationalism." During the war, commentators on the American mood predicted that at war's end the GI would exchange his fatigues for isolationist garb. Reporters for *Time* magazine who asked soldiers what they thought about the war received the answer that they "never wanted to hear of a foreign country again."[11] A servicemen's indelicate ditty went this way:

> I'm tired of these Limeys and Frogs,
> I'm fed to the teeth with these Gooks, Wops, and Wogs.
> I want to get back to my chickens and hogs,
> I don't want to leave home any more.[12]

After the war, W. Averell Harriman remarked that many Americans wanted nothing more than to "go to the movies and drink Coke," and Dean Acheson, angry over the United States' rapid postwar demobilization, defined the administration's task in 1946 as "focusing the will of 140,000,000 people on problems beyond our shores . . . [when] people are focusing on 140,000,000 other things. . . ."[13] Senator Wayne Morse of Oregon, a firm supporter of Truman's "hard-boiled policy" in 1945, feared that "sentimentalist groups" would once again gain

11. Quoted in Carl L. Becker, *How New Will the Better World Be?* (New York, 1944), p. 25.
12. Quoted in Perrett, *Days of Sadness, Years of Triumph*, p. 418.
13. Harriman and Abel, *Special Envoy*, p. 531; *Department of State Bulletin*, XIV (June 16, 1946), 1045.

control of American foreign policy.[14] "Americans can no longer sit smugly behind a mental Maginot line," implored Truman just before the end of the war.[15]

Isolationism actually evaporated quickly. "Isolationism," that vague feeling that the United States should restrict its activities overseas, especially in Europe, follow an independent or unilateral course, and mind its own business, collided with the realities of the air age and an international system which cast the United States in a starring role. The Pearl Harbor attack, said Republican Senator Arthur Vandenberg of Michigan, "ended isolationism for any realist."[16] As he put it in early 1945, when he renounced his own "isolationism" on the Senate floor, "I do not believe that any nation hereafter can immunize itself by its own exclusive action. . . . Our oceans have ceased to be moats which automatically protect our ramparts."[17] Not wishing to repeat the post–World War I debacle wherein President Woodrow Wilson launched the League of Nations and the United States then jilted it, Americans stood with Vandenberg in repudiating a failed past. Leaders and publicists of many political persuasions lectured the American people that the "horse-and-buggy days are gone," for "in a world in which a man can travel from New York to India in less time than it took Benjamin Franklin to travel from Philadelphia to New York, the attempt to escape into the Golden Age of normalcy is an invitation to chaos."[18] Such lectures, joined with the fast pace of global crises and presidential statements about the tremendous American responsibility in a world of rubble, undercut or crippled isolationist feeling. American membership in the new United Nations Organization

14. Senator Wayne Morse to Andrew Comrie, October 22, 1945, Box S-4, Wayne Morse Papers, University of Oregon Library, Eugene, Ore.
15. Quoted in Divine, *Second Chance*, p. 280.
16. Arthur H. Vandenberg, Jr., ed., *The Private Papers of Senator Vandenberg* (Boston, 1952), p. 1.
17. *Congressional Record*, XCI(January 10, 1945), 166.
18. Becker, *How New*, p. 43. See also Lester Markel, "Opinion—A Neglected Instrument," in Markel, *Public Opinion and Foreign Policy*, p. 4.

was roundly approved. Public opinion polls recorded that large majorities of Americans applauded an activist foreign policy abroad.[19] Even some of the so-called postwar isolationists, like Senator Robert Taft of Ohio, who tried to curb American programs designed to build an economic and military shield around Western Europe, seemed inconsistent as they shouted for American interventionism in Asia. As the pacifist A. J. Muste once remarked, "for isolationists these Americans do certainly get around."[20] Thus, although Truman and his officers worried about isolationism, they did not find it an obstacle to their policy of "getting tough."[21]

It was not "isolationism" which characterized American public opinion about Cold War events but ignorance or indifference. "Public opinion" suggests in a vague way that "the people" express themselves collectively on issues of national importance; yet on topics of foreign policy there was no mass public that spoke out on international relations with force or unity or that could seriously instruct or influence leaders. Most Americans read little about foreign events in their newspapers, which devoted the greater proportion of their columns to domestic topics; consequently, they were ill-informed about politics abroad. When asked to list the most significant issues before the nation, Americans catalogued domestic problems. In the Truman years, labor strikes, reconversion, price controls, housing shortages, and inflation occupied Americans. "Foreign

19. Almond, *American People and Foreign Policy*, pp. 76, 84, 208, 248; George H. Gallup, *The Gallup Poll: Public Opinion, 1935–1971* (New York, 1972; 3 vols.), I, 534.

20. Quoted in Justus D. Doenecke, "The Strange Career of American Isolationism, 1944–1954," *Peace and Change*, III(Summer–Fall 1975), 80. In 1942 the British minister in the Washington embassy, Sir Ronald Campbell, offered an explanation: "There are among the isolationists a type of people who I can easily imagine proceeding from their isolationist reasoning to a stage where they will satisfy themselves that in order to isolate themselves properly the United States must rule the roost." Quoted in Thorne, *Allies of a Kind*, p. 139.

21. For a similar conclusion, which argues that Truman administration officials were surprised to find that isolationism was weak, see May, *"Lessons" of the Past*, p. 49.

affairs!" grumbled a blue-collar worker. "That's for people who don't have to work for a living."[22]

This striking ignorance—sometimes mistaken for isolationist thought—was demonstrated in a study that the Council on Foreign Relations commissioned in March of 1947. The researchers found to their dismay that three out of every ten American voters were unaware of almost every event in United States foreign relations. They concluded further that only a quarter of the American electorate was reasonably well-informed. Sixty-five out of every one hundred voters admitted that they rarely discussed foreign affairs.[23] Other studies reported that in 1946, 43 percent of adult Americans had not followed the discussion on an American loan to Britain, that 31 percent could not even give a simple answer to a question about the purpose of the United Nations Organization, and that 58 percent had not paid attention to the major debate between the Truman administration and Henry A. Wallace which led to the latter's explosive departure from the Cabinet. In a Gallup survey for September 1949, 64 percent of those polled had neither heard nor read anything about the controversial China "White Paper."[24] Students of the relationship between foreign policy and public opinion have found these figures consistent with American tradition. "The mass public," James Rosenau has concluded, "is uninformed about either specific foreign policy issues or foreign affairs in general. Its members pay little, if any, attention to day-to-day developments in world politics."[25]

The evidence of ignorance or apathy suggests that leaders in Washington were permitted wide latitude and independence in making foreign policy. George Elsey put it too strongly when he said, "there isn't any public opinion." He would have been more

22. Quoted in Martin Kriesberg, "Dark Areas of Ignorance," in Markel, *Public Opinion and Foreign Policy*, p. 54.

23. Markel, "Opinion," p. 9.

24. Gallup, *Gallup Poll*, I, 561, 604; II, 852; Leonard S. Cottrell, Jr., and Sylvia Eberhart, *American Opinion on World Affairs in the Atomic Age* (Princeton, N.J., 1948), pp. 13–14.

25. Rosenau, *Public Opinion and Foreign Policy*, p. 35.

accurate if he had said that it was so weak that leaders were neither educated nor moved very much by it.

There was a "public opinion" that Truman and his advisers
took seriously and diligently sought to cultivate—the opinion of
the approximately 25 percent of the American people who were
attentive to foreign policy questions. Scholars have called them
variously "notables," "opinion leaders," or the "foreign policy
public." They constituted the small number of Americans who
studied the foreign news, who travelled abroad, who spoke out.
They held positions in American society that commanded
authority and insured influence—journalists, businessmen, labor
leaders, intellectuals, and members of various interest and citizen groups. They produced the "public opinion" on foreign
policy issues that counted. A Truman officer summarized the
point: "It doesn't make too much difference to the general
public what the details of a program are. What counts is how the
plan is viewed by the leaders of the community and the
nation."[26] Another State Department official remarked that "we
read the digests, we ponder the polls, and then we are likely to
be influenced by our favorite columnist."[27] The "foreign policy
public" was important, too, because it could influence a wider
audience. As someone put it, he "who mobilizes the elite, mobilizes the public."[28] The Truman administration happily found
that the elite endorsed the president's foreign policy, further en-
hancing his freedom in policymaking.[29]

To cement the alliance between the "opinion leaders" and

26. Quoted in Kensuke Yanagiya, "The Renewal of ERP: A Case
Study" (Unpublished paper, Public Affairs 520-D, Woodrow Wilson
School of Public and International Affairs, Princeton University, 1952),
p. 20.
27. Quoted in Markel, "Opinion," p. 31.
28. Almond, *American People and Foreign Policy*, p. 138.
29. See, for example, Ronald Radosh, *American Labor and United
States Foreign Policy* (New York, 1969); Thomas G. Paterson, "The
Economic Cold War: American Business and Economic Foreign Policy,
1945–1950" (Unpublished Ph.D. dissertation, University of California,
Berkeley, 1968); H. Schuyler Foster, "American Public Opinion and
U.S. Foreign Policy," *Department of State Bulletin*, XLI(November 30,
1959), 796–803.

the administration, government officials wooed them. Interest group executives were given flattering appointments on consulting bodies like the President's Committee on Foreign Aid, the Public Advisory Board of the Economic Cooperation Administration, and the Business Advisory Council of the Department of Commerce. They served as consultants to the American delegation at the founding meeting of the United Nations Organization in San Francisco. They were appointed to high office, as when Paul Hoffman of Studebaker Corporation was named to head the Economic Cooperation Administration. They were invited to appear before Congressional committees to state their views as "experts." They enjoyed special State Department briefings or attended special White House conferences like that for the Marshall Plan on October 27, 1947. Some individuals were consulted so often or sat on so many public boards that they could truly be called "external bureaucrats."[30] All in all, they were courted, sometimes because their views provided new insight, but largely because they represented a "public opinion" that mattered, that could be shaped to endorse Truman's Cold War policies.

The major task of cultivating the elite fell to the State Department's Office of Public Affairs, which was organized near the end of World War II. This agency was designed to strengthen relations with public groups and prominent individuals. It maintained ties with over two hundred organizations and drafted State Department responses to letters from opinion leaders. So that it could anticipate criticisms, it conducted polls and interviews with American voters and subscribed to over a hundred newspapers and magazines. The office also sponsored an annual conference in the Department of State to which it invited about two hundred people—usually presidents of national associations. Smaller meetings of ten to thirty participants were held each week: Usually the conferees met with middle-echelon officers, but on one occasion Secretary Acheson

30. See Chadwick F. Alger, "The External Bureaucracy in United States Foreign Affairs," *Administrative Science Quarterly*, VII(June 1962), 50–78.

himself addressed a small group to explain his controversial policy toward China. The director of the Office of Public Affairs, Francis Russell, frankly recalled that the thin line between propaganda and education was sometimes crossed.[31] Whether the office's function was education or propaganda, the chief purpose was evident: to sell the president's foreign policy to opinion leaders. That purpose was met.

A sterling example of cooperation between the government and the elite came in 1947–48, when the Committee for the Marshall Plan was organized to arouse public support for the European Recovery Program. Former Secretaries of War Henry L. Stimson and Robert Patterson joined former Assistant Secretary of State Dean Acheson to launch the committee in the fall of 1947. Working closely with the State Department, the committee staff ran newspaper ads, circulated petitions, organized letter campaigns to Congressmen, and maintained an active speaker's bureau. Groups like the Farmer's Union that were asked to tesitfy before Congressional committees were supplied with prepared texts.[32] Presidential assistant Richard E. Neustadt lauded the committee as "one of the most effective instruments for public information seen since the Second World War...."[33]

The president himself attempted to shape the public opinion that his administration wanted to hear. "A politician must be in a sense a public relations man," said Truman.[34] He used techniques common to most presidencies: He spoke at times in alarmist terms, predicting dire results if a certain policy were not carried out; he appealed to patriotism to rally Americans to his banner, often recalling the sacrifices of World War II; he created awesome and frightening images of the foreign adversary; he sketched pictures of politicial enemies like Wallace which suggested that "Reds" might someday roam the corridors of the

31. Francis Russell Oral History Interview, Truman Library.
32. See Paterson, *Soviet-American Confrontation*, pp. 221–222; Harold Stein Oral History Interview, Truman Library.
33. Neustadt, *Presidential Power*, p. 49.
34. Quoted in Manfred Landecker, *The President and Public Opinion* (Washington, D.C., 1968), p. 64.

White House.[35] Truman simplified issues and exaggerated consequences, stirring the heart rather than the mind.[36] "That is the American way," lamented New York City lawyer and former United Nations Relief and Rehabilitation Administration official Richard Scandrett. "Things are either pure black or pure white. There are no grays."[37]

Historian Thomas A. Bailey, author of a popular 1948 book entitled *The Man in the Street*, defended the president's efforts to "educate" an ignorant public: "Because the masses are notoriously short-sighted, and generally cannot see danger until it is at their throats, our statesmen are forced to deceive them into an awareness of their own long-term interests. . . ." He went on: "Deception of the people may in fact become increasingly necessary, unless we are willing to give our leaders in Washington a freer hand. . . . The yielding of some of our democratic control over foreign affairs is the price that we may have to pay for greater physical security."[38] Of course, as pollster George Gallup noted on the eve of World War II, "public opinion was influenced every time the President spoke."[39] Charles Bohlen

35. Truman and his advisers were unrelenting vis-à-vis Henry A. Wallace, practicing a highly emotional "red-baiting." To Congressman John H. Folger, the president wrote in April 1947 that Wallace "seems to have obtained his ideas of loyalty . . . from his friends in Moscow and, of course, they have no definition for that word." Several months later Clark Clifford planned strategy for the 1948 presidential campaign. His advice reflected his mentor's preference: "Every effort must be made *now* jointly and at one and the same time—although, of course, by different groups—to dissuade him [Wallace] and also to identify him in the public mind with the Communists." Truman to Folger, April 19, 1947, Box 141, President's Secretary's File, Truman Papers, Truman Library; Clark Clifford, memorandum for the President, November 17, 1947, Box 21, Clark Clifford Papers, Truman Library.

36. Historian Robert A. Divine has concluded in his study of the relationship between presidential elections and foreign policy from 1940 to 1960 that presidents have usually manipulated foreign policy subjects to gather votes: "presidential candidates . . . play politics with foreign policy; they exploit crises overseas. . . ." *Foreign Policy and U.S. Presidential Elections, 1940–1948* (New York, 1974), p. ix.

37. Richard Scandrett to Phyllis Auty, October 25, 1948, vol. 20-A, Richard Scandrett Papers, Cornell University Library.

38. Bailey, *Man in the Street*, p. 13.

39. Quoted in Yergin, *Shattered Peace*, p. 444.

noted that Cold War national security required "a confidence in the Executive where you give human nature a very large blank check."[40] Truman aide Clark Clifford correctly observed that "in time of crisis the American citizen tends to back up his President."[41]

Because the American people usually rallied around their leaders during foreign policy crises, and because the president usually succeeded in cultivating or manipulating public sentiment, it is not surprising that the public opinion the White House and the State Department heard largely matched the public opinion it worked to create. The administration in essence listened to the echo of its own words. "What the government hears," suggested one official, borrowing a metaphor from the navy, "is really the sound of its own screws, reflecting off its own rudder and coming up through its own highly selective sonar."[42]

Still, administration figures said that public opinion counted, that it guided their foreign policy. They were saying so ritualistically, out of habit and necessity, not because it was reality. One would expect high-level officials in a democratic-representative political system to say publicly that they believed that the public's views counted: That is what a public audience wanted to hear. Telling the public so actually constituted another component in the effort to create friendly opinion.

American diplomats sometimes told foreign leaders that the United States could not undertake a certain policy or program because public opinion or the American people would not countenance it. In his famous acrimonious exchange with Molotov in April 1945, Truman warned that Russian behavior would affect United States policy on foreign aid to the Soviet Union, because "he could not hope to get these measures through Congress unless there was public support for them."[43] Acting Secretary of State Joseph Grew told the Yugoslav foreign minister a month later that in matters of foreign policy "we were guided by public

40. *Ibid.*, p. 6.
41. Quoted in Walton, *Henry Wallace, Harry Truman, and the Cold War*, p. 301.
42. Charles Frankel, quoted in Cohen, *Public's Impact*, pp. 178–179.
43. *Foreign Relations, 1945*, V, 257.

opinion" and that Yugoslavia's request for foreign aid "would to a large measure depend on the impression which the American public will gain from the policies and events in the countries recently liberated."[44] In 1947 Under-Secretary of State Will Clayton said much the same thing in his attempt to persuade the British to join a European economic plan.[45] In all three examples, however, there is insufficient evidence to argue that the administration's reading of public opinion influenced its foreign economic policies. Such statements, it appears, more often than not represented a diplomatic device designed to press foreign officials rather than a political reality at home.[46]

Public opinion usually supported Truman's early Cold War policies, giving him a free hand. Even hostile opinion did not deter him from doing what he thought had to be done. Good examples are the questions of loans to Russia and Britain in the Fall of 1945. Sixty percent of the respondents in a Gallup poll disapproved of a loan to Russia (only 27 percent approved, and 13 percent had no opinion). Another Gallup poll revealed exactly the same statistics of public opposition to a loan to Britain. Nevertheless, the Truman administration proceeded, in apparent violation of "public opinion," to negotiate a $3.5 billion loan to Britain, while neglecting negotiations with the Russians, who got no loan.[47] In April of 1947, shortly after his dramatic Truman Doctrine speech, the president found that a large majority of Americans felt that the problem of aid to Greece and Turkey should be turned over to the United Nations. He never followed such a policy, again in apparent defiance of "public opinion."[48] What he and the State Department did instead was to launch an effective public campaign with the message that the United Nations was an infant organization not yet ready to take on the momentous task proposed. To quiet discon-

44. Memorandum of Conversation, May 30, 1945, vol. 7, Conversations, Joseph Grew Papers, Houghton Library, Harvard University.
45. *Foreign Relations, 1947*, III, 281.
46. See Cohen, "Relationship," for some of the ideas discussed in this paragraph.
47. Gallup, *Gallup Poll*, I, 530, 535.
48. *Ibid*, p. 639.

tent in Congress, the administration endorsed an innocuous amendment drafted by bipartisan leader Senator Arthur H. Vandenberg and the State Department staff to the effect that the United Nations could assume the task when it was ready. "I never paid any attention to the polls myself," remembered Truman, "because in my judgment they did not represent a true cross section of American opinion. . . . I also know that the polls did not represent facts but mere speculation. . . ."[49]

When the administration said that it was responding to public opinion, it usually meant that it had to deal with a special-interest group which was one issue-oriented and which, like the president, was able to exploit indifference to gain its ends.[50] Thus, in one of the rare, measureable examples of successful interest-group influence, a well-organized and vocal Jewish-American community exerted considerable pressure on vote-conscious Truman in the 1948 election, and he reacted by overruling his own State Department and backing the establishment of the new state of Israel.[51]

Even highly-charged special interest groups did not always succeed in influencing foreign policy, as the case of the Polish-Americans and United States policy toward Poland illustrates. At the Teheran Conference of 1943, President Roosevelt told Premier Stalin that he could not take part in any public agreement over Polish boundaries, because there were six to seven million Polish-Americans in the United States and that "as a

49. Truman, *Memoirs*, II, 177. Theodore C. Sorenson, one of President John F. Kennedy's chief aides is the early 1960s, has reflected that

> democratic government is not a popularity contest; and no President is obligated to abide by the dictates of public opinion. . . . Public opinion is often erratic, inconsistent, arbitrary, and unreasonable . . . [and] it rarely speaks in one loud, clear, united voice. . . . He has a responsibility to lead public opinion as well as respect it—to shape it, to inform it, to woo it, and win it. It can be his sword as well as his compass. *Decision-Making in the White House* (New York, 1963), pp. 45–46.

50. Almond, *American People and Foreign Policy*, p. 86.

51. See *Foreign Relations, 1948*, V, and the review by Thomas G. Paterson in *American Historical Review*, LXXXII(December 1977), 1356–1357.

practical man, he did not wish to lose their vote."[52] In June of 1944 a State Department official (and political appointee of Roosevelt) worried about the Soviet presence in Poland and recorded in his diary that the Poles held the political balance in Illinois and Ohio and were politically potent in Detroit, Chicago, and Buffalo[53]; at the Potsdam Conference in July of the following year, President Truman mentioned that there were six million Poles in America who could be dealt with much more easily if a free election were held in Poland.[54]

Although American diplomats were sensitive to this conspicuous political reality, American policy toward Poland was not shaped or determined by Polish-Americans. Several reasons explain this. The figure of six to seven million Polish-Americans was inflated, for it included Poles of all ages. Therefore, their voting strength was much less significant. Few Poles were in positions of national leadership from which to influence policy: There were no Americans of Polish descent in the Senate until well after World War II—although Michigan Senator Vandenberg spoke for them—and there were only ten to twelve Polish-Americans in the House. Also, political leadership in the Polish-American community itself was splintered, weakening its impact. Neither president respected the Polish-American Congress as an interest group, and they were able to reduce the effect of Polish-American opinion. FDR deftly courted Polish-American leaders in 1944 by speaking in generalities and by apparently convincing them that he agreed with them. In the election of 1944, despite differences with Roosevelt, the Poles stuck with the Democrats in overwhelming numbers. Truman grew angry with criticism from Polish-American leaders like Charles Rozmarek that the United States had sold out Poland to the Soviets, and he paid less and less attention to them. Although Rozmarek and other leaders defected in 1948 from the Democratic ranks, Polish-Americans, as ardent Democrats, on the

52. *Foreign Relations: Conferences at Cairo and Teheran*, p. 594.
53. Diary, June 13, 1944, Box 5, Breckinridge Long Papers, Library of Congress.
54. *Foreign Relations, Berlin*, II, 206.

whole voted for Truman. In short, although the Presidents and their advisers naturally worried about and courted Polish-American votes, the Polish-American community did not wield important influence in the shaping of American foreign policy.[55] Truman pursued *his* policy toward Poland.

If public opinion did not have much of an impact overall on Truman's foreign policy, can it be argued that Congress did? Congress obviously possessed powers that the amorphous public opinion lacked. In a negative and abstract sense, Congress had the power to defeat a presidential proposal. The Senate could reject a treaty if a third of its members (plus one) voted "nay," and the House of Representatives, gripping the purse strings, could refuse to appropriate funds. Both houses of Congress had the power to investigate. Administration officers had to troop into congressional hearings to answer questions from suspicious legislators, some of whom harbored stereotypes of "striped pants" diplomats. For a six-month period in 1947, the State Department expended more than a thousand man-days in describing and defending Truman's policies before congressional committees, and when he was Secretary of State, Dean Acheson spent about one-sixth of his working days in Washington meeting with congressmen.[56]

Congress can also create "watchdog" committees to oversee the execution of programs that it approved; the Senate votes on presidential appointees to diplomatic posts; the Constitution empowers the Congress to set tariffs, regulate foreign commerce

55. See Peter M. Irons, "The Test is Poland: Polish Americans and the Origins of the Cold War," *Polish-American Studies*, XXX(Autumn 1973), 5–63; John N. Cable, "Vandenberg: The Polish Question and Polish-Americans, 1944–1948," *Michigan History*, LVII(Winter 1973), 296–310; Jack L. Hammersmith, "Franklin Roosevelt, the Polish Question, and the Election of 1944," *Mid-America*, LXIX(January 1977), 5–17; Divine, *Foreign Policy and U.S. Presidential Elections*, pp. 110–112, 143; Louis L. Gerson, *The Hyphenate in Recent American Politics and Diplomacy* (Lawrence, Kan., 1964), pp. 138–140, 150–152, 161; Stephen A. Garrett, "Eastern European Ethnic Groups and American Foreign Policy," *Political Science Quarterly*, XCIII(Summer 1978), 301–323.

56. Markel, "Opinion," p. 24; Dean Acheson, *A Citizen Looks at Congress* (Westport, Conn., 1974, c. 1956), p. 65.

and immigration, and declare war; and, in extreme cases, the legislative branch can exercise its impeachment powers. In short, the "separation of powers" invests Congress with wide potential authority in making and conducting foreign policy, and any administration--if it wishes to push its programs through the legislative process—must be alert to congressional opinion. In practice, however, Congress has been largely subservient to the president in matters of foreign policy.[57]

Most presidents have reached into well-stocked arsenals for devices to augment their powers vis-à-vis Congress. Truman was a former senator, with ten years in rank, and he utilized his status as an alumnus to gain access to the upper house. He called upon his friends there, strengthening personal contacts. As president he could be found having lunch in the Senate dining room.[58] Once, on July 23, 1947, he entered the Senate chamber itself, prompting presiding officer Vandenberg to announce that the "ex-Senator from Missouri is recognized for five minutes."[59] Besides personal lobbying, Truman attempted to persuade the larger electorate, which would, it was aniticipated, in turn exercise some influence over congressmen worried about what the folks back home were feeling. The administration could further shape favorable congressional opinion by including congressmen directly in diplomatic negotiations. Thus, Senators Robert Wagner and Charles Tobey were present at the

57. Helpful studies on the role of Congress in the foreign policy process are James A. Robinson, *Congress and Foreign Policy-Making* (Homewood, Ill., 1967; rev. ed.); Arthur Schlesinger, Jr., "Congress and the Making of American Foreign Policy," *Foreign Affairs*, LI (October 1972), 78–113; Sorenson, *Decision-Making in the White House*; Robert Dahl, *Congress and Foreign Policy* (New York, 1950); Holbert N. Carroll, *The House of Representatives and Foreign Affairs* (Boston, 1966; rev. ed.); Daniel S. Cheever and H. Field Haviland, Jr., *American Foreign Policy and the Separation of Powers* (Cambridge, Mass., 1952); Rossiter, *American Presidency*; Neustadt, *Presidential Power*; Francis O. Wilcox, *Congress, the Executive, and Foreign Policy* (New York, 1971). See also many of the works cited in footnote 3 of this chapter.

58. James Reston, "Number One Voice," p. 72.

59. Quoted in Floyd M. Riddick, "The First Session of the Eightieth Congress," *American Political Science Review*, XLII(August 1948), 683.

Bretton Woods Conference, Vandenberg joined the American delegation to the United Nations Conference in San Francisco, and Vandenberg and Senator Tom Connally served at the 1946 Paris Peace Conference. Congressmen were carried by military aircraft to economically hobbled postwar Europe to encourage "aye" votes for Truman-initiated recovery programs. In June of 1949, just before the Senate approved American membership in NATO, Secretary of Defense Louis Johnson told the Cabinet that a "liberal attitude in ferrying members of Congress to Europe" would be "helpful in developing support for [the] Atlantic Pact and Arms Program."[60]

Because the conduct of foreign policy has always operated in clouds of secrecy, any administration can withhold information from Congress on grounds of national security or executive privilege. "There is a point . . . when the Executive must decline to supply Congress with information," Truman wrote, "and that is when he feels the Congress encroaches upon the Executive prerogatives."[61] Acheson believed that Congress was "dependent" upon the executive for knowledge of events—the "flow of papers"—and that "here knowledge is indeed power."[62]

While Truman was in office, initiative in foreign policy lay with the president. In essence, he decided which diplomatic topics the Congress acted upon. He sent requests for foreign aid; he delivered special messages; he outlined new programs. In short, as the famous saying has it, "the President proposes, the Congress disposes." What that often meant in the Truman period was that Congress gave legitimacy to what Truman had already decided. By announcing policies and then going to Congress to ask for endorsement, the president handed the legislative branch *faits accomplis*. By gaining the initiative in this way, he could exert considerable pressure on congressmen who did not

60. Cabinet Meeting, June 9, 1949, Notes on Cabinet Meetings, Connelly Papers. See also Ithiel de Sola Pool, Suzanne Keller, and Raymond A. Bauer, "The Influence of Foreign Travel on Political Attitudes of American Businessmen," *Public Opinion Quarterly*, XX(Spring 1956), 161–175.
61. Truman, *Memoirs*, II, 454. See also p. 478.
62. Acheson, *A Citizen Looks at Congress*, p. 53.

wish to be placed in the unenviable position of "naysayers" or "neo-isolationists"—especially on Cold War issues which he defined in exaggerated terms as matters of national survival.

The president's March 1947 request for aid to Greece and Turkey is a case in point. Once Truman had enunciated his "doctrine" before a joint session of Congress, many of its members hesitated to deny him his program. Senator Owen Brewster of Maine was reluctant "to pull the rug from under his feet," and Senator Leverett Saltonstall of Massachusetts said that Congress had to support the president, or "many people abroad who do not fully understand our system of government would look upon our failure as a repudiation of the President of the United States. American prestige abroad means more security and safety at home; this is to me a compelling reason."[63] Legislative critics questioned the apparent indiscriminate globalism of the doctrine, the bypassing of the United Nations, the aid to conservative regimes, the salvaging of the British sphere of influence, and the cost, yet sixty-seven Senators of the Republican Eightieth Congress stood with the president and only twenty-three were against. Republican Senator Henry Cabot Lodge thought that his colleagues had to decide whether or not "we are going to repudiate the President and throw the flag on the ground and stamp on it. . . ."[64] Vandenberg was particularly alert to the relationships among the president's methods, congressional responsibilities, and American foreign policy in the Cold War:

The trouble is that these "crises" never reach Congress until they have developed to a point where Congressional discretion is pathetically restricted. When things finally reach a point where a President asks us to "declare war" there is nothing left except to "declare war." In the present instance, the overriding fact is that the Presi-

63. "Should Truman's Greek and Turkish Policy Be Adopted: A Radio Discussion," *University of Chicago Roundtable*, April 20, 1947, pp. 7, 2.

64. Senate, *Legislative Origins of the Truman Doctrine*, p. 142. See also *ibid*, pp. 46, 132, 133, 136; Representative Francis Case to Harry S. Truman, May 10, 1947, Box 1278, OF 426, Truman Papers; *Congressional Record*, XCIII(April 16, 1947), 3484–3485; *New York Times*, March 18, 1947; Susan M. Hartmann, *Truman and the 80th Congress* (Columbia, Mo., 1971), pp. 60, 63, 64.

dent has made a long-delayed statement regarding Communism on-the-march which *must* be supported *if* there is any hope of ever impressing Moscow with the necessity of paying any sort of *peaceful* attention to us whatever. If we turned the President down—after his speech to the joint Congressional session—we might as well either resign ourselves to a complete Communist-encirclement and infiltration or else get ready for World War No. Three.[65]

Bipartisanship was another resource for engineering Congressional consent for the presidential foreign policy. Republicans, joining the president in his extreme depiction of the world crisis and the need to restore a broken world under Communist threat, muted their criticism of Truman's foreign policy, except that toward Asia. As Republican Senator Alexander Smith of New Jersey told Senator Robert Taft of Ohio—one of the few Republicans who vigorously questioned the bipartisan consensus: "The President and Mr. Byrnes have some tough nuts to crack and I feel it is vitally important for them to have a united nation behind them."[66] Vandenberg, one of the architects of bipartisanship, boasted to a Detroit audience in early 1949 that "during the last two years, when the Presidency and Congress represented different parties, America could only speak with unity. . . . So-called bipartisan foreign policy provided the connecting link. It did not apply to everything—for example, not to Palestine or China. But it did apply generally elsewhere." The Senator concluded: "It helped to formulate foreign policy *before* it ever reached the legislative stage."[67] Vandenberg chaired the Foreign Relations Committee during the Eightieth Congress (1947–48) and had something to say on almost every issue. He nursed presidential ambitions, became the foreign policy spokesman for his party, and wanted to be consulted by the Truman administration. A student of the diplomatic career of Dean Acheson has concluded that Acheson "unfairly considered the Senator a superficial thinker, an egotist. . . . This egotism, Acheson believed, made it possible to manipulate Vandenberg by

65. Arthur Vandenberg to Bruce Barton, March 24, 1947, Box 2, Arthur Vandenberg Papers, University of Michigan Library.
66. Quoted in Yergin, *Shattered Peace*, p. 172.
67. Vandenberg, *Private Papers*, pp. 550–551 (emphasis added).

giving him the illusion of victory on an aspect of an issue."[68]

The Truman administration deftly flattered Vandenberg, appointing him to delegations, calling upon him for advice, applauding his Cold War patriotism, agreeing to his suggestions for appointments. During the launching of the Marshall Plan, Vandenberg said he would not support it unless a distinguished panel of citizens was appointed to study it. Truman complied and named W. Averell Harriman to head the committee. Truman wanted to make Acheson the administrator of the Europeran Recovery Program, but Vandenberg disapproved. Truman thereupon consulted with the Senator and appointed one of Vandenberg's candidates, Paul Hoffman, president of Studebaker.[69] In both cases, the Marshall Plan itself was protected from serious challenge. The famous "Vandenberg Resolution" of 1948 was first suggested by and written in collaboration with the State Department. The document recommended that the United States associate itself with regional security pacts like that just formed in Western Europe under the Brussels Treaty. Writes one scholar, "the adoption of the Vandenberg Resolution [by a Senate vote of 64-4] indicates once again the executive's primacy in the identification and selection of problems which occupy the foreign policy agenda of Congress and the executive."[70] All in all, Truman officials shrewdly and easily cultivated Vandenberg, disarming a potential critic and insuring bipartisanship.

In the election of 1948, bipartisanship further greased political tracks for presidential foreign policies. As in 1944, Republican leaders pulled their punches. John Foster Dulles and Vandenberg persuaded their Republican Party colleagues, including candidate Thomas Dewey, to refrain from criticizing

68. Smith, *Acheson*, p. 407. See also Dean Acheson, "Senator Vandenberg and the Senate," in James D. Barber, ed., *Political Leadership in American Government* (Boston, 1964), pp. 74–83.

69. Paterson, *Soviet-American Confrontation*, pp. 222–224 and Neustadt, *Presidential Power*, pp. 52–53.

70. Robinson, *Congress and Foreign-Policy Making*, p. 46.

the foreign policy of the Democratic President.[71] "One of the things I tried to keep out of the campaign was foreign policy," remembered Truman.[72] He succeeded.

"Bipartisan foreign policy is the ideal for the executive," mused Dean Acheson, "because you cannot run this damned country any other way except by fixing the whole organization so it doesn't work the way it is supposed to work. Now the way to do that is to say politics stops at the seaboard—and anyone who denies that postulate is a son-of-a-bitch and a crook and not a true patriot. Now if people will swallow that, then you're off to the races."[73] Votes in the Senate on key postwar programs reveal that the Truman administration commanded the results of the "races." The Bretton Woods agreements (World Bank and International Monetary Fund) passed 61-16, United Nations Charter 89-2, ratification of the Italian peace treaty (1947) 79-10, assistance to Greece and Turkey 67-23, Rio Pact 72-1, Interim Aid to Europe 86-3, European Recovery Program 69-17, Vandenberg Resolution 64-4, NATO 82-113, and ERP Extension 70-7. Only the favorable vote on the British loan of 1946 was close—46-33.

Most congressmen debated how much to spend, not whether to spend. Sometimes they trimmed budgets and forced the executive to compromise on administrative machinery for foreign aid programs. Sometimes the president thought that he had to speak with alarm to persuade Congress to give him the votes. This was especially true in 1947–48 when the Republican Eightieth Congress sat; yet this was the same Congress that met every one of his requests for expensive foreign aid projects. Truman's tangle

71. For the election of 1948, see Michael A. Guhin, *John Foster Dulles: A Statesman and His Times* (New York, 1972), pp. 54–55, 160–161; Louis Gerson, *John Foster Dulles* (New York, 1967), pp. 52–53; Divine, *Foreign Policy and U.S. Presidential Elections*, pp. 167–276; Robert A. Divine, "The Cold War and the Election of 1948," *Journal of American History*, LIX(June 1972), 90–110.

72. Truman, *Memoirs*, II, 211.

73. Quoted in Theodore A. Wilson and Richard D. McKinzie, "White House versus Congress: Conflict or Collusion? The Marshall Plan as a Case Study" (Unpublished paper delivered to the annual meeting of the Organization of American Historians, 1973), p. 2.

with what he called the "do-nothing" Eightieth Congress
stemmed from domestic issues, not questions of international
relations. After Truman's stunning victory in the 1948 election,
Communist Mao Tse-tung's 1949 triumph in China, the emer-
gency of McCarthyism in 1950, and the outbreak of the Korean
War in June of that year, bipartisanship eroded. Still, the administration, despite congressional cuts in requests for military
assistance, got what it wanted from Congress, including aid to
Communist Yugoslavia after Tito's break with Stalin. Acheson,
no doubt a wry smile spreaking across his mustachioed face,
recalled that "many of those who demanded the dismissal of the
Secretary of State in 1950–52 joined in passing all the major
legislation he laid before the Congress. . . ."[74]

Most of the acts and treaties approved by Congress placed
immense power in the hands of the president and his subordinates—to allocate funds abroad, to direct military assistance, to
react quickly to crises, to order the use of nuclear weapons, to
negotiate tariffs, to appoint administrators. Then, too, the president circumvented Congress by making executive agreements.
Truman signed eighteen military executive agreements during his
tenure—for example, those that permitted the United States to
use an air base in the Azores (1947), to place troops in Guatemala (1947), and to hold bases in the Philippines.[75] In other important cases, Truman simply did not go to Congress to ask for
approval of his decisions. He decided to order the dropping of
the atomic bombs on Hiroshima and Nagasaki on his own, and
he alone possessed the awesome power thereafter to authorize
the use of nuclear weapons. The Berlin Blockade was met not
with a congressional program but with the president's policy of
an airlift. Moreover, Truman never went to Congress for a declaration of war during the Korean War. It was truly a "presidential" war, but Congress voted funds time and time again to continue it. Acheson explained that the administration did not ask

74. Acheson, *A Citizen Looks at Congress*, p. 75. See also Smith,
Acheson, pp. 142, 252, 408–409 and Bradford Westerfield, *Foreign Policy and Party Politics* (New Haven, 1955).
75. See Loch Johnson and James M. McCormick, "Foreign Policy
by Executive Fiat," *Foreign Policy*, No. 28 (Fall 1977), pp. 117–123.

Congress for a war declaration because it did not want to invite hearings which might produce that "one more question in cross-examination which destroys you, as a lawyer. We had complete acceptance of the President's policy by everybody on both sides of both houses of Congress." He simply did not want to answer "ponderous questions" that might have "muddled up" Truman's policy.[76]

Thus, public opinion and the Congress proved malleable, compliant, and permissive in the making of America's Cold War foreign policy. More than once President Truman successfully grasped the opportunity to free himself from political and constitutional restraints so that he could define and carry out his foreign policy preferences for dealing with the restraints and opportunities of the postwar international system. Sam Rayburn, Speaker of the House in 1940–47 and again in 1949–53, thought that it had to be that way: "America has either one voice or none, and that voice is the voice of the President—whether everybody agrees with him or not."[77] Indeed, the Soviets listened not to the voice of Congress or to the many voices of American public opinion but to the tough words of President Harry S. Truman.

76. Princeton Seminar Transcript, February 13–14, 1954, Box 66, Acheson Papers.
77. Quoted in Graber, *Public Opinion, the President, and Foreign Policy*, p. 340.

7

Suspiciousness: Soviet Foreign Policy and Its Makers

V-E DAY, PLUS TWO, brought the war-weary of Moscow into the streets. A noisy crowd of thousands gathered outside the American embassy on that May 1945 day. Above, on the fourth-floor balcony, George F. Kennan waved to the throng. The demonstrators yelled wildly. Then they watched as an embassy officer ran next door to the National Hotel, requested and received a Soviet flag, and hoisted the red banner to fly beside the American Stars and Stripes. Another boisterous roar went up. Kennan went below and shouted, in Russian, "all honor to the Soviet allies." Again, cheers echoed through the square.[1] The spirit of victory and alliance, the emotion derived from knowing that at last Hitler's rampage had been beaten back, welled up in those ecstatic Muscovites. But, as Kennan knew well, foreign policy was not made by "the people"—especially Soviet foreign policy. How much the secretive men of the Kremlin shared that spirit and emotion and how much such positive feelings would infect postwar relations were the questions of the moment. Kennan and the embassy staff tackled them with a rare expertise. Scholars have devoted lifetimes to fathoming the intentions and decisions of Josef Stalin and his Communist

1. Whitney, *Russia in My Life*, p. 98; Kennan, *Memoirs*, pp. 240–244.

cohorts. Yet all the answers carry the mark of speculation, not certainty, of guessing, not knowing.

Recognizing that national leaders respond to both external and internal stimuli when they make decisions, our purpose in this chapter is to identify the fundamental and tactical characteristics of Soviet foreign policy in the early Cold War. What were the wellsprings of Soviet behavior in the conflict-ridden international system? What internal ideas and needs might have compelled the Soviets to undertake an expansionist course and to claim great-power status? How did Soviet officials go about satisfying their fundamental ideas and needs? Like Franklin D. Roosevelt, who posed the question to the Department of State, we want to understand the "Soviet psychology."[2]

Trying to identify the ambitions of the Stalinist regime is akin to gazing into a crystal ball. Probing for the forces generating Soviet actions since the 1917 Bolshevik Revolution has been the primary, and one would have to say frustrating, function of numerous Sovietologists. The dizzying array of explanations demonstrates that there have been no pat answers, and certainly no agreement among scholars.[3] Doubt must dog any careful student of Soviet behavior. Charles Thayer, a member of the American embassy in Moscow in the 1930s, has related a fanciful story about a Kentucky mountaineer's quest for information, illustrating for us how Kremlinologists must go about the business of determining Soviet behavior, and must obviously speculate:[4]

"Where's yer paw?" he asked the boy.
"Gone fishin'."

2. Elbridge Durbrow to the White House, January 22, 1945, 861.00/1-2245, Department of State Records.

3. For the variety of interpretations and the debate among scholars, see Alexander Dallin, ed., *Soviet Conduct in World Affairs* (New York, 1960); Morton Schwartz, *The "Motive Forces" of Soviet Foreign Policy: A Reappraisal* (Denver, 1971); Daniel Bell, "Ten Theories in Search of Reality," *World Politics*, X(April 1958), 327–365; William A. Glaser, "Theories of Soviet Foreign Policy: A Classification of the Literature," *World Affairs Quarterly*, XXVII(1956–1957), 128–152.

4. Charles W. Thayer, *Diplomat* (New York, 1959), p. 179.
"How d'ye know?"

"Had his boots on and 'tain't rainin'."
"Where's yer maw?"
"Outhouse."
"How d'ye know?"
"Went out with a Montgomery Ward catalogue and she can't read."
"Where's yer sister?"
"In the hayloft with the hired man."
"How d'ye know?"
"It's after mealtime and there's only one thing she'd rather do than eat."

The American ambassador to Russia from 1946 to 1949, Walter Bedell Smith, subscribed to the dictum of a British journalist who said that "there are no experts on the Soviet Union; there are only varying degrees of ignorance."[5] This is unfortunately true, because the Soviets have been particularly secretive about their policy process. Prominent Soviet officials made few public speeches. They gave little information to journalists, or to foreign diplomats, and what they did release usually fell short of satisfactory explication. The Soviet government has also never opened its archives for the 1940s. Unlike the United States, where the curious scholar can explore, with comparatively few restrictions, rich historical documents in the Library of Congress, the National Archives, or the Harry S. Truman Library, in Russia avenues for research are blocked. We cannot study Stalin's instructions to his subordinates, Soviet position papers, minutes of Politburo meetings, Red Army contingency plans, or memoranda of conversations among Soviet diplomats.

Those students of the Soviet Union who have depicted the Kremlin as a great beast, a mellowing tiger, or a neurotic bear have so argued without the benefit of adequate and convincing evidence.[6] Their depictions may be correct, but no one can be sure. The necessarily limited evidence that they have produced

5. Smith, *My Three Years*, p. 55.

6. William Welch, *American Images of Soviet Foreign Policy: An Inquiry into Recent Appraisals from the Academic Community* (New Haven, 1970); Israel Shenker, "Hats Are off to Kremlinologists," *New York Times*, September 20, 1974.

to buttress their interpretations must be gleaned from articles in the Soviet press, a few public addresses, numerous but monotonous ideological tracts, summaries of the proceedings of international conferences, and a handful of memoirs.[7] Some analysts have piled quotation upon quotation from the pre-Cold War statements of V. I. Lenin or Stalin in an attempt to tap the inner core of the Kremlin, but the hazards therein are also obvious: Statements from the past, before the Cold War, were made in the historical context of a particular time and place, of an immediate issue. Thus, it seems that we should use historical materials or statements only from the 1940s to explain the foreign policy of that decade. Finally, by necessity, a good deal of what we know about the Soviets comes from what non-Soviets have said about them. Sources are thereby often skewed and biased; we must recognize the prejudice and guard against distortion. With all of these caveats, then, we cautiously undertake to study Soviet foreign policy and its makers.

The Soviet Union seemed determined to seize opportunities in the postwar world to expand its interests. It insisted on being treated like a great power with a major voice in world affairs. The Russians claimed that rank, they said, by virtue of their relentless fighting and tremendous human and material losses in World War II, and because of their military position in Europe at the end of the war. Long-time Soviet diplomat Maxim Litvinov complained in late 1944 that "we have never been accepted in European councils on a basis of equality. We were always outsiders."[8] Never again. They could not be taken for "fools,"

7. The Moscow journal *International Affairs* periodically prints documents and memoirs.
8. "Notes on Conversation in Moscow with Maxim Litvinov," December 6, 1944, by Edgar Snow, Box 68, President's Secretary File, Franklin D. Roosevelt Papers, Roosevelt Library. See also Molotov, *Problems of Foreign Policy*, pp. 96, 106; Vera Micheles Dean, *The United States and Russia* (Cambridge, Mass., 1948), p. 132; James L. Gormly, "In Search of a Postwar Settlement: The London and Moscow Foreign Ministers Conferences and the Origins of the Cold War" (Unpublished Ph.D. dissertation, University of Connecticut, 1977), pp. 80–81.

warned Stalin.[9] Secretary of State James F. Byrnes never took them that way. "It is obvious to me," he remarked at the London Conference in the Fall of 1945, "that Russia is out to make itself a top world power."[10]

Byrnes also commented that "there is too much difference in the ideologies of the U.S. and Russia to work out a long term program of cooperation."[11] How strongly he believed this to be true we cannot know for sure, for he spent much of his brief diplomatic career working for a higher degree of cooperation. Yet he did identify an obvious tension in the Cold War and a fundamental factor in Soviet foreign policy: Soviets and Americans agreed that ideology, be it pure nineteenth-century Karl Marx, Lenin's elaborations and amendments, or Stalin's interpretations, was a Soviet mainspring; everybody, Soviet and non-Soviet, seemed fond of quoting the pastmasters of Communist dogma.[12] Ambassador Smith allowed that "we always fall back on Lenin when we want an explanation of any of the phenomena of Soviet policy."[13] Another American diplomat reported in 1946 that "the Kremlin has hit [the] sawdust trail in revival of old-time Leninist religion."[14] A Soviet spokesman agreed that "an ideological war on a world scale is now being waged with unexampled ferocity."[15]

9. *Foreign Relations, Berlin*, I, 32.

10. Walter Brown Notes, n.d., Folder 602, Byrnes Papers.

11. Quoted in Yergin, *Shattered Peace*, p. 118.

12. See, for example, "Analysis of Soviet Strength and Weakness," by Joint Working Committee of the American Embassy, Moscow, September 1, 1946, 861.00/9-946, Box 6462, Department of State Records; James Forrestal to Clarence D. Dillon, February 11, 1947, Box 125, Forrestal Papers; "The USSR and United States Foreign Policy," May 5, 1949, Office of Public Affairs Information Memorandum No. 45, RP #106, Reports of Foreign Policy Studies Branch, Division of Historical Policy Research, Department of State Records.

13. New York State Chamber of Commerce, *Monthly Bulletin*, XLI(June 1949), 52.

14. Elbridge Durbrow in *Foreign Relations*, 1946, VI, 798.

15. Constantine Simonov in *Literaturnaia Gazeta*, November 23, 1946, reprinted in House of Representatives, Committee on Foreign Affairs, *The Strategy and Tactics of World Communism*, 80th Cong., 2nd sess. (Washington, D.C., 1948), House Document 619, Supplement I, p. 182.

The Soviet ideology—the set of frequently articulated beliefs —was official doctrine. Cultivated by the ruling Communist Party and given authority by the various agencies of the Soviet state, this dogma smacked of religious cultism, the true faith. As propaganda, the ideology was broadcast around the globe; as indoctrination, it was pressed upon Soviet citizens. The USSR's Vice-Minister of Higher Education declared emphatically that professors "bear a personal responsibility, not only for the standard of qualifications of graduating specialists, but also for their correct ideological training in Marxism-Leninism."[16] For Communists, the tenets of their thought explained the past, present, and future. Ideology can serve a host of purposes: motive force, public relations device to rally supporters, ritualism, form of communication, symbol of continuity, rationalization for other motives, model for an ideal world, or legitimizer of policy. It provides a general guide for policy-makers who, in their day-to-day deliberations, must select immediate policy courses.[17] But, as Professor Herbert S. Dinerstein has asked, "who can tell what the football coach who always predicts victory really believes?"[18]

The Soviet ideology betrayed a profound suspicion of non-Communist nations and their leaders. In Soviet thinking, the world was irrevocably divided into two competing spheres: the "Soviet camp of peace, socialism, and democracy" and the "American camp of capitalism, imperialism, and war."[19] As long as both groups of nations existed, peace was impossible. The conflict between the capitalist and Communist worlds was

16. V. Svetlov, "The Ideological Training of Students Must Be Improved," *Izvestia*, December 14, 1946, in *Soviet Press Translations*, II (March 15, 1947), 23.

17. For the functions of ideology, see John W. Spanier, *Games Nations Play* (New York, 1972), pp. 274–275; Alfred G. Meyer, "The Functions of Ideology in the Soviet Political System," *Soviet Studies*, XVII (January 1966), 273–285.

18. Herbert S. Dinerstein, *The Making of a Missile Crisis: October 1962* (Baltimore, 1976), p. 62.

19. Quoted in Robert C. Tucker, *The Soviet Political Mind: Stalinism and Post-Stalin Change* (New York, 1971; rev. ed.), p. 229. See also House, *Strategy and Tactics*, pp. 209, 216.

seen as a long-term struggle, deeply rooted in a dialectic of history. Capitalism, exploitative and expansionist, was the source of perpetual aggression and war. Conditions were such within the capitalist sphere that ambitious nations would always be grasping for more wealth—and going to war to insure success. Conflict in the international system was also insured by the class struggle within nations, by the vicious competion among capitalist states for raw materials and markets, and by the striving of colonial peoples to throw off their imperial masters. Greedy Americans and other capitalists, Communist ideologues claimed, profited from militarism, aggression, and war—"fattening on the blood of the people."[20] But the capitalist world, trapped in its unceasing conflicts, was destined to collapse. Economic havoc and depression, perhaps accompanied by war, would undercut the power of the capitalist ruling class. When economic conditions were ripe, when the capitalist leaders were down on their knees, the proletariat would seize the moment to displace them, heralding the world revolution and an end to exploitation. Communists asserted that this scenario was simply inevitable.

Until the dawning of this new, utopian time, however, the Soviets faced hostile "capitalist encirclement"—the unrelenting capitalist attempt to crush the Soviet experiment, to snuff out the flame of revolution. The Soviet task, during this long but inevitable march toward a world free from capitalist iniquity, was to build Russia into a Communist bastion and a beacon for Communists elsewhere—to establish Communism firmly in one country. Moscow, Stalin boasted in 1947, was "the champion of the movement of toiling mankind for liberation from capitalist slavery."[21] With the help of the irresistible theses of Marxism-Leninism, the Soviet Union could deepen the crisis in the capitalist camp and hurry the inevitable collapse by a variety of methods—from watchful waiting, to "peaceful coexistence," to

20. N. Voznesensky, in Barrington Moore, Jr., *Soviet Politics—The Dilemma of Power* (Cambridge, Mass., 1950), p. 372.

21. Speech of September 10, 1947, in House, *Strategy and Tactics*, p. 184.

support for violent actions by revolutionaries. The ideology permitted flexible tactics: The end was inexorable, but the means were changeable. Thus, the Soviets could even sign a pact with the Nazis and then join an alliance with capitalists in the Second World War. For certain, Soviets declared, revolution could not be exported. The conditions for rebellion were internal, peculiar to each nation. Finally, in this persistent struggle toward a noncapitalist utopia, everyone had to choose sides. Communist officials scoffed at neutralism or nonalignment in their rendition of the grand historical drama. "You are either with us, or against us," Stalin instructed a Chinese diplomat.[22] The ideology taught that for a long time most would be against.[23]

American observers pointed to Stalin's election-eve speech of February 9, 1946 as evidence that Communist ideology constituted a fundamental force driving the Soviets to expansionism and postwar uncooperativeness. H. Freeman Matthews, Director of the State Department's Office of European Affairs, thought the speech the "most important and authoritative guide to post-war Soviet policy. . . . It will henceforth be the Communist and fel-

22. Harriman and Abel, *Special Envoy*, p. 541.

23. For expressions of the Communist ideological tenets, see Molotov, *Problems of Foreign Policy*; Eugene Varga, "Anglo-American Rivalry and Partnership: A Marxist View," *Foreign Affairs*, XXV(July 1947), 583–595; B. Ponomaryov, A. Gromyko, and V. Khvostov, *History of Soviet Foreign Policy, 1917–1945* (Moscow, 1969), pp. 9–28; speeches and writings by Marx, Lenin, Stalin, Andrei Zhdanov, Molotov, and Andrei Vyshinsky in House, *Strategy and Tactics*; and various Communist statements in LaFeber, *Eastern Europe and the Soviet Union,* pp. 191–381. For discussions of the ideology, see Tucker, *Soviet Political Mind;* Waldemar Gurian, "Permanent Features of Soviet Foreign Policy," *Year Book of World Affairs, 1947* (London, 1947), pp. 1–39; William Zimmerman, "The Soviet Union," in Steven L. Spiegel and Kenneth N. Waltz, eds., *Conflict in World Politics* (Cambridge, Mass., 1971), pp. 38–54; Paul E. Zinner, "The Ideological Bases of Soviet Foreign Policy," *World Politics,* IV(July 1952), 489–511; Zbigniew Brzezinski, "Communist Ideology and International Affairs," *Journal of Conflict Resolution,* IV(September 1960), 266–290; Schwartz, *"Motive Forces"; Foreign Relations, 1946,* VI, 697–698; "X," "The Sources of Soviet Conduct;" Frederick C. Barghoorn, *The Soviet Image of the United States* (New York, 1950).

low-traveler Bible throughout the world."[24] Stalin began his address with code words drawn from Marxist-Leninist thought. World War II, he said, was "an inevitable result of the development of world economic and political forces on the basis of modern monopoly capitalism." That is, the "capitalist system of world economy conceals in itself the elements of general crisis and military clashes. . . ." The war, in brief, was not an "accident," but the result of capitalist attempts to "re-divide the 'spheres of influence' in their own favor by means of armed force." Stalin went on to applaud the durability of the Soviet system, the Five-Year Plans, and the Soviet performance in World War II and to call for a new Five-Year Plan.[25]

American leaders and publicists reacted negatively, perhaps overreacted, to this speech. The British, it seems, paid far less attention to it, but commented on the "fluttering of the dovecotes" caused by Stalin's speech in the United States.[26] It seemed clear to Americans that Stalin, the ideologue, was locked into an angry reading of world affairs.[27] Even though Stalin spoke just months later about the possibility of international cooperation with the "ruling circles" of Britain and America, other speeches in 1946 suggested that the idea of "capitalist encirclement" was fixed in the Soviet mind, that the intractable struggle between the two camps was entering yet another stage. "But even now, after the greatest victory known to history, we

24. H. Freeman Matthews to Dean Acheson, February 11, 1946, Box 2, Matthews Files, Department of State Records. See also *Foreign Relations, 1946,* VI, 695; Deane, *Strange Alliance,* p. 320; Blum, *Price of Vision,* p. 547.

25. The speech is reprinted in LaFeber, *Eastern Europe and the Soviet Union,* pp. 191–199.

26. "Political Situation in the United States," February 17, 1946, AN 423/1/45, Foreign Office Correspondence.

27. Henry A. Wallace did not agree that the speech was a simple reflection of Soviet ideology. He thought that the speech

was accounted for in some measure by the fact that it was obvious to Stalin that our military was getting ready for a war with Russia; that they were setting up bases all the way from Greenland, Iceland, northern Canada, and Alaska to Okinawa, with Russia in mind. . . . We were challenging him and his speech was taking up the challenge.

Blum, *Price of Vision,* p. 547.

cannot for one minute forget the basic fact," President Mikhail Kalinin had claimed in August, 1945, "that our own country remains the one socialist state in the world."[28] Molotov added in November that "while we are living in a 'system of states,' and while the roots of fascism and imperialist aggression have not been finally extirpated, our vigilance in regard to possible new violators of peace should not slacken. . . ."[29]

Soviet ideologues turned the pages of history to find examples —lessons—which demonstrated the veracity of their theories. To them the record of capitalist hostility was evident enough: Allied military intervention in the Russian civil war in 1918–19 and support to anti-Bolshevik forces, the creation at Versailles of a postwar *cordon sanitaire* of anti-Soviet states, refusal to recognize their government (Britain finally recognized it in 1924; the United States waited until 1933), and statements by leaders (like Senator Harry S. Truman) in the 1930s and early 1940s that fascists and Communists should fight one another, thereby ridding the burdened world of two menaces. The ghost of Hitler also haunted the Russians in the postwar period. Like Americans, they conjured up images of new Hitlers, new aggression, new wars—a replay of the 1930s. Following the dialectic of Marxism-Leninism, it seemed to the Soviets inevitable that a new round of troubles would unfold. Stalin's angry rebuke to Churchill's "Iron Curtain" speech of March 1946 suggested this line of thinking. "Mr. Churchill," charged Stalin, "now stands in the position of a firebrand of war. And Mr. Churchill is not alone here. He has friends not only in England but also in the United States of America." Indeed, Stalin snapped, "one is reminded remarkably of Hitler and his friends." Would Churchill and his friends attempt another invasion like that in the World War I era? Should they, "they will be beaten, just as they were beaten twenty-six years ago."[30]

28. Quoted in Frederick C. Barghoorn, "The Soviet Union between War and Cold War," *The Annals of the American Academy of Political and Social Science*, CCLXIII(May 1949), 4.

29. Quoted in McNeill, *America, Britain, and Russia,* pp. 653–654.

30. *New York Times*, March 14, 1946. See also Andrei Zhdanov, *The International Situation* (Moscow, 1947); Embassy of the U.S.S.R.,

All in all, the components of the Soviet ideology told Kremlin officials that they continued to face an antagonistic world bent on extinguishing both revolution and the bearer of the torch, the Soviet Union. Because of the optimism growing from certain victory in the indeterminable future, and because Soviet leaders felt a duty to preach their doctrines to others and to encourage dissident groups abroad, this ideology fed Soviet expansionism. When ideology and opportunity merged, as when Soviet troops stood guard over much of Central and Eastern Europe at the end of the war, expansionism moved from theory to reality. Although Stalin said at one point that "communism fitted Germany as a saddle fitted a cow," he also said "whoever occupies a territory imposes on it his own social system."[31]

In 1946 Maxim Litvinov (the Soviet foreign minister from 1929 to 1939) described another fundamental characteristic of Soviet foreign policy: a quest for "geographical security."[32] George F. Kennan, from his vantage point in the Moscow embassy, put the matter somewhat differently. He identified a "traditional and instinctive Russian sense of insecurity" and surmised that the Communist ideology was simply a new "vehicle" for the expression of this very Russian (as distinct from Soviet) phenomenon.[33] Although some scholars have attached more significance to ideology than to this strategic factor—national self-interest—as a wellspring of Soviet behavior in the twentieth century, we can only say that contemporaries thought the question of security worthy of considerable mention.[34] The Russian

Information Bulletin, VI(March 26, 1946), 252–253; Smith, *My Three Years*, p. 52; *Foreign Relations, 1946*, VI, 785.

31. Quoted in Deutscher, *Stalin*, p. 537, and in Djilas, *Conversations with Stalin*, p. 114.

32. *Foreign Relations, 1946*, VI, 763.

33. *Ibid.*, pp. 769–770. Edgar Snow wrote about the Russian "consciousness of vulnerability." Edgar Snow, *The Pattern of Soviet Power* (New York, 1945), p. 211.

34. For comments on security as a fundamental ingredient of Soviet foreign policy, see Becker, *How New*, pp. 68–70; Memorandum for William Leahy from the British Joint Staff Mission, September 18, 1946, Folder 46, William Leahy Papers, Naval Historical Office; Blum, *Price of Vision*, p. 503; Vera Micheles Dean, *Russia: Menace or Promise*

concern for security seemed to have necessitated expansion. We cannot know for sure if this was fuelled by fear or ambition, or both; but former State Department official Louis Halle appears to have made a good case for calling it "defensive expansion, an expansion prompted by the lack of natural defensive frontiers in a world of mortal danger on all sides. Where mountain-ramparts or impassable waters are lacking, sheer space must do in their stead."[35]

Since the early centuries of the Christian era, the Russians have suffered invasions. Mongolian intruders from the East plundered the countryside. Genghis Khan, the thirteenth-century Tartar conquerer of Kiev, earned his infamous reputation for brutality by visiting slaughter upon Russia. The Russians struck back, expanding their territory at the same time. From Ivan the Terrible (1533–84) through Peter the Great (1682–1725)— who was particularly concerned about acquiring Russian access to open seas and who won a "window on Europe" by absorbing the Baltic provinces—the Russian czars enlarged the Russian domain, in part to diminish their own country's vulnerability to attack. Still, there were more invasions and wars: The Poles in the seventeenth century, like other invaders, burned Moscow, and Napoleon led his French forces into Russia in the War of 1812; the Crimean War of the 1850s and the Russo-Japanese War of 1904–05 brought defeat to the Russians, and during World War I the Germans invaded.

The Bolsheviks, inheriting the Russian legacy, also had had to resist the invading troops of Britain, France, Japan, Italy, and the United States in 1918 and of Poland in 1920. In the harsh Brest-Litovsk Treaty of 1918, the Bolsheviks accepted a loser's peace from Germany, thereby giving up Poland, the Baltic states, and a large portion of the Ukraine—or about the equiva-

(New York, 1947), pp. 61–62; Diary, July 14, 1945, Box 17, Davies Papers; Philip E. Mosely, "Aspects of Russian Expansion," in his *Kremlin and World Politics* (New York, 1960), pp. 42–66; Ivo J. Lederer, "Russia and the Balkans," in Lederer, ed., *Russian Foreign Policy* (New Haven, 1962), pp. 417–451; Moore, *Soviet Politics*, pp. 350–394.

35. Louis J. Halle, *The Cold War as History* (New York, 1967), p. 17.

lent of the western territorial gains made since Peter the Great's day. Again, in the Second World War, Germans marched and with utter ruthlessness ravaged the Russian landscape. Awesome indeed were the losses—between fifteen and twenty million Russians died in that holocaust. Never again, Stalin told Harriman, would Russia permit the Western powers to construct a *cordon sanitaire* in Eastern Europe to threaten Russian security.[36] The Soviets proceeded to build their own security belt, which in Western parlance became known as the "iron curtain." In other words, as Litvinov remarked in a frank, unusual criticism of his own government, the Russians tried to grab "all they could while the going was good."[37]

The issue of postwar Poland epitomized the Soviet concentration on security. Poland, Soviet leaders said over and over again, was the "gateway," the "corridor," through which enemies attacked Russia. For Russia, Stalin declared, Poland was a question of "life or death."[38] In April of 1945 the Soviet dictator wrote Truman that Great Britain was shaping the postwar politics of Belgium and Greece because those countries were vital to British security: "I cannot understand why in discussing Poland no attempt is made to consider the interests of the Soviet Union in terms of security as well. . . ."[39] For Harry Hopkins, in May, Stalin repeated the point: "In the course of twenty-five years the Germans had twice invaded Russia via Poland. Neither the British nor American people had experienced such German invasions which were a horrible thing to endure. . . . It is therefore

36. W. Averell Harriman, *Peace with Russia?* (New York, 1959), p. 12. See also Hull, *Memoirs*, II, 1299.

37. Quoted in Vojtech Mastny, "The Cassandra in the Foreign Commissariat: Maxim Litvinov and the Cold War," *Foreign Affairs*, LIV (January 1976), 374.

38. Molotov in *Foreign Relations, 1945*, V, 238–239 and Stalin in *The Tehran, Yalta, and Potsdam Conferences: Documents* (Moscow, 1969), pp. 93–94.

39. Ministry of Foreign Affairs of the U.S.S.R., *Correspondence Between the Chairman of the Council of Ministers of the U.S.S.R. and the Presidents of the U.S.A. and the Prime Ministers of Great Britain During the Great Patriotic War of 1941–1945* (New York, Capricorn Books edition, 1965: *Stalin's Correspondence with Roosevelt and Truman, 1941–1945*), p. 220.

in Russia's vital interest that Poland should be strong and friendly."[40] In a public statement in March of the following year, Stalin expanded the question beyond Poland when he emphasized that the Germans had also used Finland, Rumania, Bulgaria, and Hungary to invade Russia, because those countries "had governments inimical to the Soviet Union."[41]

Why were the Russians so determined to gain a share of the authority in managing the Dardanelles, the Straits connecting the Black and Mediterranean Seas? Stalin again pointed to Russian national interest: No longer, he said at the Yalta Conference, could Russia "accept a situation in which Turkey had a hand on Russia's throat."[42] He also told Ambassador Smith that Turkey was anti-Soviet and might permit foreign control of the Straits (he thought that the Turks had done so during the war): "It is a matter of our security."[43]

The Germans, Stalin prophesied, "will recover, and very quickly. Give them twelve to fifteen years and they'll be on their feet again. And this is why the unity of the Slavs is important."[44] His prediction of another war with Germany within a generation was dead wrong, but the intensity of his feeling toward that country pointed up the centrality of the strategic factor in Soviet foreign policy. "I hate Germans," Stalin remarked to Czech Prime Minster Eduard Beneš. "The Soviet Union wants nothing else than to gain allies who will always be prepared to resist the German danger."[45]

Russia's hobbled postwar economy posed another threat to survival, and the nation's economic needs seem to have constituted a fundamental ingredient in the Soviet's outward view. Russia was a "weak great power"—before the war essentially a

40. *Foreign Relations, Berlin,* I, 39. See also Joseph Stalin, *The Great Patriotic War* (New York, 1945), pp. 152–153.

41. *New York Times,* March 14, 1946.

42. *Foreign Relations, Yalta,* p. 903.

43. Quoted in Smith, *My Three Years,* p. 53. See also *Foreign Relations, 1946,* VI, 736.

44. Quoted in Milovan Djilas, *Wartime* (New York, 1977), p. 438. See also Harriman and Abel, *Special Envoy,* p. 273.

45. Quoted in Eduard Taborsky, "Beneš and Stalin—Moscow, 1943 and 1945," *Journal of Central European Affairs,* XIII(July 1953), 179.

developing nation trying to establish an industrial base through rapid growth in Five-Year Plans and after the war a devastated country facing massive reconstruction tasks.[46] Russia's population in 1940 had been 194.1 million; at the end of the war it numbered about 170 million. Shortly after the Second World War, a British delegation visited a Moscow trade school and began asking students about their economic problems. Did their homes have heat and water? The school's director interrupted. There were more important questions. He asked pupils who had lost fathers at the front to stand up. All but one rose. The lone student explained that his father had also fought against the Germans, but had lost both his legs rather than his life.[47] Joined to this extraordinary disruption of Russia's working population was the destruction of material Russia. Over 30,000 industrial plants and 40,000 miles of railroad track were destroyed. Thousands of towns and cities had been leveled. Agricultural production was half of what it had been in 1940. Coal mines were flooded; bridges were down. The oil industry suffered shortages of steel pipe. Moreover, as if the war had not done damage enough, a killer drought struck farming regions in 1946.[48]

"One only had to visit Russia to realize how much of its policy is affected by dire need," wrote Lucius Clay, the American military governor in Germany.[49] Indeed, some observers attributed Soviet actions in international politics to their economic woes. Perhaps Soviet hyperbolic propaganda about an external enemy was stimulated by the need to rally the already

46. Dean, *United States and Russia*, p. 136.

47. V. Lelchuk, Y. Polyakov, and A. Protopopov, *A Short History of Soviet Society* (Moscow, 1971), p. 312.

48. Harry Schwartz, *Russia's Postwar Economy* (Syracuse, 1947); Deutscher, *Stalin*, pp. 573–575; Paterson, *Soviet-American Confrontation*, p. 34; Lelchuk, *et al., Short History of Soviet Society*, pp. 309–316; *New York Times*, February 9, 1946; Vera Micheles Dean, "Russia's Internal Economic Problems," *Foreign Policy Reports*, XXIII(July 1, 1947), 98–106; Whitney, *Russia in My Life*, pp. 101–102.

49. Quoted in Yergin, *Shattered Peace*, p. 298. See also Truman's talk with MacKenzie King in J.W. Pickersgill and D.F. Forster, *The MacKenzie King Record* (Toronto, 1960–1970; 4 vols.), III, 361.

burdened Russian people to overcome the war-wrought devastation. "The emotional and physical exhaustion of the Soviet masses is a greater factor than is perhaps realized anywhere outside the USSR," the State Department informed the President in 1946.[50] The Soviets also sought compensation for their losses through war booty and reparations. From Manchuria they carted machinery. In Eastern Europe they confiscated property formerly owned by Germans, including equipment used for oil production in Rumania. In Hungary, the Soviets gained control of the petroleum industry, some of which was German-operated in the war but owned by the Standard Oil Company of New Jersey. Soviet trade treaties with Bulgaria, Hungary, and Rumania proved advantageous to Russia. Soviet officials also organized joint stock companies on a fifty-fifty basis with several neighboring states, and Poland was forced to ship valuable coal to the Soviet Union.[51] The Russians, concluded a British diplomat, were pursuing an exploitative economic policy in Eastern Europe "to protect Soviet security," to gain their "rightful fruits of victory," and to insure "reconstruction and industrialization."[52] Russia also insisted on large reparations from Germany and its satellites. "Reparations for Fulfillment of the Five-Year Plan" was the slogan of one Soviet planning group.[53] In their zone in Germany, Soviet officials confiscated heavy machinery and sent newly produced goods eastward. Hungary and Rumania were assessed about $200 million each in indemnities.[54]. Economic needs may also explain why the Soviets intervened in Iran (for oil) and why they requested participation in a trusteeship for former Italian colonies in Africa (for uranium).[55] Finally, the

50. White House Summary, September 19, 1946, Department of State Records.
51. Paterson, *Soviet-American Confrontation*, ch. 5.
52. Quoted in Gormly, "In Search of a Postwar Settlement," p. 27.
53. Quoted in Robert Slusser, ed., *Soviet Economic Policy in Postwar Germany: A Collection of Papers by Former Soviet Officials* (New York, 1953), p. 49.
54. Paterson, *Soviet-American Confrontation*, chs. 5, 11.
55. For Iran and oil, see *ibid.*, pp. 177–183 and Yergin, *Shattered Peace*, pp. 179–190. As for Africa and uranium, at least Secretary Byrnes thought that the Soviet request for a trusteeship in Tripolitania was de-

chief of naval intelligence suggested in 1946 another possible expansionist effect of Russia's precarious economic status: "Maintenance of large occupational forces in Europe is dictated to a certain extent by the necessity of 'farming out' millions of men for whom living accommodations and food cannot be spared in the USSR during the current winter."[56]

Besides ideology, security, and economic needs, there was a fourth fundamental factor that helps to explain why the Soviet Union behaved as it did in world politics: military power, derived from victories over German forces in Eastern Europe, the subsequent occupation of countries in that region, and the weakness of its neighbors. These realities, this very existence of military power, thrust the Soviet Union into the affairs of Eastern Europe. Unlike the United States, the Soviets lacked economic power and did not carry much international political weight outside Eastern Europe. Molotov, for example, complained about the "voting game" which saw a majority at the United Nations Organization or international conferences cast "nays" against Soviet proposals.[57] Litvinov thought it "not unreasonable for [the] USSR to be suspicious of any forum in which she would constantly be outvoted."[58]

Yet when Americans gauged Soviet power, they did not

---

signed to afford them access to the uranium—essential to atomic development—of the Belgian Congo: "If the Soviets could get Tripolitania," said Byrnes in September 1945, "they would be in a position to head us off from the uranium. As the matter now stands we and the British have a monopoly and the Soviets want some of it." (Indigenous Soviet sources of uranium were apparently low-grade.) Byrnes quoted in Gregory F. Herkin, "American Diplomacy and the Atom Bomb, 1945–1947" (Unpublished Ph.D. dissertation, Princeton University, 1974), p. 103. Also see pp. 112, 121.

56. Thomas B. Inglis to James Forrestal, January 21, 1946, Box 24, Forrestal Papers.

57. Molotov, *Problems of Foreign Policy*, pp. 83–84. See also pp. 94, 224, 251.

58. *Foreign Relations, 1946*, VI, 764. See also Robert R. McNeal, "Roosevelt through Stalin's Spectacles," *International Journal*, XVIII (Spring 1963), 202–204.

think so much about Russian economic or political weaknesses, but rather about the huge, imposing, and battle-tested Red Army. When Secretary Byrnes mused that "somebody . . . made an awful mistake in bringing about a situation where Russia was permitted to come out of a war with the power she will have," he probably meant the power of the Red Army in Eastern Europe.[59] American military officials projected that, should war break out between the United States and Russia, Red Army forces could probably march deep into Western Europe before Russia could be stopped and punished.[60]

Western observers overestimated the size of the Soviet armed forces. This happened in part because the Kremlin, secretive as always, did not publicize its own demobilization program and in part because outsiders, in making their own military plans, tended, as always, to think the worst about the potential enemy's intentions and wherewithal. In March of 1948, for example, the Central Intelligence Agency and other intelligence groups from the military branches reported that Soviet troops were "combat ready," but predicted that the USSR would not resort to war that year. The secret report concluded, however, that "we have no access to the thinking or decisions of the Kremlin and little contact with lower echelons of Soviet officialdom."[61] The Soviet armed forces apparently shrank from their wartime peak of about 11.3 million persons to about 2.8 million in 1948.[62] Contemporary estimates ran as high as 5 mil-

59. Quoted in Yergin, *Shattered Peace*, p. 118.
60. "Joint Basic Outline War Plan ('Pincher')," by Joint War Plans Committee, JWPC 423/3, April 27, 1946, Geographic File 381-USSR, Joint Chiefs of Staff Records.
61. "Possibility of Direct Soviet Military Action During 1948," Central Intelligence Agency, April 2, 1948, CD 21-1-26, Records of the Office of the Secretary of Defense, Modern Military Branch, National Archives.
62. Brzezinski, "Competitive Relationship," p. 161; Yergin, *Shattered Peace*, pp. 270, 467; *The Soviet Army* (Moscow, 1971), p. 313. For a study which thinks that these figures are deflated, see Thomas W. Wolfe, *Soviet Power and Europe, 1945–1970* (Baltimore, 1970), pp. 10–11.

lion persons in arms.[63] It even appears that much of the Soviet army's equipment was broken or obsolete; as late as 1950 half of its transportation was horse-drawn.[64]

Overrated or not, the Red Army was probably the largest military grouping in Europe, and its standing, the fear it aroused in others, derived not only from its own size but from the fact that Russia's neighbors were so weak. The roughly half a million Russian soldiers who occupied Eastern Europe and part of Germany permitted Moscow to manipulate politics, and hence to orient the foreign policies of its neighbors. The Red Army did not always have to intervene in a blatant fashion; its mere presence was symbolic of Soviet hegemony. Few could forget, as Stalin bragged in early 1946, that this was the "very army which utterly routed the German army that but yesterday struck terror into the armies of European states."[65]

Still, the Soviet military establishment did reveal weaknesses. The Soviet navy lacked carriers and a modern fleet, the air force was insignificant, and a Soviet atomic bomb was not successfully exploded until 1949. The American chief of naval intelligence suggested that Russia was unlikely to launch a military attack, because the "Red Fleet is incapable of any important offensive or amphibious operations," because "a strategic air force is practically nonexistent either in material or concept," and because "economically, the Soviet Union is exhausted. The people are undernourished, industry and transport are in an advanced state of deterioration, enormous areas have been devastated, thirty per cent of the population has been dislocated."[66]

63. See *New York Times*, May 12, 1947 (5 million); Edgar O'Ballance, *The Red Army* (New York, 1964), p. 189 (3 to 5 million); Major General Milton B. Persons to Charles Eaton, November 22, 1947, Tray 18831, Committee on Foreign Affairs, House of Representatives Records, National Archives (4 million).

64. O'Ballance, *Red Army*, p. 192.

65. LaFeber, *Eastern Europe and the Soviet Union*, p. 194.

66. Thomas B. Inglis to James Forrestal, January 21, 1946, Box 24, Forrestal Papers. For similar statements see Ambassador Smith in C. L. Sulzberger, *A Long Row of Candles* (New York, 1969), p. 313; Memorandum by the Chief of Staff, U.S. Army, to Joint Chiefs of Staff, July 28, 1947, Box 166, Central File 471.6, Joint Chiefs of Staff Records;

Compared to the non-Communist world, Russia was, said Kennan, the "weaker force."[67] In early 1948 Stalin complained privately to Yugoslav leaders that their support for the Greek Communist rebels in a civil war wracking the Near East country was dangerous to Soviet security. "What do you think, that Great Britain and the United States—the United States, the most powerful state in the world—will permit you to break their line of communication in the Mediterranean! Nonsense. And we have no navy."[68]

The Soviets drew some measure of military power from geography. The vast land mass of Russia, as Napoleon and Hitler learned, could swallow invaders from the west, bitter cold winters wearing them down. Retreating Russian armies abandoned and even destroyed their towns, waiting for the eventual day of counterattack and retribution. Also, in the nuclear age, it was not clear that the atomic bomb could be easily employed as a weapon against Russia. Target sites were widely dispersed, requiring a large number of bombs which would probably have to be delivered with synchronization.[69] As it was, no military tests of power ensued: The Red Army did not move westward, and American atomic bombs did not rain their terror on Russian cities.

A working committee of the American embassy in Moscow in 1946 delineated historical, ideological, geographic, and economic factors to explain the "dynamic, expanding" character of the Soviet Union. The committee, which included two men who would later become leading academic scholars of Soviet politics (Robert Tucker and Frederick Barghoorn), advanced another

---

Truman in Pickersgill and Forster, *MacKenzie King Record*, IV, 31; *Foreign Relations, 1948*, III, 157; Yergin, *Shattered Peace*, p. 467; Eayers, *In Defence of Canada*, p. 334.

67. *Foreign Relations, 1946*, VI, 707. Although recognizing the superior power of the Red Army, Zbigniew Brzezinski has concluded that for the period 1945–47, "the Soviet position in the world was still very inferior to that of the United States." Zbigniew Brzezinski, "The Competitive Relationship," in Charles Gati, ed., *Caging the Bear: Containment and the Cold War* (Indianapolis, 1974), p. 160.

68. Djilas, *Conversations with Stalin*, p. 182.

69. Morgenthau, *Politics Among Nations*, pp. 107–108.

fundamental ingredient, an "institutional" mainspring: totalitarianism.[70] The Soviets themselves, of course, never mentioned this characteristic. It emanated from outside observers
who did not believe that Russia's fears, ideology, or strategic-economic needs were sufficient to account for the general Soviet
suspiciousness of and hostility toward other nations. The Soviets, argued some analysts, exaggerated threats. Why? The highly
speculative answer read that the maintenance of Stalinist totalitarianism—"a Frankenstein dictatorship worse than any of the
others, Hitler included," Truman said—needed external enemies
to deflect domestic criticism from the repressive regime.[71] Stalin's centralized one-man, one-party government, insisting on
ideological purity and holding a monopoly of enforcing power,
therefore really feared internal critics more than external capitalists: The Kremlin heated up passions against the latter in order
to silence its dissidents at home, to perpetuate its dreadful treat-
ment of the Russian people, and to urge the common people to
accept further sacrifice. "The regime of ruthless dictatorship, of
rule by police terror, imposed and maintained by Stalin from the
early thirties on," concluded Thomas Whitney, a foreign service
officer in Moscow, "required the presence of an external enemy
in order that there should be justification for repression and
terror."[72]

Whitney and others believed that Hitler was a real threat to
the Soviets in the 1930s, but that in the late 1940s the Soviets
invented the myth of "capitalist encirclement" and an "imperialist" United States as an enemy. This theoretical argument placed
too much emphasis on the passivity of the United States in the
postwar period and discounted any suggestion that American
behavior might have influenced Soviet behavior. "The basic
problem," Acheson declared, "is that the very nature of the
police state and of the Russian police state is such that it must

70. "Analysis of Soviet Strength and Weakness," Joint Working
Committee of the American Embassy, Moscow, September 1, 1946,
861.00/9-946, Department of State Records.
71. Quoted in Truman, *Truman*, p. 306.
72. Whitney, *Russia in My Life*, p. 105.

continue an aggressive expansionist foreign policy. . . . It just must do that. It can't do anything else."[73] Journalist Walter Lippmann, like many others, penned an affirmative answer in 1947 to this question: "Does not the maintenance of the dictatorship in Russia depend upon maintaining a state of tension and insecurity to justify it?"[74]

The peculiar needs and fears of the totalitarian government, it was further suggested, perpetuated a Russian tradition: intense suspiciousness of all foreigners. Thus, American diplomats in Moscow were treated like potential enemies, spied upon, followed, isolated from the Russian people, and made to suffer indignities at the hands of petty Soviet bureaucrats. Journalists had to submit all stories for clearance to suspicious and capricious censors. The Soviets only reluctantly, after much obstruction, would permit American pilots to land at Russian airfields during the war. Russian women who had married American men were often not permitted to leave the country to join their husbands in the United States. Russian soldiers and diplomats who had visited other nations in the course of their wartime duties came home to suspicions of disloyalty, interrogations by the secret police, and the ever-present hidden microphone. Stalin sought to detect any traces of ideological flabbiness, or worse, any evidence that the "enemy" had recruited them.[75] When Senator Wayne Morse of Oregon visited Vienna in 1946, he grew impatient with Soviet travel restrictions which required a ride from the airport to city center that took over an hour, rather than the few minutes it should have taken. "Each of these

73. "American Foreign Policy," transcript of proceedings, June 4, 1947, Box 93, Records of the United States Mission to the United Nations, Department of State Records. See also *Foreign Relations, 1946*, I, 1168.

74. Walter Lippmann, "The Stassen Interview," *Washington Post*, May 6, 1947. See also "X", "Sources of Soviet Conduct;" Schwartz, "*Motive Forces*," pp. 34–37; Ulam, *Expansion and Coexistence*, pp. 398–403; Harriman and Abel, *Special Envoy*, p. 521; Stimson and Bundy, *On Active Service*, p. 639; Louis Fischer, *The Great Challenge* (London, 1947), p. 254.

75. Harriman and Abel, *Special Envoy*, pp. 214, 308, 317, 547; Ulam, *Stalin*, pp. 633–634; Whitney, *Russia in My Life*, p. 23.

little incidents standing alone is not of great significance," he told a New York audience, "but when multiplied by many such incidents their cumulative effect helps produce the war of nerves which is developing in Europe."[76]

Even Communists in other countries were suspect. If they did not hew to the Moscow line, if they betrayed a sense of independence, if they did not wholly share the Kremlin's dark view of capitalists, and if they pursued different means than those prescribed by Stalin to reach the proletarian revolution, the totalitarian regime seemed again to be threatened and the wayward had to be disciplined. Stalin gave no aid to the Greek rebels, lectured and then broke relations with that independent Yugoslav Communist, Josip Broz Tito, and only half-heartedly supported the Communists of Mao Tse-tung in the Chinese civil war. Stalin "helped revolutions up to a certain point—as long as he could control them—but he was always ready to leave them in the lurch whenever they slipped out of his grasp," concluded Yugoslav Milovan Djilas after several conversations with the Russian despot.[77] To discourage any centrifugal inclinations in the Communist world, then, Stalin exaggerated the capitalist danger.[78] In short, totalitarian requirements necessitated international conflict.

This identification of totalitarianism as a linchpin of Soviet behavior in the Cold War, it must be repeated, rests at a higher level of conjecture than that for the other fundamental factors discussed. As we have noted, we simply cannot be certain about any of the apparent inner drives propelling the expansionist course followed by the suspicious leaders of the Soviet Union. The several "fundamentals" all seem to have been ingredients in the policy mix; at least, all were outlined by contemporaries. No careful scholar, necessarily wary because of deficient Soviet sources, should venture to claim that one factor was more important than another.

76. Speech by Wayne Morse, January 8, 1947, Box 0-3, Morse Papers.
77. Djilas, *Conversations with Stalin*, p. 132.
78. See Joseph R. Starobin, "Origins of the Cold War: The Communist Dimension," *Foreign Affairs*, XLVII(July 1969), 681–696.

Assessing the tactical factors of Soviet foreign policy also presents difficulties. The evidence is one-sided, coming from non-Soviets who sat across the negotiating table from their grim Communist counterparts. The Soviets themselves seldom commented on their own diplomatic style or method, and we can only surmise that differences in style contributed to postwar conflict. Some diplomats simply disliked other diplomats, found it nearly impossible to carry on negotiations with them, and stood back, seldom trusting. That Truman never met again with Stalin after Potsdam, that an American President did not sit down with a Soviet Premier for the period 1945–55, may not have been in itself a cause of Cold War tension, but it certainly meant that an obstacle blocked the road to diplomatic solutions. Negotiations can prove fruitless, of course, and summit conferences have often been superficial public shows of momentary cooperativeness, yet contact and communication are essential to the business of diplomacy. When they are absent—when, for example, Harriman thought that the Russians were "barbarians" and "world bullies" and Acheson became convinced that any discussion with the Soviets was futile—patient, low-key diplomacy gives way to name-calling, impatience, and bickering over minor matters.[79] In brief, people who do not get along cannot move negotiations along to mutually beneficial results. What we can say for sure is that the Soviet diplomatic style and governmental organization did not serve to reduce conflict. American leaders thought that they insured confrontation.

Once, when Stalin and Harriman were discussing Poland, the ambassador warned that American public opinion, which he said the president had to listen to, would turn anti-Soviet unless an independent Polish state was established. Stalin replied that *he* had to worry about *Soviet* public opinion. Harriman shot back, "you know how to handle your public opinion."[80] It appears that Stalin was indeed the primary decisionmaker and shaper of "public opinion" in Soviet Russia. At times, internal debate

79. Memorandum of Conversation with Harriman, July 17, 1945, Box 18, Davies Papers; *Foreign Relations, 1944,* IV, 989.
80. Harriman and Abel, *Special Envoy,* p. 316.

occurred. Kremlin leaders, for example, apparently differed over policy toward Germany (whether to take reparations in the form of plant equipment or freshly produced goods).[81] Litvinov privately took the rare step of criticizing his government's foreign policy to an American journalist, as well as to others.[82] Eminent economist Eugene S. Varga strayed from strict Soviet ideology to argue that because of the American federal government's intervention in the economy, the expected postwar depression in the capitalist world might be delayed and war within the capitalist sphere might not even be inevitable.[83] However, Stalin, or at least those who were privileged to be in his inner circle, apparently decided the outcome of debates and how long dissent would be tolerated. Litvinov was dropped from power, and Varga was publicly chastised and forced to recant. Moreover, in the summer of 1946 Andrei Zhdanov, a member of the Politburo, pushed for uniformity of thought when he began a government-approved purge of the intelligentsia that lasted with wrenching effect until his death in 1948.[84]

Stalin's closest cohorts, a "set of inside advisers of whom we know little or nothing," reported Kennan, seemed to have been the members of the Politburo, the executive committee of the Communist Party and the supreme policymaking organ.[85] "He is a decent fellow," Truman once commented about Stalin. "But Joe is a prisoner of the Politburo. He can't do what he wants to."[86] Ambassador Smith thought that the Russian leader was "chairman of the board," suggesting thereby that he had to consider the views of the other Politburo "directors."[87] Stalin

81. See Slusser, *Soviet Economic Policy.*
82. See Mastny, "Cassandra in the Foreign Commissariat."
83. Shulman, *Stalin's Foreign Policy Reappraised,* pp. 32–33; *Soviet Views on the Post-War World Economy* (Washington, 1948); Frederick C. Barghoorn, "The Varga Discussion and Its Significance," *American Slavic and East European Review,* III(October 1948), 214–236.
84. Ulam, *Expansion and Coexistence,* p. 402; Deutscher, *Stalin,* p. 579.
85. *Foreign Relations, 1946,* VI, 722.
86. *Public Papers, Truman, 1948,* p. 329. See also notes from interview with Harry S. Truman, August 30, 1949, Box 85, Daniels Papers.
87. Smith, *My Three Years,* p. 55.

was a "moderating influence" in the Kremlin, concluded Truman.[88] Indeed, some Americans believed, with considerable speculation, that Stalin was not altogether a free man and that when he did exercise his authority, he attempted to curb the hostile excesses of his Politburo advisers.[89] We cannot know for sure.

As for Stalin himself, contemporaries and later scholars alike agree that he demonstrated monstrous qualities, as evidenced by the ghastly purges of the 1930s and the terror of everyday political life in Russia. Callousness marked his entire political career. Even his infrequent attempts at humor lent credence to the popular opinion that he was cold-bloodedly cruel. "Bring the machine guns. Let's liquidate the diplomats," he once joked in the presence of Charles de Gaulle, Georges Bidault, and Harriman, none of whom was amused.[90] The Russian premier was suspicious, it appears, of everyone. "He saw enemies everywhere," his daughter recalled.[91] Although some commentators years after Stalin's death (1953) surmised that he was paranoid, contemporaries did not think him insane or irrational.[92] Instead, they thought him a sober, if fearful, "realist" who calculated—who, as he put it, preferred arithmetic to algebra.[93]

88. Campbell and Herring, *Diaries of Stettinius*, p. 440 (October 22, 1945).

89. Edward R. Stettinius, Jr., *Roosevelt and the Russians* (New York, 1949), p. 309; Harriman and Abel, *Special Envoy*, pp. 344, 444.

90. Harriman and Abel, *Special Envoy*, p. 377.

91. Svetlana Alliluyeva, *Twenty Letters to a Friend* (New York, 1967), p. 196.

92. For the paranoia thesis, see Schlesinger, "Origins of the Cold War" and Tucker, *Soviet Political Mind*. For criticism of this view, see William A. Williams, "The Cold War Revisionists," *The Nation*, CCV (November 13, 1967), 492–495; Yergin, *Shattered Peace*, pp. 51–52; Melvin Croan in "Origins of the Post-War Crisis—A Discussion," *Journal of Contemporary History*, III(April 1968), 233–237, reprinted in Thomas G. Paterson, *The Origins of the Cold War* (Lexington, Mass., 1974; 2nd ed.), pp. 230–234.

93. Anthony Eden, *The Reckoning* (Boston, 1965), pp. 336–337; Harriman in *Foreign Relations, Berlin*, I, 61; Truman, *Memoirs*, I, 263; Blum, *Price of Vision*, pp. 172, 347; Philip E. Mosely, "Across the Green Table from Stalin," *Current History*, XV(September 1948), 129–133, 167; Dixon, *Double Diploma*, p. 140.

Kennan wrote years later that "merciless as he could be, and little as his purposes may have coincided with ours, Stalin was entirely rational in his external policies. . . ."[94]

Much the same sort of assessment was attached to Stalin's chief negotiator, V. M. Molotov, the Commissar for Foreign Affairs from 1939 to 1949 and again from 1953 to 1956, who was noted for his "extraordinary firmness" and "pungency."[95] This stern man, who peered through his pince-nez and "laughed with his mouth not his eyes," was universally disliked.[96] Truman thought that labor leader John L. Lewis and Molotov were "principal contenders for top rating as walking images of Satan."[97] "Stone Ass," as Molotov was impolitely called, was considered by some to be more intransigent than Stalin. In June of 1945 Harriman complained to Truman that "Molotov did not report to Stalin accurately. . . . It is also clear that Molotov is far more suspicious of us and less willing to view matters in our mutual relations from a broad standpoint than is Stalin."[98] American diplomats sought to skirt Molotov, to go directly to Stalin, who seemed more flexible. When Hopkins went to Moscow in May 1945, for example, he attempted, through direct talks with Stalin, to change the Soviet position on the veto in the United Nations. The Soviets wanted the veto to cover everything, including discussion, whereas the American position was that the veto should be used only to strike down actions. Molotov had stood utterly firm on the question. As Stalin listened to Hopkins and heard what Molotov had been arguing, he gruffly turned on his foreign secretary, uttered "that's nonsense," and immediately accepted the American position.[99]

94. George F. Kennan, "The United States and the Soviet Union, 1917–1976," *Foreign Affairs*, LIV(July 1976), 681.

95. Authors of the *Diplomatichesky Slovar* in W. Gottlieb, "A Self-Portrait of Soviet Foreign Policy," *Soviet Studies*, III(October 1951), 187.

96. Clement Attlee on Molotov in Williams, *Twilight of Empire*, p. 59. See also Campbell and Herring, *Diaries of Stettinius*, p. 449; Pickersgill, *MacKenzie King Record*, I, 432.

97. Quoted in Donovan, *Conflict and Crisis*, p. 209.

98. *Foreign Relations, Berlin*, I, 61.

99. Quoted in Bohlen, *Witness to History*, p. 220.

Whether observers were commenting on Stalin, Molotov, or other Soviet officials, the pervasive judgment was that the Soviet diplomatic style inhibited the negotiating process and eroded goodwill. The Soviets were thought to be rude, untrustworthy, excessively suspicious, devious, unreceptive to gestures of kindness, and too dependent upon direct instructions from the Kremlin.[100] It seems that few of the experienced diplomats of the Commissariat of Foreign Affairs survived the purges of the 1930s. Many of the new members of the diplomatic service had little university education or liberal arts background, having been schooled in technical institutes. Furthermore, many had not travelled abroad and were not proficient in foreign languages.[101] Some, like Soviet ambassador to the United Nations Andrei Vyshinsky, had been stalwarts of Stalinist ruthlessness in the purges—and Americans could not easily forget that he had blood on his hands. The polished Acheson, who found talking to the Russians a particularly arduous trial, snidely suggested that Russian diplomats went to schools "where naturally coarse manners were made intentionally offensive, and where the students were trained in a technique of intellectual deviousness designed to frustrate any discussion."[102] Whether so trained or whether simply stupid, the Russians developed their own "get-tough" style which obstructed negotiations. To American officials, who had little bargaining experience with the

100. For comments on the Soviet diplomatic style, see Raymond Dennett and Joseph E. Johnson, eds., *Negotiating with the Russians* (Boston, 1951); Philip E. Mosely, "Some Soviet Techniques of Negotiation," in Mosely, *Kremlin and World Politics*, pp. 3–41; Mosely, "Across the Green Table"; Stephen Kertesz, "Reflections on Soviet and American Negotiating Behavior," *Review of Politics*, XIX (January 1957), 3–36; Gordon A. Craig, "Techniques of Negotiation," in Lederer, *Russian Foreign Policy*, pp. 351–373; James B. Reston, "Negotiating with the Russians," *Harper's Magazine*, CXCV (August 1947), 97–106; House of Representatives, Committee on Government Operations, *The Soviet Approach to Negotiation: Selected Writing* (Washington, D.C., 1969).
101. Teddy J. Uldricks, "The Impact of the Great Purges on the People's Commissariat of Foreign Affairs," *Slavic Review*, XXXVI (June 1977), 187-203.
102. Dean Acheson, *Sketches from Life* (Westport, Conn., 1974), pp. 91–92.

Soviets before World War II, it seemed that their Soviet opposites were deliberately hindering the business of diplomacy.
"They don't know how to behave," Truman remarked. "They're
like bulls in a china shop. They're only twenty-five years old.
We're over one hundred years old and the British are centuries
older. We've got to teach them how to behave."[103]

Truman also concluded that the Soviets were "touchy,"
easily slighted, and over-sensitive to any hint that they were not
representatives of a great nation.[104] At the Potsdam Conference, for example, the British, American, and Russian chiefs of
staff gathered to discuss military questions. American Admiral
William Leahy rapped the gavel on the table and called the
meeting "to order." The Soviet delegate, upon hearing the trans-
lation of these opening remarks, abruptly rose to his feet, grumbled that he and his colleagues had been insulted, and demanded
to know who was "out of order."[105] Months later, Trygve Lie,
Secretary General of the United Nations, toured devastated
Russia and at one luncheon bestowed what he thought was
praise upon his Soviet hosts: that they ranked first in army
strength, second in wealth and industry, and third in sea power.
The angry Soviets interpreted these words to mean that Lie was
telling them they were not a great power.[106]

The Soviets also bargained hard in negotiations. Truman
saw them as "pigheaded."[107] They often repeated their positions endlessly, prolonging meetings. "Jimmy," an impatient and
perturbed Truman complained to Byrnes at Potsdam after hearing one of Stalin's *nyets*, "do you realize that we have been here
seventeen whole days. Why, in seventeen days you can decide
anything!"[108] Soviet diplomats balked at compromise, perhaps

103. Quoted in Walton, *Wallace, Truman and the Cold War*, p. 41.
104. Harry S. Truman to Eleanor Roosevelt, May 10, 1945, Box
4560, Eleanor Roosevelt Papers.
105. Leslie Hollis, *One Marine's Tale* (London, 1956), pp. 144–145.
106. Lie, *In The Cause of Peace*, p. 223.
107. Quoted in Alfred Steinberg, *The Man from Missouri* (New
York, 1962), p. 259.
108. Quoted in Truman, *Truman*, p. 279. For an example of the
repetitiveness of the Soviet method, see Harrison Salisbury, *Russia on
the Way* (New York, 1946), p. 381.

fearful of having to explain any divergence from precise instructions to a suspicious Kremlin. "I must talk to my government" was a common, and annoying, utterance from Soviet diplomats at crucial moments in negotiations.[109] The seemingly timid Soviet diplomats took on the appearance of messenger boys.[110] They also threatened to walk out of meetings—and occasionally did—and they sometimes changed positions with an abruptness that baffled. They could run hot and cold; President Roosevelt noted the "Russian habit of sending him a friendly note on Monday, spitting in his eye on Tuesday, and then being nice again on Wednesday."[111] A common expression among diplomatic officers in the Moscow embassy was that when trading with the Russians you had to buy the same horse twice, because they kept bringing up points that others thought were settled.[112] Secretary Marshall deplored another Soviet tactic in negotiations: The Soviets would say to him, "you did not deny our statement so obviously it must be correct."[113] The harshest judgment was that Soviet diplomats were liars, not to be trusted.[114]

Stalin apparently described himself as a "rude old man."[115] Non-Soviet diplomats could only agree that that description was appropriate for much of the Soviet foreign service. Hugh Dalton, British chancellor of the exchequer, pronounced the Russians a

109. Vyshinsky in Campbell and Herring, *Diaries of Stettinius*, p. 453.

110. See Isador Lubin's comments in "American-Soviet Relations," Discussion Meeting Report, October 2, 1947, Records of Groups, vol. XIV, Council on Foreign Relations Files; General Osborn in *ibid.*, April 5, 1948; and Charles Bohlen in Memorandum of Background Press and Radio Conference, May 11, 1948, Box 8, Bohlen Files.

111. Blum, *Price of Vision*, p. 245.

112. Harriman and Abel, *Special Envoy*, p. 412.

113. *Foreign Relations, 1948*, V, Part 1, 164.

114. For contemporary comments on the Soviets as dishonest and lying diplomats, see Truman in Donovan, *Conflict and Crisis*, p. 62; Leahy in Journal, August 1, 1945, Box 19, Davies Papers; John R. Deane, "Negotiating on Military Assistance, 1943–1945," in Dennett and Johnson, *Negotiating*, pp. 8, 27; Baruch in Bernstein, "Quest for Security," p. 1042; *Foreign Relations, 1948*, V, 164.

115. Smith, *My Three Years*, p. 60.

"bad mannered people." He compared them to a "pup which is not yet housetrained." Indeed, "they bounce about and bark and knock things over and misbehave themselves generally and the next day are puzzled if one is still resentful."[116] Acheson's conclusion bears repeating: "You cannot sit down with them."[117] What is more, he seldom did, for he believed that the fundamental dynamics of the Soviet Union and the tactics of its officials militated against serious accommodation in the escalating Cold War.

116. Hugh Dalton Diary, October 5, 1946, Hugh Dalton Papers, London School of Economics, London, England. For other comments, mostly critical, on the Soviet diplomatic style, see Harry S. Truman to Eleanor Roosevelt, December 21, 1948, Box 4560, Eleanor Roosevelt Papers; Blum, *Price of Vision*, p. 451; Memorandum of telephone conversation, December 6, 1946, Box 30, Warren Austin Papers, University of Vermont Library, Burlington, Vermont; William Leahy, *I Was There* (New York, 1950), p. 349; Cabinet Meeting, October 11, 1946, Notes on Cabinet Meetings, Connelly Papers; Dean, *United States and Russia*, p. 49; "An American's Opinion on Iran," June 20, 1946, 891.00/6-2046, Department of State Records; Acheson in *New York Times*, October 13, 1971; Digest of Meeting, April 10, 1947, Records of Meetings, vol. VIII, Council of Foreign Relations Files; Walter Johnson, ed., *Papers of Adlai Stevenson* (Boston, 1972–1977; 7 vols.), II, 301; Sulzberger, *A Long Row of Candles*, p. 364.
117. Senate, *Legislative Origins of the Truman Doctrine*, p. 95.

8

Bipolarity: The World in 1950

~~~~~~

AN AMERICAN B-29 equipped with sensitive instruments, flying over the North Pacific in September of 1949, detected unusually high radioactivity in the atmosphere. A study of the data led to a startling conclusion: The Soviets had exploded an atomic bomb. "This is now a different world," muttered Senator Vandenberg.[1] Their nuclear monopoly erased, American officials huddled, worried about the future. Would the Soviets use the weapon to blackmail Western Europe, to intimidate other nations which had not yet gravitated to one of the two poles of the Cold War? Then came further distressing news. Mao Tse-tung's Communist victory in late 1949 in China—which was assumed by Americans to have become a tool of the Soviet Union—and the signing of the Sino-Soviet Treaty of Friendship and Alliance in February 1950 seemed to indicate that Moscow was enjoying a new and threatening surge of power.

Yet from the Kremlin in late 1949 and early 1950 came a call for "peaceful coexistence." From the Soviet perspective, decisions in the American sphere of influence—the creation of NATO, the launching of the expensive Mutual Defense Assistance Program, and Western steps toward a united command in Europe—signalled an American thrust to roll back the Soviet sphere. Now, at mid-century, might not the Americans react to

1. Quoted in LaFeber, *America, Russia, and the Cold War*, p. 86.

the Soviet atomic detonation and Mao's success by taking aggressive steps against Russia and its orbit? Perhaps, thought some Soviet officials. In preparation, they tightened their sphere, escalating political violence and purges in Eastern Europe to expunge any Titoist tendencies.[2]

Officials of the Truman administration pondered the changed world of late 1949 and early 1950. How should they respond to the perceived Soviet advances? Advice was not wanting. From Britain Winston Churchill recommended a summit conference. United Nations leaders called for Soviet-American negotiations. Communist censors permitted journalist Harrison Salisbury to send dispatches from Russia which reported that Soviet diplomats were entertaining ideas of bilateral talks. Yet President Truman and Secretary Acheson eschewed negotiations. They wanted no part of "appeasement"; they would not be taken in by the Soviet "Trojan dove," announced Acheson.[3] Nor, he said, would the United States "pull down the blinds and sit in the parlor with a loaded shotgun, waiting."[4] Indeed, recognizing the destabilizing impact of the Second World War on the international system, which contributed to "breeding grounds of conflict," Acheson vowed publicly in early 1950 that America was "playing for keeps" in a global contest with the USSR and would go around the world creating "situations of strength."[5]

While these public rumblings echoed between the major antagonists, secret, momentous decisions were being made in Washington. In January, 1950, Truman ordered the production of the hydrogen bomb, the "super." In February, following the advice set out in a National Security Council Paper of the previous December that the United States should create "friendly and independent" Asian states to "contain and reduce the power of the U.S.S.R.," the United States extended diplomatic recognition to the French-backed, anti-Communist Bao Dai government

2. Shulman, *Stalin's Foreign Policy Reappraised*, pp. 104–138; Ulam, *Expansion and Coexistence*, pp. 498–503.

3. Acheson, *Present at the Creation*, pp. 378–379.

4. *Department of State Bulletin*, XXII(June 26, 1950), 1038.

5. *Ibid.*, p. 1037; *Department of State Bulletin*, XXII(March 20, 1950), 427–428.

in Indochina—signalling a new and ultimately costly American commitment in Asia.[6] The president directed the State and Defense departments to review American military and foreign policy. In April there emerged National Security Council Paper No. 68 (NSC-68), a blunt plea for a much-expanded American defense establishment and an activist containment doctrine. Describing "a shrinking world of polarized power," this significant document advised the president that the United States had to "take new and fateful decisions" to develop "a successfully functioning system among the free nations." NSC-68 depicted an aggressive Communism on a global march. Relief from this menace was not imminent; only when the Soviet system itself decayed would the Kremlin's "design" be frustrated and world peace be achieved. The United States had to follow two courses: first, the development of "a healthy international community," and second, the containment of the Soviet system. This combination of expansionism and containment could be realized only if the United States launched a costly program of military spending, necessitating higher defense budgets from Congress and increased taxes. A "consensus" in the American public, NSC-68 advised, would have to be cultivated to back this dramatic build-up.[7]

Of course, one question was how to "sell" the recommendations of NSC-68 to the American people. As an Acheson aide recalled, "we were sweating over it, and then—with regard to NSC 68—thank God Korea came along."[8] The Korean War, which broke out in June when the Soviet-equipped forces of North Korea moved into American-backed South Korea, was a "we-told-you-so" event. It seemed to confirm all the worst assumptions about Soviet aggressive proclivities, even though

6. NSC 48/2 quoted in Roger Dingman, "1950: The Fate of a Grand Design," *Pacific Historical Review*, XLVII(August 1978), 465. See also Gary R. Hess, "The First American Commitment in Indochina: The Acceptance of the 'Bao Dai Solution', 1950," *Diplomatic History*, II(Fall 1978), 331–350.

7. NSC-68, "United States Objectives and Programs for National Security," April 14, 1950, in *Foreign Relations, 1950*, I, 237–292.

8. Edward W. Barrett in Princeton Seminars, October 10–11, 1953, Box 65, Acheson Papers.

there still is no firm answer as to whether the Soviets started that
war.[9] It was simply assumed to be the Soviet probing of a "situation of weakness" which might spread elsewhere. The United
States came to the aid of the embattled member of its sphere of
influence, South Korea, made further commitments to the
French in Indochina, to the Philippines, and to Chiang on Formosa, and began to act upon the counsel of NSC-68.

Thus, by mid-1950 the conflict-ridden postwar international
system which emerged from the slaughter and dislocation of
World War II had become essentially bipolar, with competing
and warring spheres of influence. Two great nations, power
"vacuums," massive economic disorder, political turmoil rocking
governments on all continents, colonial revolts, disintegrating
empires, newly independent states, fledgling international organizations, the atomic bomb, a shrinking interdependent globe—all
insured tension in the fashioning of the postwar international
system. The United States and the Soviet Union sought in this
unstable environment to satisfy their particular needs and ideas,
to expand their divergent interests and principles.

If Americans were universalist on behalf of an ideology link-
ing peace, prosperity, democracy, and the open door, Russians
preached a univcrsal message of inevitable proletarian revolution. If America's political heritage championed ideals that
Americans thought others should adopt—and should be encouraged to adopt—totalitarianism may have stimulated Soviet exag-
gerations of an external threat, and hence an imperative for
pressing others abroad to conform politically. If the Russians
conjured up the ghost of Hitler, predicting a relentless duel with
the capitalist menace, Americans also drew lessons from the past
which suggested a renewed struggle with Hitler-like aggression.
If Americans reached for foreign outposts and markets to meet
their strategic-economic needs, the Soviets found as well that
their security and economy required expansionism. If the Soviet

9. Robert R. Simmons, *The Strained Alliance: Peking, Pyongyang,
Moscow and the Politics of the Korean Civil War* (New York, 1975),
pp. 102–136; Edmund S. Wehrle and Donald F. Lach, *International Politics in East Asia Since World War II* (New York, 1975), pp. 86–92.

Union commanded regional authority in Eastern Europe through the power of the Red Army, the United States held impressive and influential power—economic, political, and military—on a global scale.

In the pursuit of their objectives, leaders in Moscow and Washington conducted diplomacy with a personality and style that annoyed their opposites and obstructed negotiations. Soviet and American diplomats who eyed one another across the bargaining table harbored strong dislikes, betraying considerable suspiciousness and distrust. And the American and Soviet political systems were such that diplomacy rested in the hands of Truman and Stalin and their immediate advisers, who faced few domestic restraints and were thus able to define the character of the postwar confrontation.

Thus, as we have seen, a combination of systemic, fundamental, and tactical factors merged to make the Cold War and to divide the world into recognizable spheres of influence. To attempt to rank these factors, to argue that one was more important than another, would be a futile intellectual exercise. They were intertwined, they fed one another, they were inseparable.

The history of international relations in succeeding decades is the story of the disintegration of the bipolar configuration, the growing diffusion of world power among several states, and the determined efforts of the United States and the Soviet Union to preserve and expand their spheres of influence. American covert and overt interventions in Iran, Guatemala, Lebanon, Cuba, Dominican Republic, and Vietnam and Soviet intrusions into Hungary, Czechoslovakia, and Africa, among others, in the 1950s, 1960s, and 1970s bear witness to the enduring nature of the global Soviet-American contest which lodged itself as a prominent feature of world politics. An explanation of how and why the Cold War started has been the purpose of this book. To others belongs the task of finding the means for reducing its potential for harm, if not for destruction. For that assignment an historical perspective—an understanding of the Cold War's beginnings—is imperative.

Appendix: The Events of 1944-50

〰〰〰〰〰〰〰〰〰〰〰〰〰〰〰〰〰〰〰〰〰〰〰〰〰〰〰〰〰

1944

June Allied invasion at Normandy, France

July Bretton Woods Conference (World Bank and International Monetary Fund)

August–October Dumbarton Oaks Conference (United Nations)

October Churchill-Stalin spheres-of-influence agreement at Moscow

1945

February Yalta Conference

March Pro-Soviet government took power in Rumania

April President Roosevelt's death; Truman became president

May Germany surrendered; Harry Hopkins mission to Moscow

June Pro-Soviet government organized in Poland; UN Charter signed in San Francisco

July Atomic bomb test at Alamogordo, New Mexico; Byrnes became secretary of state

July–August Potsdam Conference

August Atomic bombs dropped on Hiroshima and Nagasaki; Japan surrendered

September Vietnam Republic declared by Ho Chi Minh

September–October London Foreign Ministers meeting

November General Marshall appointed to China mission

December Moscow Foreign Ministers meeting; US granted Britain $3.5 billion loan; Byrnes received Ethridge report on Soviet intrusions in Eastern Europe

1946

January–April   Crisis over Iran
January   People's Republic of Albania (Communist) proclaimed; USSR protested British interference in Greece
February   Stalin's election speech
March   Churchill's "Iron Curtain" speech; Jordan became independent
April   All-out civil war in China between Mao's Communists and Chiang's Nationalists; failure of Marshall's truce in China; USS *Missouri* visited Athens
May   Renewed civil war in Greece; US called for free elections in Rumania; General Clay halted reparations to Soviet zone of Germany
June   Baruch Plan for control of atomic weapons
July   Philippines became independent; US protested that USSR was economically stripping Hungary
August   Russia sought influence over Straits from Turkey; US backed Turkey; US protested absence of democracy in Poland
September   Wallace forced to resign from cabinet; Clifford report to Truman on Soviet-American relations
October   US called for free elections in Rumania
November   Republicans won Congressional elections; China and US signed treaty of friendship and commerce; US protested rigged elections in Rumania which gave victory to Communists
November–December   New York Foreign Ministers meeting
December   Britain and US fused their zones in Germany

1947

January   Marshall became secretary of state; Polish Communists won rigged elections; US charged violation of Yalta pledge in Poland
February   Peace treaties signed in Paris for Italy, Bulgaria, Rumania, Hungary, and Finland; British sent notes to US on withdrawal from Greece and on Turkey's need for aid
March   Truman Doctrine speech
March–April   Moscow Foreign Ministers meeting
April   UN approved US as trustee for Pacific islands

May   Truman signed bill for aid to Greece and Turkey; Communists took power in Hungary

June   Marshall's speech at Harvard on need for European recovery

July   Russia refused at Paris to participate in Marshall Plan; publication of Kennan's "X" article in *Foreign Affairs*; National Security Act passed (creation of Defense Department, National Security Council, and Central Intelligence Agency)

August   India and Pakistan became independent

September   Rio Pact organized in Latin America

October   USSR created Cominform

November–December   London Foreign Ministers meeting

December   Brussels Conference on European defense; Interim Aid to Europe bill signed by Truman; King Michael abdicated in Rumania

1948

January   Burma became independent

February   Brussels Treaty signed; Ceylon became independent; Communists took power in Czechoslovakia

March   USSR protested Western obstruction in Germany and refused to meet again in Allied Control Council

April   Truman signed European Recovery Act of $5.3 billion; Committee of European Economic Cooperation organized to oversee Marshall Plan; Organization of American States established

May   State of Israel created and immediately recognized by US

June   Poland signed trade agreement with USSR; Yugoslavia was expelled from the Cominform

July   Berlin blockade and airlift

August   Republic of Korea proclaimed (South Korea—pro-West)

September   People's Democratic Republic of Korea proclaimed (North Korea—Communist)

November   Truman elected president

1949

January   Point Four program recommended by Truman; USSR created Council of Economic Assistance (Comecon); Acheson became Secretary of State

April NATO formed

May Constitution for West Germany written; Berlin blockade lifted

June French created puppet government in Vietnam under Bao Dai

July Truman signed NATO Treaty

August US issued "White Paper" on Chiang's failure in China

September Federal Republic of Germany established (West Germany); USSR exploded atomic device

October People's Republic of China (Communist) proclaimed; Greek civil war ended with defeat of leftists and Communists; Truman approved $1.3 billion Mutual Defense Assistance Act

December Chiang's government installed in Formosa; Indonesia gained independence from the Dutch; on Stalin's seventieth birthday Soviet government called for "peaceful coexistence"; Shah of Iran joined Truman in statement of US-Iranian solidarity

1950

January Truman authorized development of hydrogen bomb

January–August Russia boycotted United Nations Security Council

February Senator McCarthy began his charges that Truman administration was Communist-influenced; USSR and China signed treaty of friendship and defense; U.S. reorganized Bao Dai in Vietnam

April National Security Council Paper 68 (NSC-68) prepared

May US extended military assistance to France to fight Vietnamese rebels

June Outbreak of the Korean War

Sources

≋≋≋≋≋≋≋≋≋≋≋≋≋≋≋≋≋≋≋≋≋≋≋≋≋≋≋≋≋≋≋≋≋≋≋≋≋

Guides to the Literature and Documents

The footnotes for this book and the citations presented below should be supplemented by other guides to the vast literature on the Cold War. Among them are Wilton B. Fowler, ed., *American Diplomatic History Since 1890* (Northbrook, Ill., 1975); Thomas G. Paterson, ed., *The Origins of the Cold War* (Lexington, Mass., 1974); Walter LaFeber, *America, Russia, and the Cold War, 1945–1975* (New York, 1976; 3rd ed.); William J. Stewart, ed., *The Era of Franklin D. Roosevelt: A Selected Bibliography* (Hyde Park, N.Y., 1974); Frank Friedel, ed., *Harvard Guide to American History* (Cambridge, Mass., 1974; 2 vols.); Margaret L. Stapleton, *The Truman and Eisenhower Years, 1945–1960* (Metuchen, N.J., 1973); Thomas T. Hammond, ed., *Soviet Foreign Relations and World Communism* (Princeton, 1965); Leo Okinshevich, comp., *United States History and Historiography in Postwar Soviet Writings, 1945–1970* (Santa Barbara, Cal., 1976); Council on Foreign Relations, *The Foreign Affairs 50-Year Bibliography* (New York, 1972); David F. Trask *et al.*, *A Bibliography on United States—Latin American Relations Since 1810* (Lincoln, Neb., 1968); and the forthcoming *Guide to the Foreign Relations of the United States*, edited by Richard Burns and sponsored by the Society for Historians of American Foreign Relations.

Useful historiographical works include Alexander DeConde, *American Diplomatic History in Transformation* (Washington, D.C., AHA Pamphlets, 1976); David F. Trask, "Writings on American Foreign Relations: 1957 to the Present," in John Braeman *et al.*, eds.; *Twentieth-Century American Foreign Policy* (Columbus, Ohio, 1971); Robert Griffith, "Truman and the Historians," *Wisconsin Magazine of History*, LIX(Autumn 1975), 20–50; Greg Cashman and Arthur N. Gilbert, "Some Analytical Approaches to the Cold War Debate," *History Teacher*, X(February 1977), 263–280; Norman A. Graebner, "Cold War Origins and the Continuing

Debate: A Review of Recent Literature," *Journal of Conflict Resolution*, XIII(March 1969), 123–132; Warren F. Kimball, "The Cold War Warmed Over," *American Historical Review*, LXXIX (October 1974), 1119–1136; Michael Leigh, "Is There a Revisionist Thesis on the Origins of the Cold War?" *Political Science Quarterly*, LXXXIX(March 1974), 101–116; Robert J. Maddox, *The New Left and the Origins of the Cold War* (Princeton, 1973); David S. Patterson, "Recent Literature on Cold War Origins," *Wisconsin Magazine of History*, LV(Summer 1972), 320–329; J.L. Richardson, "Cold War Revisionism: A Critique," *World Politics*, XXIV(July 1972), 579–612; Robert B. Schulzinger, "Moderation in Pursuit of Truth Is No Virtue; Extremism in Defense of Moderation Is a Vice," *American Quarterly*, XXVII(May 1975), 222–236; Richard S. Kirkendall, ed., *The Truman Period as a Research Field* (Columbia, Mo., 1974); William Welch, *American Images of Soviet Foreign Policy: An Inquiry into Recent Appraisals from the Academic Community* (New Haven, 1970); and the essays by Roland N. Stromberg, Barton J. Bernstein, and Thomas A. Krueger in "The Continuing Cold War: A Symposium," *Reviews in American History*, I(December 1973), 445–470.

The voluminous American government documents—Congressional hearings, departmental pamphlets, speeches, and more—can be located through U.S. Superintendent of Documents, *Monthly Catalog of U.S. Government Publications* (Washington, D.C.; vol. for each year). The volumes of the *Public Papers of the Presidents: Harry S. Truman* (Washington, D.C., 1961–66; 8 vols.), reprint speeches, press conference remarks, and other utterances. The *Department of State Bulletin* includes addresses, articles, and other materials from foreign affairs officers, and the Department of State's *Foreign Relations of the United States* series prints significant diplomatic correspondence. Particularly useful for verbatim remarks on a host of issues are the formerly secret post-1945 executive session hearings of the Senate Foreign Relations Committee and the House Committee on Foreign Affairs, which were published by these bodies, beginning in the early 1970s in their "historical series." The *Congressional Record* prints debates in the House and Senate. A very good collection of documents is Walter LaFeber, ed., *The Dynamics of World Power: Eastern Europe and the Soviet Union* (New York, 1973; vol. 2 of four volumes edited by Arthur M. Schlesinger, Jr.).

Alan Meckler and Ruth McMullin, comps., *Oral History Collections* (New York, 1975), is the best source for finding transcripts of oral history interviews with leading participants in the making of foreign policy after World War II. The various Presidential libraries maintain lists of their oral histories as well.

Unpublished Personal Papers, Official Records, and Oral Histories

Much of my previously published scholarship has drawn heavily upon unpublished sources. Many of these materials are mentioned in my book, *Soviet-American Confrontation*, and although some of them may not be cited herein, they have held cumulative and informative value for *On Every Front*.

At the Harry S. Truman Library of Independence, Missouri, truly a fine institution with a dedicated and generous staff, there were several collections that proved useful for this study. The Dean Acheson Papers include the "Princeton Seminars," recorded verbatim conversations—often free-wheeling—that were held in the early 1950s among the former Secretary of State and some of his former aides. The George V. Allen Papers consist largely of the ambassador's "memoirs" of his post in Iran. The William L. Clayton Papers are helpful for economic foreign policy. The papers of Truman's White House assistant, Clark Clifford, cover a host of Cold War topics, including the development of the Truman Doctrine and the Marshall Plan. The Committee for the Marshall Plan Records at the Truman Library reveal the workings of an influential organization. In the Matthew J. Connelly Papers are notes of Cabinet meetings—some of which are fragmentary, some extensive. Another of Truman's aides, George M. Elsey, left a valuable set of personal papers, including drafts of key speeches. Policy toward India, Greece, and Iran can be gleaned from the papers of Ambassador Henry F. Grady. For the origins of the Point Four program, the papers of Benjamin Hardy are valuable. A speechwriter, Joseph Jones, especially noteworthy for his contributions in 1947, has also deposited his papers in Independence. The papers of Secretary of the Treasury John W. Snyder hold materials on a variety of issues, including the World Bank, Export-Import Bank, and the Marshall Plan. The voluminous Harry S. Truman Papers were researched in various categories: Official File, Personal File, Files of Assistants, Confidential File, and President's Secretary's File. When at the

Truman Library, I also examined the papers of the following: Clinton P. Anderson, Stanley Andrews, Thomas C. Blaisdell, Frederick J. Lawton, David D. Lloyd, Edwin A. Locke, and J. Howard McGrath. The library also houses some selected documents—transcripts and notes on press conferences—of the Senate Foreign Relations Committee. Finally, the records of the President's Air Policy Committee, President's Committee on Foreign Aid (Harriman Committee), and President's Materials Policy Commission provided a good amount of documentation.

The National Archives, Washington, D.C., is the depository for rich diplomatic and military documents. Within the Diplomatic Branch, I researched the Department of State Records: central decimal files, H. Freeman Matthews Files, John D. Hickerson Files, Loy Henderson Files, Charles E. Bohlen Files, Moscow Post Files (available at the records center in Suitland, Maryland), and United States Mission to the United Nations Files. Especially informative for high-level discussions were the Committee of Three Records. Helpful in determining which issues the Department of State thought the President should concentrate on, day-to-day, was the White House Daily Summary—a brief synopsis of diplomatic telegrams, organized by country or program. The Department of State's Top Secret Daily Staff Summary was a review of key telegrams; the Secretary's Top Secret Weekly Summary for the years 1947–1948 were read by Secretary Marshall and initialed; and the Secretary's Weekly Summary for 1947–1948 consisted of long analyses of trends and events. These three summaries permit the scholar to assess the relative importance that the Secretary of State's staff assigned to global issues. The records of the Policy Planning Staff include that body's reports and some correspondence. Various research reports of the Foreign Policy Studies Branch, Division of Historical Policy Research in the Department of State yielded useful material. I also dug into the massive International Trade Files of the Records of International Conferences, Commissions, and Expositions and the records of Interdepartmental and Intradepartmental Committees (such as the State-War-Navy Coordinating Committee, or SWNCC, Greek-Turkish Aid Committee, USSR Country Committee, and Committee on Post-War Problems).

In the Modern Military Branch of the National Archives are the records of the Joint Chiefs of Staff, including materials on war plans, Soviet capabilities, and American defense, the White House Records of William D. Leahy, miscellaneous reports of the Central Intelligence Agency, and numbered reports of the National Security Council. The Old Navy and Army Branch, Department of the Navy Records, provided me with the correspondence of Secretaries James F. Forrestal and John L. Sullivan. At the Suitland, Maryland, center, I studied a variety of Military Attache (Army Intelligence) and Naval Attache (Department of the Navy) reports. In the Legislative, Judicial, and Fiscal Branch, I used the records of the House of Representatives (various committees) and Senate (committee documents).

Among the collections that I consulted at the Library of Congress, Manuscript Division, Washington, D.C., were those of Charles E. Bohlen, Senator Tom Connally (rather thin), Joseph E. Davies (especially the diaries and memoranda), Herbert Feis (on policy and the writing of history), Felix Frankfurter (correspondence with many prominent people), Harold L. Ickes, William D. Leahy (his diary), Breckinridge Long (especially his diary), Secretary of War Robert P. Patterson, Eric Sevareid (correspondence and news analyses), and Senator Robert A. Taft. The Naval Historical Center, Washington Navy Yard, provided the opportunity to study the Command Files, the Chief of Naval Operations Records, and the papers of William D. Leahy. In the Chamber of Commerce Library, Washington, D.C., I researched minutes of meetings of the Chamber of Commerce of the United States.

The Franklin D. Roosevelt Library, Hyde Park, New York, houses the massive Franklin D. Roosevelt Papers, wherein I studied documents in the President's Secretary's File, Official File, and Personal File. The Eleanor Roosevelt Papers are rich on many subjects and include often frank correspondence with President Truman. Other useful collections at Hyde Park were the Adolf A. Berle Papers, Oscar Cox Papers, Louis Fischer Papers (noteworthy for interviews with diplomats), Harry Hopkins Papers, Isador Lubin Papers, and the Harold Smith Papers (diary).

The Public Record Office, London, England, is the depository for extremely valuable British sources on postwar international affairs. The Foreign Office Correspondence, compared to U.S. Department of State records a model of orderliness and fullness, provided provocative and sometimes effusive commentary on American and Soviet policies and Cold War crises. The Cabinet Records included accounts of meetings. The Records of the Prime Minister's

Office proved valuable. At the London School of Economics I went through the diaries of Hugh Dalton.

Among the papers that I consulted at the Sterling Library, Yale University, New Haven, Connecticut, were those of Henry L. Stimson, Chester Bowles, Hanson Baldwin, Walter Lippmann, and Arthur Bliss Lane. At Harvard University, Cambridge, Massachusetts, the Joseph C. Grew Papers provided material for 1945. For the George F. Kennan Papers, James V. Forrestal Papers, Bernard M. Baruch Papers, John Foster Dulles Papers, Arthur Krock Papers, and Senator H. Alexander Smith Papers, I used the excellent research facilities of the Princeton University Library, Princeton, New Jersey. At the University of Vermont Library, Burlington, are the papers of Warren R. Austin, ambassador to the United Nations. Clemson University, Clemson, South Carolina, houses the papers of Secretary of State James F. Byrnes, wherein the Walter Brown Notes are instructive. The papers of Senator Wayne L. Morse, University of Oregon Library, Eugene, include typically outspoken comments in letters. The University of Michigan Library, Ann Arbor, provided me with some materials from the Senator Arthur H. Vandenberg Papers. In Chapel Hill, the University of North Carolina Library holds the papers of Jonathan Daniels (especially useful were his notebooks) and Congressman Carl T. Durham. For aspects of Soviet-American relations, I consulted the Richard B. Scandrett, Jr., Papers and the thin papers of Congressman Sterling Cole at Cornell University, Ithaca, New York.

Two collections in New York City contain valuable sources for the early Cold War period. The bulky Records of the United Nations Relief and Rehabilitation Administration (UNRRA) at the United Nations Library provde massive documentation of the dislocations wrought by the Second World War. At the offices of the Council on Foreign Relations, scholars can research the files of that body. Revealing and instructive were "Records of Groups" (such as those studying Soviet-American relations or the Marshall Plan) and "Records of Meetings," wherein the commentary of prominent Americans, official and public, is recorded.

Among the oral history transcripts that I read from the Truman Library were interviews with George M. Elsey, John D. Hickerson, Harry N. Howard, Francis Russell, Harold Stein, Theodore Achilles, Willis C. Armstrong, David E. Bell, Winthrop G. Brown, George McGhee, Mark Ethridge, Loy W. Henderson, Paul Hoffman, Edwin

A. Locke, Jr., H. Freeman Matthews, Jack K. McFall, Charles S. Murphy, James W. Riddleberger, Durward V. Sandifer, and Joseph C. Satterthwaite. The Truman Library also holds numerous oral histories about the Marshall Plan, some of which were conducted by the Library staff, some by Ellen Clayton Garwood, and some by Harry B. Price.

Published Works and Unpublished Dissertations

THE POSTWAR WORLD, THE COLD WAR,
AND AMERICAN DIPLOMACY

For the general characteristics of an "international system" and the traits of the postwar structure, see footnote 3 of chapter 2. I found the following particularly helpful: Raymond F. Hopkins and Richard W. Mansbach, *Structure and Process in International Politics* (New York, 1973); Marshall R. Singer, *Weak States in a World of Power: The Dynamics of International Relationships* (New York, 1972); and Alan Henrikson, "The Map as an 'Idea': The Role of Cartographic Imagery During the Second World War," *American Cartographer*, II(April 1975), 19–53. See also Morton A. Kaplan, *System and Process in International Politics* (New York, 1957), John Spanier, *Games Nations Play* (New York, 1972), and Harold and Margaret Sprout, *Foundations of International Politics* (Princeton, 1962). Definitions of "sphere of influence" can be found in Geddes W. Rutherford, "Spheres of Influence: An Aspect of Semi-Suzerainty," *American Journal of International Law*, XX(April 1926), 300–325, and Frederick L. Schuman, "Spheres of Influence," *Encyclopedia of the Social Sciences* (New York, 1944; 15 vols.), XIV, 297–299.

The disintegration of colonial empires and the American response, especially in Asia, are treated in Robert J. McMahon, "The United States and Decolonization in Southeast Asia: The Case of Indonesia, 1945–1949" (Unpublished Ph.D. dissertation, University of Connecticut, 1977); George C. Herring, "The Truman Administration and the Restoration of French Sovereignty in Indochina," *Diplomatic History*, I(Spring 1977), 97–117; Walter LaFeber, "Roosevelt, Churchill, and Indochina, 1942–45," *American Historical Review*, LXXX(December 1975), 1277–1295; Christopher Thorne, "Indochina and Anglo-American Relations, 1942–1945," *Pacific Historical Review*, XLV(February 1976), 73–96;

Gary R. Hess, "Franklin Roosevelt and Indochina," *Journal of American History*, LIX(September 1972), 353–368; Stewart C. Easton, *The Rise and Fall of Western Colonialism* (New York, 1964); Rupert Emerson, *From Empire to Nation: The Rise to Self-Assertion of Asian and African Peoples* (Cambridge, Mass., 1962); Lisle A. Rose, *Roots of Tragedy: The United States and the Struggle for Asia, 1945–1953* (Westport, Conn., 1976); Rudolf von Albertini, *Decolonization* (Garden City, N.Y., 1971); and William R. Louis, *Imperialism at Bay: The United States and the Decolonization of the British Empire, 1941–1945* (New York, 1978).

Among the many overviews of the Cold War and its origins are Walter LaFeber, *America, Russia, and the Cold War, 1945–1975* (New York, 1976; 3rd ed.); Seyom Brown, *The Faces of Power* (New York, 1968); Lynn Miller and Ronald Pruessen, eds., *Reflections on the Cold War* (Philadelphia, 1974); William A. Williams, *Tragedy of American Diplomacy* (New York, 1962, 1971); Richard J. Barnet, *Intervention and Revolution* (New York, 1968), *Roots of War* (New York, 1972), and *The Giants* (New York, 1977); Daniel Yergin, *Shattered Peace* (Boston, 1977); Stephen Ambrose, *Rise to Globalism* (Baltimore, 1976; rev. ed.); J. William Fulbright, "Reflections: In Thrall to Fear," *New Yorker*, XLVII(January 8, 1972), 41–62; Franz Schurmann, *The Logic of World Power* (New York, 1974); Gabriel Kolko, *The Politics of War* (New York, 1968), *The Limits of Power* (New York, 1972), and *Roots of American Foreign Policy* (Boston, 1969); William H. McNeill, *America, Britain, and Russia* (London, 1953); Robert W. Tucker, *The Radical Left and American Foreign Policy* (Baltimore, 1971); Paul Y. Hammond, *Cold War and Détente* (New York, 1975; 2nd ed.); George F. Kennan, "The United States and the Soviet Union, 1917–1976," *Foreign Affairs*, LIV(July 1976), 670–690; Louis Halle, *The Cold War as History* (New York, 1967); James A. Nathan and James K. Oliver, *United States Foreign Policy and World Order* (Boston, 1976); Herbert Feis, *From Trust to Terror* (New York, 1970); Marshall D. Shulman, *Beyond the Cold War* (New Haven, 1966); John L. Gaddis, *The United States and the Origins of the Cold War, 1941–1947* (New York, 1972) and *Russia, The Soviet Union, and the United States: An Interpretive History* (New York, 1978); Lisle Rose, *After Yalta* (New York, 1973); Arthur Schlesinger, Jr., "Origins of the Cold War," *Foreign Affairs*, XLVI(October 1967), 22–52; Adam Ulam, *The Rivals*

(New York, 1971); Barton J. Bernstein, ed., *Politics and Policies of the Truman Administration* (Chicago, 1970); Lloyd C. Gardner, *Architects of Illusion* (Chicago, 1970); and Kirkendall, *The Truman Period as a Research Field.* Essays representative of the different schools of thought are collected in Paterson, *Origins of the Cold War.*

For particular conferences, see Diane Shaver Clemens, *Yalta* (New York, 1970); Herbert Feis, *Between War and Peace: The Potsdam Conference* (Princeton, 1960); Charles L. Mee, Jr., *Meeting at Potsdam* (New York, 1975); and James L. Gormly, "In Search of a Postwar Settlement: The London and Moscow Conferences and the Origins of the Cold War" (Unpublished Ph.D. dissertation, University of Connecticut, 1977).

Representative works on the decision to use the A-bomb and its impact are anthologized in Barton J. Bernstein, ed., *The Atomic Bomb* (Boston, 1976), which includes some of his own extensive work on this topic, and Paul R. Baker, ed., *The Atomic Bomb* (Hinsdale, Ill., 1976; 2nd rev. ed.). The following provide a variety of interpretations: Martin J. Sherwin, *A World Destroyed: The Atomic Bomb and the Grand Alliance* (New York, 1975); Herbert Feis, *The Atomic Bomb and the End of World War II* (Princeton, 1966); Gregory F. Herkin, "American Diplomacy and the Atom Bomb, 1945–1947" (Unpublished Ph.D. dissertation, Princeton University, 1974); and Gar Alperovitz, *Atomic Diplomacy* (New York, 1965). Richard Hewlett and Oscar Anderson, *The New World* (University Park, Pa., 1962), and Richard Hewlett and Francis Duncan, *Atomic Shield* (University Park, Pa., 1970), are the official histories of American atomic development. The destruction of Hiroshima is recounted in Michihiko Hachiya, *Hiroshima Diary* (Chapel Hill, N.C., 1955; trans. by Warner Wells); John Hersey, *Hiroshima* (New York, 1946); John Tolland, *The Rising Sun* (New York, 1970); and William L. Laurence, *Dawn Over Zero* (New York, 1946).

The creation of the United Nations Organization is studied specifically in Thomas Campbell, *Masquerade Peace* (Tallahassee, Fla., 1973). Robert A. Divine, *Second Chance: The Triumph of Internationalism in the United States During World War II* (New York, 1967) presents the debate at home. John G. Stoessinger, *The United Nations and the Superpowers* (New York, 1970; 2nd ed.), Frederick H. Gareau, *The Cold War, 1947 to 1967: A Quantitative Study* (Denver, 1968–69), and Edward T. Rowe, "The United States, the United Nations, and the Cold War," *International Organization*, XXV(Winter 1971), 59–78, demonstrate the weighty American position within the institution. For information about America's first Ambassador to the United Nations, see George T. Mazuzan, *Warren R. Austin at the U.N., 1946–1953* (Kent, Ohio, 1977). Also useful is Alvin Z. Rubinstein and George Ginsburgs, eds., *Soviet and American Policies in the United Nations: A Twenty-Five-Year Perspective* (New York, 1971).

The economic havoc and human suffering visited by the Second World War on a global scale and the task of relief are detailed in George Woodbridge, *UNRRA: The History of the United Nations Relief and Rehabilitation Administration* (New York, 1950; 3 vols.). The war-wrought economic dislocations in Europe are described in Richard Mayne, *Recovery of Europe* (Garden City, N.Y., 1973); Robert Kaiser, *Cold Winter, Cold War* (New York, 1974); Arnold J. Toynbee, ed., *The Realignment of Europe* (London, 1955); Gordon Wright, *The Ordeal of Total War* (New York, 1968); Alan S. Milward, *War, Economy and Society, 1939–1945* (Berkeley, Cal., 1977); Peter Calvocoressi and Guy Wint, *Total War* (New York, 1972); and David Irving, *The Destruction of Dresden* (New York, 1963). Some of the tragedy is captured in Joy Davidman, ed., *War Poems of the United Nations* (New York, 1943). George C. Herring, Jr., *Aid to Russia, 1941–1946* (New York, 1973) tells the troubled history of Lend-Lease aid to the Soviet Union. Thomas G. Paterson, *Soviet-American Confrontation* (Baltimore, 1973) discusses the European reconstruction crisis, American assistance programs, United States loan policy, and antagonisms with the Soviet sphere. For background, see Lloyd C. Gardner, *Economic Aspects of New Deal Diplomacy* (Madison, Wis., 1964). Richard N. Gardner, *Sterling-Dollar Diplomacy* (New York, 1969; rev. ed.) specializes in Anglo-American economic relations. For the founding and workings of the World Bank, consult Alfred E. Eckes, Jr., *A Search for Solvency: Bretton Woods and the International Monetary System, 1941–1971* (Austin, Tex., 1975), and Edward S. Mason and Robert E. Asher, *The World Bank Since Bretton Woods* (Washington, D.C., 1973). Also useful are Mira Wilkins, *The Maturing of Multinational Enterprise: American Business Abroad from 1914 to 1970* (Cambridge, Mass., 1974), and David Baldwin, *Economic Development and American Foreign Policy* (Chicago, Ill. 1966).

Joseph M. Jones, *The Fifteen Weeks* (New York, 1955) is an

insider's account of the formulation of the Truman Doctrine. Richard Freeland, *The Truman Doctrine and the Origins of McCarthyism* (New York, 1972) probes growing American anti-Communism, as do Athan Theoharis, *Seeds of Repression: Harry S Truman and the Origins of McCarthyism* (Chicago, 1971), and Robert Griffith and Athan Theoharis, eds., *The Specter* (New York, 1974).

The Marshall Plan and European reconstruction are treated in Harry Price, *The Marshall Plan and Its Meaning* (Ithaca, N.Y. 1955); Warren Hickman, *Genesis of the European Recovery Program* (Geneva, 1949); Hadley Arkes, *Bureaucracy, the Marshall Plan, and the National Interest* (Princeton, 1973); David Wightman, *Economic Co-operation in Europe* (New York, 1956); and in the forthcoming works by Theodore Wilson and Richard McKenzie on postwar foreign aid and by Immanuel Wexler on the European Recovery Program.

Thomas G. Paterson, ed., *Containment and the Cold War* (Reading, Mass., 1973), and Charles Gati, ed., *Caging the Bear* (Indianapolis, Ind., 1974), trace the complex history of the containment doctrine. Walter Lippmann's *The Cold War* (New York, 1947) was a contemporary critique. The ideas and influence of George F. Kennan, especially as they relate to the development of the containment doctrine, are discussed in Thomas G. Paterson, "The Search for Meaning;" in Frank Merli and Theodore A. Wilson, eds., *Makers of American Diplomacy* (New York, 1974), pp. 553–588; C. Ben Wright, "Mr. 'X' Containment," *Slavic Review*, XXV (March 1976), 1–31; John L. Gaddis, "Containment: A Reassessment," *Foreign Affairs*, LV(July 1977), 873–887; and Eduard M. Mark, "The Question of Containment," *Foreign Affairs*, LVI (January 1978), 430–441. Thomas H. Etzold and John L. Gaddis, eds., *Containment: Documents on American Policy and Strategy, 1945–1950* (New York, 1978) presents some of the most important high-level papers.

The Soviet sphere in Eastern Europe is studied in Paterson, *Soviet-American Confrontation*; Lynn Etheridge Davis, *The Cold War Begins* (Princeton, 1974); Stephan Kertesz, ed., *The Fate of East Central Europe* (Notre Dame, Ind., 1956); Margaret Dewar, *Soviet Trade with Eastern Europe, 1945–49* (London, 1951); Bennett Kovrig, *The Myth of Liberation* (Baltimore, 1972); Robert Lee Wolff, *The Balkans in Our Time* (2nd ed., New York, 1979); Paul Zinner, *Communist Strategy and Tactics in Czechoslovakia,*

1918–1948 (New York, 1963); and Ygael Gluckstein, *Stalin's Satellites in Europe* (Boston, 1952). For Greece, see John O. Iatrides, *Revolt in Athens* (Princeton, N.J. 1972); Francis F. Lincoln, *United States' Aid to Greece, 1947–1962* (Germantown, Tenn., 1975); and Stephen Xydis, *Greece and the Great Powers* (Thessalonike, Greece, 1963). For issues regarding postwar Germany, I have used John Gimbel, *The American Occupation of Germany* (Stanford, 1968) and *The Origins of the Marshall Plan* (Stanford, Cal., 1976); Bruce Kuklick, *American Policy and the Division of Germany* (Ithaca, N.Y. 1972); John H. Backer, *Priming the German Economy: American Occupational Policies, 1945–1948* (Durham, N.C., 1971); Michael Balfour and John Mair, *Four Power Control in Germany and Austria, 1945–1946* (London, 1956); Manuel Gottlieb, *The German Peace Settlement and the Berlin Crisis* (New York, 1960); Robert Slusser, ed., *Soviet Economic Policy in Postwar Germany* (New York, 1953); Eugene Davidson, *The Death and Life of Germany* (New York, 1959); and Jean Smith, *The Defense of Berlin* (Baltimore, 1963).

Internal developments and great-power competition in Asia are treated in Christopher Thorne, *Allies of a Kind: The United States, Britain and the War against Japan, 1941–1945* (New York, 1978); Akira Iriye, *The Cold War in Asia* (Englewood Cliffs, N.J., 1974); Yōnosuke Nagai and Akira Iriye, eds., *The Origins of the Cold War in Asia* (New York, 1977); Herbert Feis, *The China Tangle* (Princeton, 1953) and *Contest Over Japan* (New York, 1967); Tang Tsou, *America's Failure in China, 1941–1950* (Chicago, 1963); Edmund S. Wehrle and Donald F. Lach, *International Politics in East Asia since World War II* (New York, 1975); Edward Friedman and Mark Selden, eds., *America's Asia* (New York, 1971); Warren I. Cohen, *America's Response to China* (New York, 1971); James Fetzer, "Senator Vandenberg and the American Commitment to China, 1945–1950," *The Historian*, XXXVI(February 1974), 283–303; George Kahin and John Lewis, *The United States and Vietnam* (New York, 1969; rev. ed.); Lawrence S. Wittner, "MacArthur and the Missionaries: God and Man in Occupied Japan," *Pacific Historical Review*, XL(February 1971), 77–98; Howard Schonberger, "The Japan Lobby in American Diplomacy, 1947–1952," *Pacific Historical Review*, XLVI(August 1977), 327–359; Robert R. Simmons, *The Strained Alliance: Peking, Pyongyang, Moscow and the Politics of the Korean Civil War* (New York,

1975); Edwin O. Reischauer, *The United States and Japan* (Cambridge, Mass., 1950); E. J. Kahn, Jr., *The China Hands* (New York, 1975); and Russell D. Buhite, " 'Major Interests': American Policy Toward China, Taiwan, and Korea, 1945–1950," *Pacific Historical Review*, XLVII(August 1978), 425–451.

For NATO and questions of defense, see the essays in Lawrence Kaplan, ed., *NATO and the Policy of Containment* (Boston, 1968); Richard F. Haynes, *The Awesome Power: Harry S. Truman as Commander in Chief* (Baton Rouge, La., 1973); Robert Osgood, *NATO: The Entangling Alliance* (Chicago, 1962); Vincent Davis, *Postwar Defense Policy and the U.S. Navy, 1943–1946* (Chapel Hill, N.C., 1966); Robert G. Albion and Robert H. Connery, *Forrestal and the Navy* (New York, 1962); Warner R. Schilling *et al.*, *Strategy, Politics, and Defense Budgets* (New York, 1962); and Michael S. Sherry, *Preparing for the Next War: American Plans for Postwar Defense, 1941–1945* (New Haven, Conn. 1977).

The United States presence in Latin America is discussed in Donald Dozer, *Are We Good Neighbors?* (Gainesville, 1959); Gerald K. Haines, "Under the Eagle's Wing: The Franklin Roosevelt Administration Forges an American Hemisphere," *Diplomatic History*, I(Fall 1977), 373–388); David Green, *The Containment of Latin America* (Chicago, 1971); Stephen G. Rabe, "The Elusive Conference: United States Economic Relations With Latin America, 1945–1952," *Diplomatic History*, II (Summer 1978), 279–294; and J. Fred Rippy, *Globe and Hemisphere* (Chicago, 1958). Tensions in the Middle East are explored in George Kirk, *The Middle East, 1945–1950* (London, 1954), and George Lenczowski, *Russia and the West in Iran, 1918–1948* (Ithaca, N.Y. 1949). Canadian foreign policy is covered in James Eayers, *In Defence of Canada* (Toronto, 1972).

For the acrimonious experience of Soviet-American negotiations, I found the following useful: Stephen D. Kertesz, "Reflections on Soviet and American Negotiating Behavior," *Review of Politics*, XIX(January 1957), 3–36; Philip E. Mosely, "Across the Green Table from Stalin," *Current History*, XV(September 1948), 129–133; Raymond Dennett and Joseph E. Johnson, eds., *Negotiating with the Russians* (Boston, 1951); Philip E. Mosely, "Some Soviet Techniques of Negotiation," in Mosely, *The Kremlin and World Politics* (New York, 1960); Gordon A. Craig, "Techniques of

Negotiation," in Ivo J. Lederer, ed., *Russian Foreign Policy* (New Haven, Conn., 1962), pp. 351–373; James B. Reston, "Negotiating with the Russians," *Harper's Magazine*, CXCV(August 1947), 97–106; and U.S. Congress, Committee on Government Operations, *The Soviet Approach to Negotiation: Selected Writing* (Washington, D.C., 1969).

Among the many contemporary commentaries I found informative on the difficult transition from wartime to peacetime are William T. R. Fox, *The Super-Powers* (New York, 1944); Carl L. Becker, *How New Will the Better World Be?* (New York, 1944); Joseph M. Jones, *A Modern Foreign Policy for the United States* (New York, 1944); Howard K. Smith, *The State of Europe* (New York, 1949); Bernard Brodie, ed., *The Absolute Weapon* (New York, 1946); Harrison Salisbury, *Russia on the Way* (New York, 1946); John Gunther, *Behind the Iron Curtain* (New York, 1949); Walter Lippmann, "A Year of Peacemaking," *The Atlantic*, CLXXVIII(December 1946), 35–40; Louis Fischer, *The Great Challenge* (London, 1947); Vera M. Dean, *Russia: Menace or Promise* (New York, 1947); Americans for Democratic Action, *Toward Total Peace* (Washington, D.C., 1947); Henry A. Wallace, *Toward World Peace* (New York, 1948); Emil Lengyel and Joseph C. Harsch, "Eastern Europe Today and American Policy in Eastern Europe," Foreign Policy Association *Headline Series*, No. 77 (September–October 1949); Sumner Welles, *The Time for Decision* (New York, 1944); Walter Lippman, *U.S. War Aims* (Boston, 1944); Herbert Feis, *Petroleum and American Foreign Policy* (Stanford, Cal., 1944); Bernard Brodie, *Foreign Oil and American Security* (New Haven, Conn., 1947); and Edgar Snow, *The Pattern of Soviet Power* (New York, 1945).

Other studies of early Cold War questions include Athan Theoharis, "The Origins of the Cold War: A Revisionist Interpretation," *Peace and Change*, IV(Fall 1976), 3–11, and "Roosevelt and Truman at Yalta," *Political Science Quarterly*, LXXXVII(June 1972), 210–241; Robert Donovan, *Conflict and Crisis* (New York, 1977); Zbigniew Brzezinski, "The Competitive Relationship," in Gati, *Caging the Bear*, pp. 157–193; Lowell T. Young, "Franklin D. Roosevelt and America's Islets: Acquisition of Territory in the Caribbean and in the Pacific," *The Historian*, XXXV(February 1973), 205–220; Alfred D. Sander, "Truman and the National Security Council: 1945–1947," *Journal of American History*, LIX(September

1972), 369–388; Les K. Adler and Thomas G. Paterson, "Red Fascism: The Merger of Nazi Germany and Soviet Russia in the American Image of Totalitarianism, 1930's–1950's," *American Historical Review*, LXXV(April 1970), 1046–1064; Russell Buhite, "Soviet-American Relations and the Repatriation of Prisoners of War, 1945," *The Historian*, XXV(May 1973), 384–397; Mark Elliot, "The United States and Forced Repatriation of Soviet Citizens, 1944–1947," *Political Science Quarterly*, LXXXVIII(June 1973), 253–275; Thomas G. Paterson, "Foreign Aid Under Wraps: The Point Four Program," *Wisconsin Magazine of History*, LVI (Winter 1972–73), 119–126; Dennis Brogan, "The Illusion of American Omnipotence," *Harper's Magazine*, CCV(December 1952), 21–28; Urie Bronfenbrenner, "The Mirror Image in Soviet-American Relations: A Social Psychologist's Report," *Journal of Social Issues*, XVII(1961), 45–56; Norman A. Graebner, "Global Containment: The Truman Years," *Current History*, LIII(August 1969), 77–84; Thomas A. Krueger, "The Social Origins of Recent American Foreign Policy," *Journal of Social History*, VII(Fall 1973), 98–101; Eduard M. Mark, "The Interpretation of Soviet Foreign Policy in the United States, 1928–1947" (Unpublished Ph.D. dissertation, University of Connecticut, 1978), Theodore Wright, "The Origins of the Free Elections Dispute in the Cold War," *Western Political Quarterly*, XIV(December 1961), 850–864; Robert L. Messer, "Paths Not Taken: The United States Department of State and Alternatives to Containment, 1945–1946," *Diplomatic History*, I(Fall 1977), 297–319; and Albert Resis, "The Churchill–Stalin 'Percentages' Agreement on the Balkans, Moscow, October 1944," *American Historical Review*, LXXXIII(April 1978), 368–387.

AMERICAN LEADERS

For President Franklin D. Roosevelt, see Samuel Roseman, ed., *Public Papers and Addresses of Franklin D. Roosevelt* (New York, 1938–50; 13 vols.); Francis L. Loewenheim, Harold Langley, and Manfred Jonas, eds., *Roosevelt and Churchill: Their Secret Wartime Correspondence* (New York, 1975); Robert E. Sherwood, *Roosevelt and Hopkins* (New York, 1948); James MacGregor Burns, *Roosevelt: The Soldier of Freedom* (New York, 1970); Robert A. Divine, *Roosevelt and World War II* (Baltimore, 1969);

Herbert Feis, *Churchill, Roosevelt, Stalin* (Princeton, 1957); Robert Dallek, "Franklin Roosevelt as World Leader," *American Historical Review*, LXXVI(December 1971), 1503–1515; and Warren F. Kimball, "Churchill and Roosevelt: The Personal Equation," *Prologue*, VI(Fall 1974), 169–182.

Harry S. Truman and his administration are the subject of Harry S. Truman, *Memoirs* (Garden City, N.Y., 1955–56; 2 vols.); Margaret Truman, *Harry S. Truman* (New York, 1973); John L. Gaddis, "Harry S. Truman and the Origins of Containment," in Merli and Wilson, *Makers of American Diplomacy*, pp. 493–522; Bert Cochran, *Harry Truman and the Crisis Presidency* (New York, 1973); Jonathan Daniels, *The Man of Independence* (Philadelphia, 1950); Alfred Steinberg, *The Man from Missouri* (New York, 1962); and Richard E. Neustadt, *Presidential Power* (New York, 1960). Arthur M. Schlesinger, *The Imperial Presidency* (Boston, 1973), treats Roosevelt and Truman, among others.

For the secretaries of state, consult Cordell Hull, *Memoirs* (New York, 1948; 2 vols.); Edward R. Stettinius, Jr., *Roosevelt and the Russians* (Garden City, N.Y., 1949); Thomas M. Campbell and George C. Herring, eds., *The Diaries of Edward R. Stettinius, Jr., 1943–1946* (New York, 1975); James F. Byrnes, *Speaking Frankly* (New York, 1947) and *All in One Lifetime* (New York, 1958); George Curry, *James F. Byrnes* (New York, 1965); Robert Ferrell, *George C. Marshall* (New York, 1966); Dean Acheson, *Present at the Creation* (New York, 1969) and *Sketches from Life* (New York, 1961); Gaddis Smith, *Dean Acheson* (New York, 1972); David S. McLellan, *Dean Acheson* (New York, 1976); Ronald Steel, "Commissar of the Cold War [Acheson]," *New York Review of Books*, February 12, 1970, pp. 17–21; and Transcript, Eric Sevareid's "A Conversation with Dean Acheson," CBS Television Network, September 28, 1969.

For autobiographical studies by diplomats who were deeply involved in Soviet-American relations, see Charles Bohlen, *Witness to History, 1929–1969* (New York, 1973), and *The Transformation of American Foreign Policy* (New York, 1969); George F. Kennan, *Memoirs, 1925–1950* (Boston, 1967); Elie Abel and W. Averell Harriman, *Special Envoy to Churchill and Stalin, 1941–1946* (New York, 1975); W. Averell Harriman, *Peace With Russia?* (New York, 1959); Walter Bedell Smith, *My Three Years in Moscow*

(Philadelphia, 1950); John R. Deane, *The Strange Alliance* (New York, 1947); Thomas P. Whitney, *Russia in My Life* (London, 1963); and Charles W. Thayer, *Diplomat* (New York, 1959).

Other American memoirs include William Leahy, *I Was There* (New York, 1950); Robert Murphy, *Diplomat Among Warriors* (Garden City, N.Y., 1964); Henry Stimson and McGeorge Bundy, *On Active Service in Peace and War* (New York, 1948); Arthur Bliss Lane, *I Saw Poland Betrayed* (Indianapolis, 1948); Philip C. Jessup, *The Birth of Nations* (New York, 1973); Jonathan Daniels, *White House Witness* (New York, 1975); Lucius Clay, *Decision in Germany* (Garden City, N.Y., 1950); Chester Bowles, *Promises to Keep* (New York, 1971); O. Edmund Clubb, *The Witness and I* (New York, 1974); Douglas MacArthur, *Reminiscences* (New York, 1964); William J. Sebald, *With MacArthur in Japan* (New York, 1965); and Alfred C. Oppler, *Land Reform in Occupied Japan: A Participant Looks Back* (Princeton, N.J., 1976).

Diaries are the core of Walter Millis, ed., *The Forrestal Diaries* (New York, 1951); John M. Blum, *From the Morgenthau Diaries* (Boston, 1959–67; 3 vols.) and *The Price of Vision: The Diary of Henry A. Wallace* (Boston, 1973); Arthur Vandenberg, Jr., *The Private Papers of Senator Vandenberg* (Boston, 1952); Adolf A. Berle, *Navigating the Rapids* (New York, 1973; and C. L. Sulzberger, *A Long Row of Candles* (New York, 1969).

Other works presenting the views of prominent Americans on the issues of the early Cold War years include Jean Smith, ed., *The Papers of General Lucius Clay: Germany, 1945–1949* (Bloomington, Ind., 1974; 2 vols.); James T. Patterson, *Mr. Republican: A Biography of Robert A. Taft* (Boston, 1972); Richard J. Walton, *Henry Wallace, Harry Truman, and the Cold War* (New York, 1976); Samuel Walker, *Henry A. Wallace and American Foreign Policy* (Westport, Conn., 1976); Norman Markowitz, *The Rise and Fall of the People's Century* [on Wallace] (New York, 1973); David E. Lilienthal, *Journals* (New York, 1964–76; 6 vols.); Frederick Dobney, ed., *Selected Papers of Will Clayton* (Baltimore, 1971); Clinton P. Anderson, *Outsider in the Senate* (New York, 1970); Leo Crowley in *Milwaukee Journal*, August 17–22, 24–27, 1969; Clark M. Eichelberger, *Organizing for Peace: A Personal History of the Founding of the United Nations* (New York, 1977); Walter Johnson, ed., *The Papers of Adlai Stevenson* (Boston, 1972–77; 7 vols.); Arthur Krock, *Memoirs* (New York, 1968); F. Ross

Peterson, *Prophet Without Honor: Glen Taylor and the Fight for American Liberalism* (Lexington, Ky., 1974); Charles Sawyer, *Concerns of a Conservative Democrat* (Carbondale, Ill., 1968); Martin Weil, *A Pretty Good Club: The Founding Fathers of the U.S. Foreign Service* (New York, 1978); Townsend Hoopes, *The Devil and John Foster Dulles* (Boston, 1973); Henry H. Adams, *Harry Hopkins* (New York, 1977); Otis Carey, ed., *War-Wasted Asia: Letters, 1945–46* (Toyko, 1975); H. Stuart Hughes, "The Second Year of the Cold War: A Memoir and an Anticipation," *Commentary*, XLVIII(August 1969), 27–32; Herbert Feis, *Three International Episodes: Seen from E.A.* (New York, 1947); Michael A. Guhin, *John Foster Dulles: A Statesman and His Times* New York, 1972); and Louis Gerson, *John Foster Dulles* (New York, 1967).

WORLD LEADERS

Josef Stalin is the subject of a few works, many of them necessarily based upon scarce sources or public statements: Milovan Djilas, *Conversations with Stalin* (New York, 1962); Adam B. Ulam, *Stalin* (New York, 1973); Isaac Deutscher, *Stalin: A Political Biography* (New York, 1967); Alexander Dallin, "Allied Leadership in the Second World War: Stalin," *Survey*, XXI(Winter–Spring, 1975), 11–19; William O. McCagg, Jr., *Stalin Embattled, 1943–1948* (Detroit, Mich., 1978); Robert H. McNeal, "Roosevelt Through Stalin's Spectacles," *International Journal*, XVIII(Spring 1963), 194–206; and Svetlana Alliluyeva, *Twenty Letters to a Friend* (New York, 1967). Stalin's own words can be read in *J. V. Stalin on Post-War International Relations* (London, 1947); Josef Stalin, *The Great Patriotic War of the Soviet Union* (New York, 1945); *Correspondence Between the Chairman of the Council of Ministers of the U.S.S.R. and the Presidents of the U.S.A. and the Prime Ministers of Great Britain during the Great Patriotic War of 1941–1945* (New York, Capricorn Books edition, 1965). His outlook is also reflected in the records of conferences that he attended, including *The Tehran, Yalta, and Potsdam Conferences: Documents* (Moscow, 1969). Other Soviet leaders and their views can be studied in V. M. Molotov, *Problems of Foreign Policy* (Moscow, 1949); Georgei Zhukov, *Memoirs of Marshal Zhukov* (New York, 1971); Vojtech Mastny, "The Cassandra in the Foreign Commissariat: Maxim Litvinov and the Cold War," *Foreign Affairs*, LIV(Janu-

ary 1976), 366–376; and U.S. Congress, Committee on Foreign
Affairs, *The Strategy and Tactics of World Communism* (Washington, D.C., 1948).

Compared to Soviet biographical materials, British works are
numerous. For memoirs, see Winston S. Churchill, *Triumph and
Tragedy* (Boston, 1953); Piers Dixon, *Double Diploma* (London,
1968); Clement Attlee, *As It Happened* (New York, 1954); Hugh
Dalton, *High Tide and After* (London, 1962); Anthony Eden, *Full
Circle* (London, 1960), and *The Reckoning* (London, 1965); Harold Macmillan, *The Blast of War, 1939–1945* (London, 1967) and
Tides of Fortune, 1945–1955 (New York, 1969); Maurice Peter-
son, *Both Sides of the Curtain* (London, 1950); Lord Strang, *Home
and Abroad* (London, 1956); Hastings Ismay, *The Memoirs of
General, the Lord Ismay* (London, 1960); and Leslie Hollis, *One
Marine's Tale* (London, 1956). Useful diaries include David Dilks,
ed., *The Diaries of Sir Alexander Cadogan, 1938–45* (London,
1971), and Arthur Bryant, *Triumph in the West* (Garden City,
N.Y., 1959). Other studies of British leaders are Francis Williams,
Twilight of Europe: Memoirs of Prime Minister Clement Attlee
(New York, 1962); Alan Bullock, *The Life and Times of Ernest
Bevin* (London, 1960–67; 2 vols.); and Lord Moran, *Churchill*
(Boston, 1966).

For other individuals see Josip Tito, *Selected Speeches and Articles, 1941–1961* (Zagreb, 1963); Konrad Adenauer, *Memoirs* (Chicago, 1966); Hubert Ripka, *Czechoslovakia Enslaved* (London,
1950); Trygve Lie, *In the Cause of Peace* (New York, 1954); Lester B. Pearson, *Mike: Memoirs* (Toronto, 1972–75); 3 vols.);
Milovan Djilas, *Wartime* (New York, 1977); and J. W. Pickersgill
and D. F. Forster, *The MacKenzie King Record* (Toronto, 1960–
70; 4 vols.).

THE AMERICAN DOMESTIC SETTING

The United States at the end of World War II is described in
Jack Goodman, ed., *While You Were Gone* (New York, 1946);
Richard Polenberg, *War and Society: The United States, 1941–1945*
(Philadelphia, 1972); Richard E. Lingerman, *Don't You Know
There's a War On?* (New York, 1970); John M. Blum, *V Was for
Victory* (New York, 1976); and Geoffrey Perrett, *Days of Sad-
ness, Years of Triumph* (Baltimore, 1974). David M. Potter, *Peo-*

ple of Plenty: Economic Abundance and the American Character (Chicago, 1954), provides a useful analysis.

The relationship between public opinion, the president, and the making of foreign policy is the subject of Bernard C. Cohen, *The Public's Impact on Foreign Policy* (Boston, 1973), *The Influence of Non-Governmental Groups on Foreign Policy Making* (Boston, 1959), and "The Relationship Between the Public Opinion and Foreign Policy Maker," in Melvin Small, ed., *Public Opinion and Historians* (Detroit, Mich., 1970), pp. 65–80; Walter LaFeber, "American Policy-Makers, Public Opinion, and the Outbreak of the Cold War, 1945–50," in Nagai and Iriye, *The Origins of the Cold War in Asia,* pp. 43–65; Ralph B. Levering, *The Public and American Foreign Policy, 1918–1978* (New York, 1978) and *American Opinion and the Russian-American Alliance, 1939–1945* (Chapel Hill, N.C., 1976); Lester Markel *et al., Public Opinion and Foreign Policy* (New York, 1949); Gabriel Almond, *The American People and Foreign Policy* (New York, 1950); James N. Rosenau, ed., *Domestic Sources of Foreign Policy* (New York, 1967), *Public Opinion and Foreign Policy* (New York, 1961), and *National Leadership and Foreign Policy* (Princeton, 1963); H. Schuyler Foster, "American Public Opinion and U.S. Foreign Policy," *Department of State Bulletin,* XLI(November 30, 1959), 796–803; Thomas A. Bailey, *The Man in the Street* (New York, 1948); Blair Bolles, "Who Makes Our Foreign Policy," Foreign Policy Association *Headline Series,* No. 62 (March–April 1947), 5–86; Doris A. Graber, *Public Opinion, the President, and Foreign Policy* (New York, 1968); Manfred Landecker, *The President and Public Opinion* (Washington, 1968); Michael Leigh, *Mobilizing Consent: Public Opinion and American Foreign Policy, 1937–1947* (Westport, Conn., 1976); and William R. Caspary, "U.S. Public Opinion during the Onset of the Cold War," *Peace Research Society (International) Papers,* IX(1968), 25–46.

Polling data is presented in Hadley Cantril and Mildred Strunk, *Public Opinion, 1935–1946* (Princeton, 1951); George Gallup, *The Gallup Poll, 1935–1971* (New York, 1972; 3 vols.); and Leonard S. Cottrell and Sylvia Eberhart, *American Opinion on World Affairs in the Atomic Age* (Princeton, 1948). *Fortune* magazine and the *Public Opinion Quarterly* regularly reported polls on foreign policy questions.

Executive-legislative relations are examined in James A. Robinson, *Congress and Foreign Policy-Making* (Homewood, Ill., 1967; rev. ed.); Edgar E. Robinson, ed., *Powers of the President in Foreign Affairs, 1945–65* (San Francisco, 1966); Arthur Schlesinger, Jr., "Congress and the Making of American Foreign Policy," *Foreign Affairs*, LI(October 1972), 78–113, and *The Imperial Presidency*; James Nathan, "The Roots of the Imperial Presidency: Public Opinion, Domestic Institutions, and Global Interests," *Presidential Studies Quarterly*, V(Winter 1975), 63–74; David N. Farnsworth, *The Senate Committee on Foreign Relations* (Urbana, Ill., 1961); Loch Johnson and James M. McCormick, "Foreign Policy by Executive Fiat," *Foreign Policy*, No. 28 (Fall 1977), 117–123; Daniel S. Cheever and H. Field Haviland, Jr., *American Foreign Policy and the Separation of Powers* (Cambridge, Mass., 1952); Holbert N. Carroll, *The House of Representatives and Foreign Affairs* (Boston, 1966; rev. ed.); H. Bradford Westerfield, *Foreign Policy and Party Politics* (New Haven, Conn., 1955); Theodore Sorensen, *Decision-Making in the White House* (New York, 1963); Robert Dahl, *Congress and Foreign Policy* (New York, 1950); Clinton Rossiter, *The American Presidency* (New York, 1956); Dean Acheson, "Arthur Vandenberg and the Senate," in James D. Barber, ed., *Political Leadership in American Government* (Boston, 1964), pp. 74–83; Francis O. Wilcox, *Congress, the Executive, and Foreign Policy* (New York, 1971); and Susan M. Hartmann, *Truman and the 80th Congress* (Columbia, Mo., 1971).

For interest groups, see Ronald Radosh, *American Labor and United States Foreign Policy* (New York, 1969); Thomas G. Paterson, "The Economic Cold War: American Business and Economic Foreign Policy, 1945–1950" (Unpublished Ph.D. dissertation, University of California, Berkeley, 1968); Ross Koen, *The China Lobby in American Politics* (New York, 1974); Louis Gerson, *The Hyphenate in Recent American Politics and Diplomacy* (Lawrence, Kan., 1964); John Snetsinger, *Truman, the Jewish Vote, and the Creation of Israel* (Stanford, 1974); Roscoe Baker, *The American Legion and American Foreign Policy* (New York, 1954); Peter M. Irons, "The Test is Poland: Polish Americans and the Origins of the Cold War," *Polish-American Studies*, XXX(Autumn 1973), 5–63; John N. Cable, "Vandenberg: The Polish Question and Polish-Americans, 1944–1948," *Michigan History*, LVII(Winter 1973), 296–310, and Jack L. Hammersmith, "Franklin Roosevelt, the Polish Question, and the Election of 1944," *Mid-America*, LXIX(January 1977), 5–17; and Stephan A. Garrett, "Eastern European Ethnic Groups and American Foreign Policy," *Political Science Quarterly*, XCIII(Summer 1978), 301–323.

Other helpful studies cover the American domestic setting and foreign policy: Robert A. Divine, *Foreign Policy and U.S. Presidential Elections, 1940–1960* (New York, 1974; 2 vols.), and "The Cold War and the Election of 1948," *Journal of American History*, LIX(June 1972), 90–110; Thomas G. Paterson, ed., *Cold War Critics* (Chicago, 1971); Ronald Radosh, *Prophets on the Right: Profiles of Conservative Critics of American Globalism* (New York, 1974); Athan Theoharis, *The Yalta Myths* (Columbia, Mo., 1970); Justus D. Doenecke, "The Strange Career of American Isolationism, 1944–1954," *Peace and Change*, III(Summer-Fall 1975), 79–83; Eric Goldman, *The Crucial Decade—and After, 1945–1960* (New York, 1971); and Alonzo Hamby, *Beyond the New Deal* (New York, 1973). Ernest R. May, *"Lessons" of the Past* (New York, 1973), discusses the importance of previous experiences in shaping foreign policy.

For the view that the foreign affairs bureaucracy can develop a life of its own, one that is sometimes independent from that of the president, see Graham Allison, *Essence of Decision* (Boston, 1971), and "Conceptual Models and the Cuban Missile Crisis," *American Political Science Review*, LXII(September 1969), 689–718; and Graham Allison and Morton H. Halperin, "Bureaucratic Politics: A Paradigm and Some Policy Implications," *World Politics*, XXIV(Spring 1972), Supplement, 40–79. Studies critical of the bureaucratic model, which argue that the President dominates the decision-making process, include Robert J. Art, "Bureaucratic Politics and American Foreign Policy: A Critique," *Policy Studies*, IV(December 1973), 467–490, and Stephen D. Krasner, "Are Bureaucracies Important? (Or Allison Wonderland)," *Foreign Policy*, No. 7 (Summer 1972), 159–179. Other useful works on the politics of bureaucracy are Morton H. Halperin, *Bureaucratic Politics and Foreign Policy* (Washington, 1974); Morton H. Halperin and Arnold Kanter, eds., *Readings in American Foreign Policy: A Bureaucratic Perspective* (Boston, 1973); Morton H. Halperin, "Why Bureaucrats Play Games," *Foreign Policy*, No. 2 (Spring 1971), 70–90; Alexander George, "Washington Foreign Policy," *American Political Science Review*, LXV(September

1972), 769–781; Leslie H. Gelb and Morton H. Halperin, "Diplomatic Notes: The Ten Commandments of the Foreign Affairs Bureaucracy," *Harper's Magazine*, CCXLIV(June 1972), 28–37; Chadwick F. Alger, "The External Bureaucracy in United States Foreign Affairs," *Administrative Science Quarterly*, VII(June 1962), 50–78; Irving L. Janis, *Victims of Groupthink* (Boston, 1972); and James C. Thomson, Jr., "Getting Out and Speaking Out," *Foreign Policy*, No. 13 (Winter 1973–74), 49–69.

THE SOVIET UNION AND ITS FOREIGN POLICY

For a lengthy overview, see Adam B. Ulam, *Expansion and Coexistence* (New York, 1974). Russia's diplomacy in the Cold War is recounted in Vera Micheles Dean, *The United States and Russia* (Cambridge, Mass., 1948); Philip E. Mosely, *The Kremlin and World Politics* (New York, 1960); Ivo J. Lederer, ed., *Russian Foreign Policy* (New Haven, 1962); W. Gottlieb, "A Self-Portrait of Soviet Foreign Policy," *Soviet Studies*, III(October 1951), 185–205; Marshall Shulman, *Stalin's Foreign Policy Reappraised* (New York, 1966); Thomas Wolfe, *Soviet Power and Europe* (Baltimore, 1970); and George F. Kennan, *Russia and the West Under Lenin and Stalin* (Boston, 1960). For the war years, see Vojtech Mastny, *Russia's Road to the Cold War: Stalin's War Aims, 1941–1945* (New York, 1978). *Soviet Press Translations* reprinted a variety of *Pravda* and *Izvestia* articles, among others, for the late 1940s.

For the wellsprings of Soviet behavior in world affairs, the following are representative of the variety of interpretation: Robert D. Warth, *Soviet Russia in World Politics* (New York, 1963); Morton Schwartz, *The "Motive Forces" of Soviet Foreign Policy: A Reappraisal* (Denver, Colo. 1971); Alexander Dallin, ed., *Soviet Conduct in World Affairs* (New York, 1960); William A. Glaser, "Theories of Soviet Foreign Policy: A Classification of the Literature," *World Affairs Quarterly*, XXVII(1956–57), 128–152; Nathan Leites, *The Operational Code of the Politburo* (New York, 1951); Alfred G. Meyer, "The Functions of Ideology in the Soviet Political System," *Soviet Studies*, XVII(January 1966), 273–285; Daniel Bell, "Ten Theories in Search of Reality," *World Politics*, X(April 1958), 327–365; R. S. Tarn, "Continuity in Russian Foreign Policy," *International Journal*, V(Autumn 1950), 283–298; Robert C. Tucker, *The Soviet Political Mind* (New York,

1971); Adam Ulam, "Soviet Ideology and Soviet Foreign Policy," *World Politics*, XI(January 1959), 153–172; Barrington Moore, Jr., *Soviet Politics: The Dilemma of Power* (Cambridge, Mass., 1950); Paul Zinner, "The Ideological Bases of Soviet Foreign Policy," *World Politics*, IV(July 1952), 489–511; William Zimmerman, "The Soviet Union," in Steven L. Spiegel and Kenneth N. Waltz, eds., *Conflict in World Politics* (Cambridge, Mass., 1971).

Other studies of the Soviet Union include Frederick C. Barghoorn, "The Soviet Critique of American Foreign Policy," *Journal of International Affairs*, V(Winter 1951), 5–14, "The Varga Discussion and Its Significance," *American Slavic and East European Review*, III(October 1948), 214–236, and *The Soviet Image of the United States* (New York, 1950); Victor L. Issraelian, *The Anti-Hitler Coalition* (Moscow, 1971); Edgar O'Ballance, *The Red Army* (New York, 1964); B. Ponomaryov *et al.*, *History of Soviet Foreign Policy, 1917–1945* (Moscow, 1969); Alexander Werth, *Russia at War, 1941–1945* (New York, 1964); Robert D. Warth, "Stalin and the Cold War: A Second Look," *South Atlantic Quarterly*, LIX(Winter 1960), 1–12; Joseph R. Starobin, "Origins of the Cold War: The Communist Dimension," *Foreign Affairs*, XLVII (July 1969), 681–696; *The Soviet Army* (Moscow, 1971); Harry Schwartz, *Russia's Postwar Economy* (Syracuse, 1947); and Teddy J. Uldricks, "The Impact of the Great Purges on the People's Commissariat of Foreign Affairs," *Slavic Review*, XXXVI(June 1977), 187–203.

Index